GAME
HACKING

Developing Autonomous Bots for Online Games

by Nick Cano

**no starch
press**

San Francisco

Printed in USA

First printing

20 19 18 17 16   1 2 3 4 5 6 7 8 9

ISBN-10: 1-59327-669-9
ISBN-13: 978-1-59327-669-0

Publisher: William Pollock
Production Editor: Laurel Chun
Cover Illustration: Ryan Milner
Interior Design: Octopod Studios
Developmental Editor: Jennifer Griffith-Delgado
Technical Reviewer: Stephen Lawler
Copyeditor: Rachel Monaghan
Compositor: Laurel Chun
Proofreader: Paula L. Fleming
Indexer: BIM Creatives, LLC

For information on distribution, translations, or bulk sales, please contact No Starch Press, Inc. directly:
No Starch Press, Inc.
245 8th Street, San Francisco, CA 94103
phone: 415.863.9900; info@nostarch.com
www.nostarch.com

Library of Congress Cataloging-in-Publication Data

Cano, Nick, author.
  Game hacking : developing autonomous bots for online games / by Nick Cano.
        pages cm
  Includes index.
  Summary: "A hands-on guide to hacking computer games. Shows programmers how to dissect computer games and create bots to alter their gaming environment. Covers the basics of game hacking, including reverse engineering, assembly code analysis, programmatic memory manipulation, persistent hacks, responsive hacks, and code injection."-- Provided by publisher.
  ISBN 978-1-59327-669-0 -- ISBN 1-59327-669-9
  1. Intelligent agents (Computer software) 2. Internet programming. 3. Internet games--Programming. 4. Hacking. I. Title.
  QA76.76.I58C36 2016
  005.8--dc23
                                        2015036294

About the Author

Nick Cano wrote his first scripts for open source game servers when he was 12 and started a business selling his bots when he was 16. He has been a part of the game-hacking community ever since and advises game developers and designers on best practices to protect their games against bots. Nick also has years of experience in detecting and defending against malware, and he has spoken at many conferences about his research and tools.

About the Technical Reviewer

Stephen Lawler is the founder and president of a small computer software and security consulting firm. He has been actively working in information security for over 10 years, primarily in reverse engineering, malware analysis, and vulnerability research. He was a member of the Mandiant malware analysis team and assisted with high-profile computer intrusions affecting several Fortune 100 companies. Stephen also developed and teaches the Practical ARM Exploitation class, which has been offered at BlackHat and several other security conferences for the past five years.

BRIEF CONTENTS

CONTENTS IN DETAIL

PART 1
TOOLS OF THE TRADE

1
SCANNING MEMORY USING CHEAT ENGINE   3

5
ADVANCED MEMORY FORENSICS   97

6
READING FROM AND WRITING TO GAME MEMORY   119

PART 3
PROCESS PUPPETEERING

7
CODE INJECTION   133

12
STAYING HIDDEN

FOREWORD

Nick is great. We first hit it off in all the right and wrong ways, as you can imagine. I've been in the security field a while; he's a little younger. I've had the schooling, whereas he's not much for college. I'm a faith guy, and he's not. The interesting thing is that none of that matters; we've had a blast anyway. Age, race, gender, degrees—when it comes to gaming, hacking, and coding, no one cares!

Nick gets it done. He's fun. He's brilliant. He's hard working. And probably most pertinent: he's one of the rare few who understand the intersection of gaming, hacking, and coding. He's worked in this niche and created profitable bots.

In this first-of-its-kind book, Nick walks you through what it means to pull apart games. He teaches you the software investigation tools and tricks of the trade. You'll learn about game internals, how to pull them apart, and how to modify play. For example, Nick teaches how to avoid anti-cheat so that you can automate play. Wouldn't it be cool to have your own bot that collects experience, gold, items, and more—all while you're away?

Ever wonder how the cheaters cheat? Ever wanted to patch or protect your game? Grab a coffee, crack open your laptop, and enjoy.

Blessings to you and yours,

Dr. Jared DeMott
Security Expert & Software Builder

ACKNOWLEDGMENTS

Writing this book was an amazing journey, and I couldn't have done it alone. No Starch Press has been extremely supportive and worked closely with me to take this book from concept to reality. In particular, I'd like to thank my developmental editor, Jennifer Griffith-Delgado, and my production editor, Laurel Chun. Bill Pollock, Tyler Ortman, Alison Law, and the rest of the team at No Starch are wonderful people, and I'm pleased to have worked with them.

Thanks to copyeditor Rachel Monaghan, proofreader Paula L. Fleming, and technical reviewer Stephen Lawler. Thanks also to my friends Cavitt "synt4x" Glover and Vadim Kotov, who took the time to skim some chapters before submission, and to Jared DeMott for writing the book's foreword.

I'd like to thank all of the people on TPForums who took me in when I was just a naive kid and helped me learn how to hack games. In particular, I owe my thanks to Joseph "jo3bingham" Bingham, Ian Obermiller, and jeremic, who all had a significant influence on my progression as a hacker, and to TPForums founder Josh "Zyphrus" Hartzell, who helped me find my confidence and skills when my future looked its bleakest.

Thanks also to my entire forum staff and every customer who has ever used my bots. And finally, thanks to my family, friends, and colleagues, who have been fun and supportive and helped shape me into the man I am today.

INTRODUCTION

A common misconception in the world of online gaming is the idea that the only game you can play is the one in the title. In fact, game hackers enjoy playing the game that hides behind the curtain: a cat-and-mouse game of wits between them and the game developers. While game hackers work to reverse engineer game binaries, automate aspects of game play, and modify gaming environments, game developers combat the hacker-designed tools (normally referred to as *bots*) using anti-reversing techniques, bot detection algorithms, and heuristic data mining.

As the battle between game hackers and developers has progressed, the technical methods implemented by both parties—many of which resemble techniques utilized by malware developers and antivirus vendors—have evolved, becoming more complex. This book highlights the fight put up by game hackers, and the advanced methods they have engineered to manipulate games while simultaneously eluding game developers in the dark corners of their own software.

Although the book focuses on teaching you to develop tools that would likely be considered a nuisance or even malicious by gaming companies, you'll find that many of the techniques are useful for development of tools that are perfectly benign and neutral. Furthermore, the knowledge of how these techniques are implemented is key for the game developers working to prevent their use.

Prerequisites for the Reader

This book does not aim to teach you software development, and therefore assumes that you have, at minimum, a solid software development background. This background should include familiarity with native Windows-based development, as well as light experience with game development and memory management. While these skills will be enough for you to follow this book, experience with x86 assembly and Windows internals will ensure that details of more advanced implementations are not lost on you.

Furthermore, since all the advanced hacks discussed in this book rely on code injection, an ability to write code in a native language like C or C++ is a must. All of the example code in this book is written in C++ and can be compiled with Microsoft Visual C++ Express Edition. (You can download MSVC++ Express Edition from *http://www.visualstudio.com/en-US/products/visual-studio-express-vs.*)

NOTE *Other languages that compile to native code, such as Delphi, are also capable of injection, but I will not discuss them in this book.*

A Brief Game Hacking History

Since the dawn of online PC gaming in the early 1980s, an ongoing war of wits between game hackers and game developers has been taking place. This seemingly endless struggle has prompted game developers to devote countless hours toward preventing hackers from taking their games apart and greasing between the gears. These hackers, who fight back with their sophisticated stealth implementations, have many motivations: customized graphics, better performance, ease of use, autonomous play, in-game asset acquisition, and, of course, real-life profit.

The late 1990s and early 2000s were the golden age of game hacking, when online PC games became advanced enough to draw large crowds but were still simple enough to easily reverse engineer and manipulate. Online games that came out during this time, such as *Tibia* (January 1997), *Runescape* (January 2001), and *Ultima Online* (September 1997), were heavily targeted by bot developers. The developers of these games and others like them still struggle today to control the massive communities of bot developers and bot users. The game developers' lack of action and the hackers' tenacity have not only completely shattered the economies within the games, but have also produced a thriving for-profit industry focused around bot development and bot defense.

In the years since the golden age, more mature game companies started taking bot defense very seriously. These companies now have dedicated teams focused on developing bot prevention systems, and many also view bots as a legal matter and will not hesitate to banish players who use bots and sue the bot developers who provided them. As a result, many game hackers have been forced to develop advanced stealth techniques to keep their users safe.

This war wages on, and the numbers on both sides of the fight will continue to grow as online gaming becomes more prevalent over the coming years. Major game developers are pursuing hackers with endless determination, even slamming some game hacking giants with multimillion-dollar lawsuits. This means that game hackers who are serious about their business must either target smaller gaming companies, or anonymously market their products from the shadows in order to escape prosecution. For the foreseeable future, game hacking and bot development will continue to grow into a larger and more lucrative industry for those game hackers bold enough to take the risks.

Why Hack Games?

Aside from its obvious allure and challenging nature, game hacking has some practical and profitable purposes. Every day, thousands of novice programmers experiment with small-scale game hacking as a way to automate monotonous tasks or perform menial actions. These script kiddies will use automation tools like AutoIt for their small, relatively harmless hacks. On the other hand, professional game hackers, backed by their large toolkits and years of programming experience, will devote hundreds of hours to the development of advanced game hacks. These types of game hacks, which are the focus of this book, are often created with the intent of making large amounts of money.

Gaming is a huge industry that generated $22.4 billion in sales in 2014, according to the Entertainment Software Association. Of the tens of millions of players who play games daily, 20 percent play massively multiplayer online role-playing games (MMORPGs). These MMORPGs often have thousands of players who trade virtual goods within thriving in-game economies. Players often have a need for in-game assets and are willing to buy these assets with real-world money. Consequently, MMORPG players end up developing large communities that provide gold-for-cash services. These services often go as far as enforcing exchange rates from in-game gold to real-world currencies.

To take advantage of this, game hackers will create bots that are capable of automatically farming gold and leveling characters. Then, depending on their goal, hackers will either set up massive gold farms and sell their in-game profits, or perfect and sell their software to players who wish to seamlessly obtain levels and gold with minimal interference. Due to the massive communities surrounding popular MMORPGs, these game hackers can make between six and seven figures annually.

While MMORPGs provide the largest attack surface for hackers, they have a relatively small audience overall. About 38 percent of gamers favor real-time strategy (RTS) and massive online battle arena (MOBA) games, and another 6 percent play primarily first-person shooter (FPS) games. These competitive player versus player (PvP) games collectively represent 44 percent of the gaming market and provide great rewards to determined game hackers.

PvP games are often episodic in nature; each match is an isolated game, and there's typically not much profitable progression for botting away from keyboard (AFK). This means that, instead of running gold farms or creating autonomous bots to level up characters, hackers will create reactive bots that assist players in combat.

These highly competitive games are about skill and tactics, and most players participate to prove their ability to themselves and others. As a consequence, the number of people seeking bots for PvP-type games is substantially lower than you'd find in the grind-heavy world of MMORPGs. Nevertheless, hackers can still make a pretty penny selling their PvP bots, which are often much easier to develop than full-fledged autonomous bots.

How This Book Is Organized

This book is split into four parts, each of which focuses on a different core aspect of game hacking. In **Part 1: Tools of the Trade**, you'll get a box full of tools to help you hack games.

- **Chapter 1: Scanning Memory Using Cheat Engine** will teach you how to scan a game's memory for important values using Cheat Engine.

- In **Chapter 2: Debugging Games with OllyDbg**, you'll get a crash course in debugging and reverse engineering with OllyDbg. The skills you learn here will be extremely useful when you start making advanced bots and injecting code.

- To wrap up, **Chapter 3: Reconnaissance with Process Monitor and Process Explorer**, will teach you how to use two reconnaissance tools to inspect how games interact with files, other processes, the network, and the operating system.

The online resources for each chapter in Part 1 include custom binaries I created to give you a safe place to test and hone your newly discovered skills.

Once you're comfortable with every wrench and hammer, **Part 2: Game Dissection**, will teach you how to get under the hood and figure out how games work.

- In **Chapter 4: From Code to Memory: A General Primer**, you'll learn what a game's source code and data look like once compiled into a game binary.

- **Chapter 5: Advanced Memory Forensics** builds on the knowledge you'll gain from Chapter 4. You'll learn how to scan memory and use debugging to seamlessly locate tricky memory values and dissect complex classes and structures.

- Finally, **Chapter 6: Reading from and Writing to Game Memory** shows you how to read and modify data within a running game.

These chapters provide lots of in-depth proof-of-concept example code that you can use to verify everything you read.

In **Part 3: Process Puppeteering**, you'll become a puppeteer as you learn how to turn any game into a marionette.

- Building on the skills from Parts 1 and 2, **Chapter 7: Code Injection** describes how to inject and execute your own code in the address space of a game.

- Once you've mastered injection, **Chapter 8: Manipulating Control Flow in a Game** will teach you how to use injection to intercept, modify, or disable any function call made by a game, and will wrap up with some useful real-world examples for the common libraries Adobe AIR and Direct 3D.

To complement your puppeteering classes, these chapters are accompanied by thousands of lines of production-ready code that you can use as a boilerplate library for a future bot.

In **Part 4: Creating Bots**, you'll see how to combine your toolbox, dissection abilities, puppeteering skills, and software engineering background to create powerful bots.

- **Chapter 9: Using Extrasensory Perception to Ward Off Fog of War** explores ways to make a game display useful information that isn't exposed by default, such as the locations of hidden enemies and the amount of experience you earn per hour.

- **Chapter 10: Responsive Hacks** shows code patterns you can use to detect in-game events, like decreases in health, and to make bots that react to those events faster than human players.

- **Chapter 11: Putting It All Together: Writing Autonomous Bots** reveals how bots that play games without human interaction work. Automated bots combine control theory, state machines, search algorithms, and mathematical models, and this chapter is a crash course in those topics.

- In **Chapter 12: Staying Hidden**, you'll learn about some of the high-level techniques you can use to escape and evade any system that would interfere with your bots.

As you've probably come to expect, these chapters have lots of example code. Some of the hacks shown in this part are built on example code from previous chapters. Others explore succinct, straightforward design patterns you can use to create your own bots. Once you've finished all four parts of this book, you'll be sent off into the virtual world with your new superpower.

About the Online Resources

You'll find many additional resources for this book at *https://www.nostarch .com/gamehacking/*. These resources include compiled binaries to test your skills, a considerable amount of example code, and quite a few snippets of production-ready game hacking code. These resources go hand-in-hand with the book, and it really isn't complete without them, so make sure to download them before you continue.

How to Use This Book

This book should be used first and foremost as a guide to get you started in game hacking. The progression is such that the content of each chapter introduces new skills and abilities that build on all previous chapters. As you complete chapters, I encourage you to play with the example code and test your skills on a real game before continuing your reading. This is important, as some covered topics will have use cases that don't become evident until you're 10 feet deep in the mud.

Once you've finished the book, I hope it can still be useful to you as a field manual. If you come across some data structure you're unsure of, maybe the details in Chapter 5 can help. If you reverse engineer a game's map format and are ready to create a pathfinder, you can always flip to Chapter 11, study the content, and use some of the example code as a starting point. Although it's impossible to anticipate all the problems you might face when you're hacking away, I've tried to ensure you'll find some answers within these pages.

A NOTE FROM THE PUBLISHER

This book does not condone piracy, violating the DMCA, infringing copyright, or breaking in-game Terms of Service. Game hackers have been banned from games for life, sued for millions of dollars, and even jailed for their work.

PART 1

TOOLS OF THE TRADE

1

SCANNING MEMORY USING CHEAT ENGINE

The best game hackers in the world spend years personalizing expansive arsenals with custom-built tools. Such potent toolkits enable these hackers to seamlessly analyze games, effortlessly prototype hacks, and effectively develop bots. At the core, however, each unique kit is built from the same four-piece powerhouse: a memory scanner, an assembler-level debugger, a process monitor, and a hex editor.

Memory scanning is the gateway to game hacking, and this chapter will teach you about Cheat Engine, a powerful memory scanner that searches a game's operating memory (which lives in RAM) for values like the player's level, health, or in-game money. First, I'll focus on basic memory scanning, memory modification, and pointer scanning. Following that, we'll dive into Cheat Engine's powerful embedded Lua scripting engine.

NOTE *You can grab Cheat Engine from* http://www.cheatengine.org/. *Pay attention when running the installer because it will try to install some toolbars and other bloatware. You can disable those options if you wish.*

Why Memory Scanners Are Important

Knowing a game's state is paramount to interacting with the game intelligently, but unlike humans, software can't determine the state of a game simply by looking at what's on the screen. Fortunately, underneath all of the stimuli produced by a game, a computer's memory contains a purely numeric representation of that game's state—and programs can understand numbers easily. Hackers use memory scanners to find those values in memory, and then in their programs, they read the memory in these locations to understand the game's state.

For example, a program that heals players when they fall below 500 health needs to know how to do two things: track a player's current health and cast a healing spell. The former requires access to the game's state, while the latter might only require a button to be pressed. Given the location where a player's health is stored and the way to read a game's memory, the program would look something like this pseudocode:

```
// do this in some loop
health = readMemory(game, HEALTH_LOCATION)
if (health < 500)
    pressButton(HEAL_BUTTON)
```

A memory scanner allows you to find HEALTH_LOCATION so that your software can query it for you later.

Basic Memory Scanning

The memory scanner is the most basic, yet most important, tool for the aspiring game hacker. As in any program, all data in the memory of a game resides at an absolute location called a *memory address*. If you think of the memory as a very large byte array, a memory address is an index pointing to a value in that array. When a memory scanner is told to find some value x (called a *scan value*, because it's the value you're scanning for) in a game's memory, the scanner loops through the byte array looking for any value equal to x. Every time it finds a matching value, it adds the index of the match to a result list.

Due to the sheer size of a game's memory, however, the value of x can appear in hundreds of locations. Imagine that x is the player's health, which is currently 500. Our x uniquely holds 500, but 500 is not uniquely held by x, so a scan for x returns all variables with a value of 500. Any addresses not related to x are ultimately clutter; they share a value of 500 with x only by chance. To filter out these unwanted values, the memory scanner allows you to rescan the result list, removing addresses that no longer hold the same value as *x*, whether *x* is still 500 or has changed.

For these rescans to be effective, the overall state of the game must have significant *entropy*—a measure of disorder. You increase entropy by changing the in-game environment, often by moving around, killing creatures, or switching characters. As entropy increases, unrelated addresses are less likely to continue to arbitrarily hold the same value, and given enough entropy, a few rescans should filter out all false positives and leave you with the true address of *x*.

Cheat Engine's Memory Scanner

This section gives you a tour of Cheat Engine's memory-scanning options, which will help you track down the addresses of game state values in memory. I'll give you a chance to try the scanner out in "Basic Memory Editing" on page 11; for now, open Cheat Engine and have a look around. The memory scanner is tightly encapsulated in its main window, as shown in Figure 1-1.

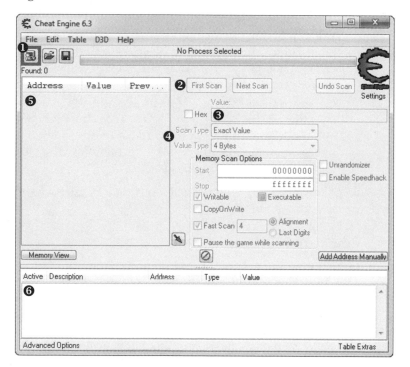

Figure 1-1: Cheat Engine main screen

To begin scanning a game's memory, click the Attach icon ❶ to attach to a process and then enter the scan value (referred to as *x* in our conceptual scanner) you want to locate ❸. By attaching to a process, we're telling

Cheat Engine to prepare to operate on it; in this case, that operation is a scan. It helps to also tell Cheat Engine what kind of scan to run, as I'll discuss next.

Scan Types

Cheat Engine allows you to select two different scan directives, called Scan Type and Value Type ❹. Scan Type tells the scanner how to compare your scan value with the memory being scanned using one of the following scan types:

Exact Value Returns addresses pointing to values equal to the scan value. Choose this option if the value you are looking for won't change during the scan; health, mana, and level typically fall into this category.

Bigger Than Returns addresses pointing to values greater than the scan value. This option is useful when the value you're searching for is steadily increasing, which often happens with timers.

Smaller Than Returns addresses pointing to values smaller than the scan value. Like Bigger Than, this option is useful for finding timers (in this case, ones that count down rather than up).

Value Between Returns addresses pointing to values within a scan value range. This option combines Bigger Than and Smaller Than, displaying a secondary scan value box that allows you to input a much smaller range of values.

Unknown Initial Value Returns all addresses in a program's memory, allowing rescans to examine the entire address range relative to their initial values. This option is useful for finding item or creature types, since you won't always know the internal values the game developers used to represent these objects.

The Value Type directive tells the Cheat Engine scanner what type of variable it's searching for.

Running Your First Scan

Once the two scan directives are set, click **First Scan** ❷ to run an initial scan for values, and the scanner will populate the results list ❺. Any green addresses in this list are *static*, meaning that they should remain persistent across program restarts. Addresses listed in black reside in *dynamically allocated memory*, memory that is allocated at runtime.

When the results list is first populated, it shows the address and real-time value of each result. Each rescan will also show the value of each result during the previous scan. (Any real-time values displayed are updated at an interval that you can set in Edit ▶ Settings ▶ General Settings ▶ Update interval.)

Next Scans

Once the results list is populated, the scanner enables the Next Scan ❷ button, which offers six new scan types. These additional scan types allow you to compare the addresses in the results list to their values in the previous scan, which will help you narrow down which address holds the game state value you're scanning for. They are as follows:

Increased Value   Returns addresses pointing to values that have increased. This complements the Bigger Than scan type by keeping the same minimum value and removing any address whose value has decreased.

Increased Value By   Returns addresses pointing to values that have increased by a defined amount. This scan type usually returns far fewer false positives, but you can use it only when you know exactly how much a value has increased.

Decreased Value   This option is the opposite of Increased Value.

Decreased Value By   This option is the opposite of Increased Value By.

Changed Value   Returns addresses pointing to values that have changed. This type is useful when you know a value will mutate, but you're unsure how.

Unchanged Value   Returns addresses pointing to values that haven't changed. This can help you eliminate false positives, since you can easily create a large amount of entropy while ensuring the desired value stays the same.

You'll usually need to use multiple scan types in order to narrow down a large result list and find the correct address. Eliminating false positives is often a matter of properly creating entropy (as described in "Basic Memory Scanning" on page 4), tactically changing your scan directives, bravely pressing Next Scan, and then repeating the process until you have a single remaining address.

When You Can't Get a Single Result

Sometimes it is impossible to pinpoint a single result in Cheat Engine, in which case you must determine the correct address through experimentation. For example, if you're looking for your character's health and can't narrow it down to fewer than five addresses, you could try modifying the value of each address (as discussed in "Manual Modification with Cheat Engine" on page 8) until you see the health display change or the other values automatically change to the one you set.

Cheat Tables

Once you've found the correct address, you can double-click it to add it to the *cheat table pane* ❻; addresses in the cheat table pane can be modified, watched, and saved to cheat table files for future use.

For each address in the cheat table pane, you can add a description by double-clicking the Description column, and you can add a color by right-clicking and selecting Change Color. You can also display the values of each address in hexadecimal or decimal format by right-clicking and selecting Show as hexadecimal or Show as decimal, respectively. Lastly, you can change the data type of each value by double-clicking the Type column, or you can change the value itself by double-clicking the Value column.

Since the main purpose of the cheat table pane is to allow a game hacker to neatly track addresses, it can be dynamically saved and loaded. Go to **File ▸ Save** or **File ▸ Save As** to save the current cheat table pane to a *.ct* document file containing each address with its value type, description, display color, and display format. To load the saved *.ct* documents, go to **File ▸ Load**. (You'll find many ready-made cheat tables for popular games at *http://cheatengine.org/tables.php.*)

Now that I've described how to scan for a game state value, I'll discuss how you can change that value when you know where it lives in memory.

Memory Modification in Games

Bots cheat a game system by modifying memory values in the game's state in order to give you lots of in-game money, modify your character's health, change your character's position, and so on. In most online games, a character's vitals (such as health, mana, skills, and position) are held in memory but are controlled by the game server and relayed to your local game client over the Internet, so modifying such values during online play is merely cosmetic and doesn't affect the actual values. (Any useful memory modification to an online game requires a much more advanced hack that's beyond Cheat Engine's capabilities.) In local games with no remote server, however, you can manipulate all of these values at will.

Manual Modification with Cheat Engine

We'll use Cheat Engine to understand how the memory modification magic works.

To modify memory manually, do the following:

1. Attach Cheat Engine to a game.
2. Either scan for the address you wish to modify or load a cheat table that contains it.
3. Double-click on the Value column for the address to open an input prompt where you can enter a new value.
4. If you want to make sure the new value can't be overwritten, select the box under the Active column to *freeze* the address, which will make Cheat Engine keep writing the same value back to it every time it changes.

This method works wonders for quick-and-dirty hacks, but constantly changing values by hand is cumbersome; an automated solution would be much more appealing.

Trainer Generator

Cheat Engine's trainer generator allows you to automate the whole memory modification process without writing any code.

To create a *trainer* (a simple bot that binds memory modification actions to keyboard hotkeys), go to **File ▸ Create generic trainer Lua script from table**. This opens a Trainer generator dialog similar to the one shown in Figure 1-2.

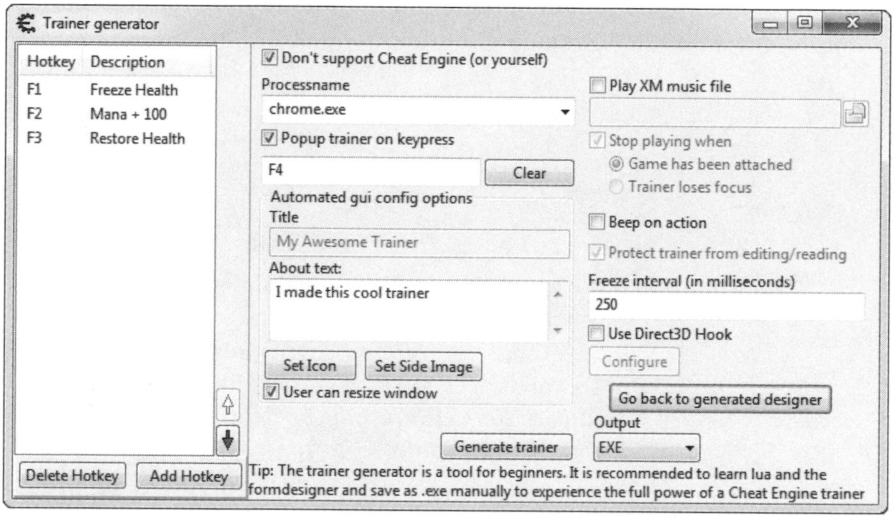

Figure 1-2: Cheat Engine Trainer generator dialog

There are a number of fields to modify here:

Processname   The name of the executable the trainer should attach to. This is the name shown in the process list when you attach with Cheat Engine, and it should be autofilled with the name of the process Cheat Engine is attached to.

Popup trainer on keypress   Optionally enables a hotkey—which you set by entering a key combination in the box below the checkbox—to display the trainer's main window.

Title   The name of your trainer, which will be displayed on its interface. This is optional.

About text   The description of your trainer, to be displayed on the interface; this is also optional.

Freeze interval (in milliseconds)   The interval during which a freeze operation overwrites the value. You should generally leave this at 250, as lower intervals can sap resources and higher values may be too slow.

Once these values are configured, click **Add Hotkey** to set up a key sequence to activate your trainer. You will be prompted to select a value from your cheat table. Enter a value, and you will be taken to a Set/Change hotkey screen similar to Figure 1-3.

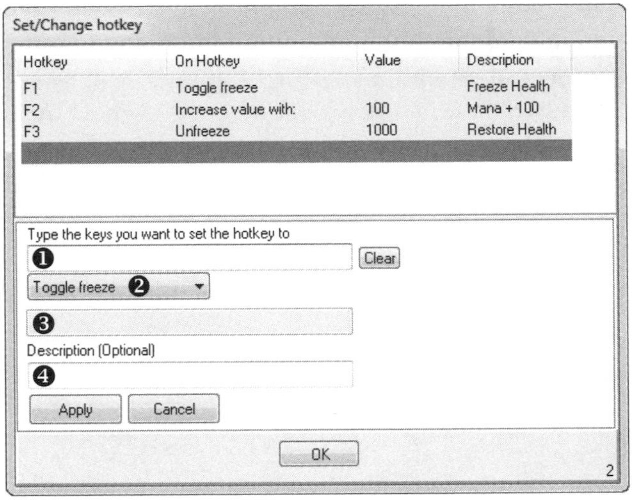

Figure 1-3: Cheat Engine Set/Change hotkey screen

On this screen, place your cursor in the box labeled Type the keys you want to set the hotkey to ❶ and enter the desired key combination. Next, choose the desired action from the drop-down menu ❷; your options should appear in the following order:

Toggle freeze   Toggles the freeze state of the address.

Toggle freeze and allow increase   Toggles the freeze state of the address but allows the value to increase. Any time the value decreases, the trainer overwrites it with its previous value. Increased values will not be overwritten.

Toggle freeze and allow decrease   Does the opposite of Toggle freeze and allow increase.

Freeze   Sets the address to frozen if it's not frozen already.

Unfreeze   Unfreezes the address if it's frozen.

Set value to   Sets the value to whatever you specify in the value box ❸.

Decrease value with   Decreases the value by the amount you specify in the value box ❸.

Increase value with   Does the opposite of Decrease value with.

Finally, you can set a description for the action ❹. Click **Apply**, then **OK**, and your action will appear in the list on the Trainer generator screen. At this point, Cheat Engine runs the trainer in the background, and you can simply press the hotkeys you configured to execute the memory actions.

To save your trainer to a portable executable, click **Generate trainer**. Running this executable after the game is launched will attach your trainer to the game so you can use it without starting Cheat Engine.

Now that you know your way around Cheat Engine's memory scanner and trainer generator, try modifying some memory yourself.

BASIC MEMORY EDITING

Download the files for this book from *https://www.nostarch.com/gamehacking/*, and run the file *BasicMemory.exe*. Next, start up Cheat Engine and attach to the binary. Then, using only Cheat Engine, find the addresses for the x- and y-coordinates of the gray ball. (Hint: Use the 4 Bytes value type.)

Once you've found the values, modify them to place the ball on top of the black square. The game will let you know once you've succeeded by displaying the text "Good job!" (Hint: Each time the ball is moved, its position—stored as a 4-byte integer—in that plane is changed by 1. Also, try to look only for static [green] results.)

Pointer Scanning

As I've mentioned, online games often store values in dynamically allocated memory. While addresses that reference dynamic memory are useless to us in and of themselves, some static address will always point to another address, which in turn points to another, and so on, until the tail of the chain points to the dynamic memory we're interested in. Cheat Engine can locate these chains using a method called *pointer scanning*.

In this section, I'll introduce you to pointer chains and then describe how pointer scanning works in Cheat Engine. When you have a good grasp of the user interface, you can get some hands-on experience in "Pointer Scanning" on page 18.

Pointer Chains

The chain of offsets I've just described is called a *pointer chain* and looks like this:

```
list<int> chain = {start, offset1, offset2[, ...]}
```

The first value in this pointer chain (start) is called a *memory pointer*. It's an address that starts the chain. The remaining values (offset1, offset2, and so on) make up the route to the desired value, called a *pointer path*.

This pseudocode shows how a pointer chain might be read:

```
int readPointerChain(chain) {
❶    ret = read(chain[0])
     for i = 1, chain.len - 1, 1 {
         offset = chain[i]
         ret = read(ret + offset)
     }
     return ret
}
```

This code creates the function readPointerPath(), which takes a pointer chain called chain as a parameter. The function readPointerPath() treats the pointer path in chain as a list of memory offsets from the address ret, which is initially set to the memory pointer at ❶. It then loops through these offsets, updating the value of ret to the result of read(ret + offset) on each iteration and returning ret once it's finished. This pseudocode shows what readPointerPath() looks like when the loop is unrolled:

```
list<int> chain = {0xDEADBEEF, 0xAB, 0x10, 0xCC}
value = readPointerPath(chain)
// the function call unrolls to this
ret = read(0xDEADBEEF) //chain[0]
ret = read(ret + 0xAB)
ret = read(ret + 0x10)
ret = read(ret + 0xCC)
int value = ret
```

The function ultimately calls read four times, on four different addresses—one for each element in chain.

NOTE *Many game hackers prefer to code their chain reads in place, instead of encapsulating them in functions like* readPointerPath()*.*

Pointer Scanning Basics

Pointer chains exist because every chunk of dynamically allocated memory must have a corresponding static address that the game's code can use to reference it. Game hackers can access these chunks by locating the pointer chains that reference them. Because of their multitier structure, however, pointer chains cannot be located through the linear approach that memory scanners use, so game hackers have devised new ways to find them.

From a reverse engineering perspective, you could locate and analyze the assembly code in order to deduce what pointer path it used to access the value, but doing so is very time-consuming and requires advanced tools. *Pointer scanners* solve this problem by using brute-force to recursively iterate over every possible pointer chain until they find one that resolves to the target memory address.

The Listing 1-1 pseudocode should give you a general idea of how a pointer scanner works.

```
   list<int> pointerScan(target, maxAdd, maxDepth) {
❶      for address = BASE, 0x7FFFFFFF, 4 {
           ret = rScan(address, target, maxAdd, maxDepth, 1)
           if (ret.len > 0) {
               ret.pushFront(address)
               return ret
           }
       }
       return {}
   }
   list<int> rScan(address, target, maxAdd, maxDepth, curDepth) {
❷      for offset = 0, maxAdd, 4 {
           value = read(address + offset)
❸          if (value == target)
               return list<int>(offset)
       }
❹      if (curDepth < maxDepth) {
           curDepth++
❺          for offset = 0, maxAdd, 4 {
               ret = rScan(address + offset, target, maxAdd, maxDepth, curDepth)
❻              if (ret.len > 0) {
                   ret.pushFront(offset)
❼                  return ret
               }
           }
       }
       return {}
   }
```

Listing 1-1: Pseudocode for a pointer scanner

This code creates the functions pointerScan() and rScan().

pointerScan()

The pointerScan() function is the entry point to the scan. It takes the parameters target (the dynamic memory address to find), maxAdd (the maximum value of any offset), and maxDepth (the maximum length of the pointer path). It then loops through every 4-byte aligned address ❶ in the game, calling rScan() with the parameters address (the address in the current iteration), target, maxAdd, maxDepth, and curDepth (the depth of the path, which is always 1 in this case).

rScan()

The rScan() function reads memory from every 4-byte aligned offset between 0 and maxAdd ❷, and returns if a result is equal to target ❸. If rScan() doesn't return in the first loop and the recursion is not too deep ❹, it increments curDepth and again loops over each offset ❺, calling itself for each iteration.

If a self call returns a partial pointer path ❻, rScan() will prepend the current offset to the path and return up the recursion chain ❼ until it reaches pointerScan(). When a call to rScan() from pointerScan() returns a pointer path, pointerScan() pushes the current address to the front of the path and returns it as a complete chain.

Pointer Scanning with Cheat Engine

The previous example showed the basic process of pointer scanning, but the implementation I've shown is primitive. Aside from being insanely slow to execute, it would generate countless false positives. Cheat Engine's pointer scanner uses a number of advanced interpolations to speed up the scan and make it more accurate, and in this section, I'll introduce you to the smorgasbord of available scanning options.

To initiate a pointer scan in Cheat Engine, right-click on a dynamic memory address in your cheat table and click **Pointer scan for this address**. When you initiate a pointer scan, Cheat Engine will ask you where to store the scan results as a *.ptr* file. Once you enter a location, a Pointerscanner scanoptions dialog similar to the one shown in Figure 1-4 will appear.

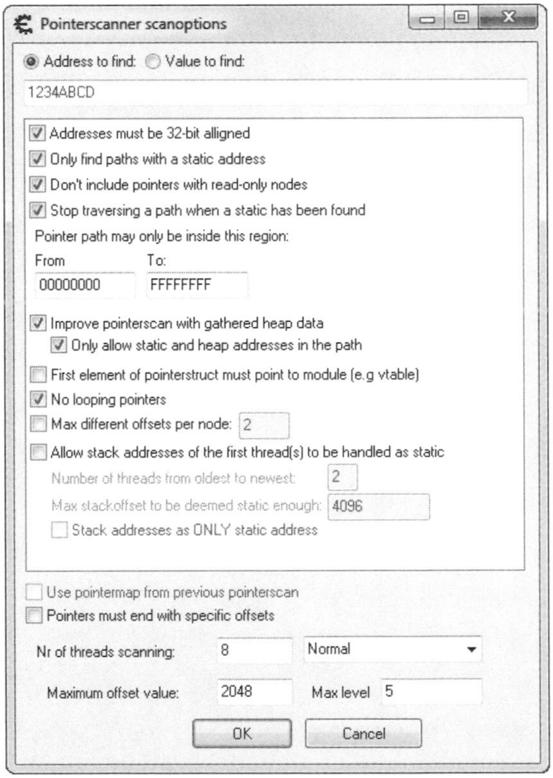

Figure 1-4: Cheat Engine Pointerscanner scanoptions dialog

The Address to find input field at the top displays your dynamic memory address. Now carefully select from among Cheat Engine's many scan options.

Key Options

Several of Cheat Engine's scan options typically retain their default values. Those options are as follows:

Addresses must be 32-bits aligned   Tells Cheat Engine to scan only addresses that are multiples of 4, which greatly increases the scan speed. As you'll learn in Chapter 4, compilers align data so that most addresses will be multiples of 4 anyway by default. You'll rarely need to disable this option.

Only find paths with a static address   Speeds up the scan by preventing Cheat Engine from searching paths with a dynamic start pointer. This option should *always* be enabled because scanning for a path starting at another dynamic address can be counterproductive.

Don't include pointers with read-only nodes   Should also always be enabled. Dynamically allocated memory that stores volatile data should never be read-only.

Stop traversing a path when a static has been found   Terminates the scan when it finds a pointer path with a static start address. This should be enabled to reduce false positives and speed up the scan.

Pointer path may only be inside this region   Can typically be left as is. The other options available to you compensate for this large range by intelligently narrowing the scope of the scan.

First element of pointerstruct must point to module   Tells Cheat Engine not to search heap chunks in which virtual function tables are not found, under the assumption that the game was coded using object orientation. While this setting can immensely speed up scans, it's highly unreliable and you should almost always leave it disabled.

No looping pointers   Invalidates any paths that point to themselves, weeding out inefficient paths but slightly slowing down the scan. This should usually be enabled.

Max level   Determines the maximum length of the pointer path. (Remember the maxDepth variable in the example code in Listing 1-1?) This should be kept around 6 or 7.

Of course, there will be times when you'll need to change these options from the settings described. For example, failing to obtain reliable results with the No looping pointers or Max level settings typically means that the value you're looking for exists in a dynamic data structure, like a linked list, binary tree, or vector. Another example is the Stop traversing a path when a static has been found option, which in rare cases can prevent you from getting reliable results.

Situational Options

Unlike the previous options, your settings for the remaining ones will depend on your situation. Here's how to determine the best configuration for each:

Improve pointerscan with gathered heap data   Allows Cheat Engine to use the heap allocation record to determine offset limits, effectively speeding up the scan by weeding out many false positives. If you run into a game using a custom memory allocator (which is becoming increasingly common), this option can actually do the exact opposite of what it's meant to do. You can leave this setting enabled in initial scans, but it should be the first to go when you're unable to find reliable paths.

Only allow static and heap addresses in the path   Invalidates all paths that can't be optimized with heap data, making this approach even more aggressive.

Max different offsets per node   Limits the number of same-value pointers the scanner checks. That is, if n different addresses point to 0x0BADF00D, this option tells Cheat Engine to consider only the first m addresses. This can be extremely helpful when you're unable to narrow down your result set. In other cases, you may want to disable it, as it will miss many valid paths.

Allow stack addresses of the first thread(s) to be handled as static   Scans the call stacks of oldest m threads in the game, considering the first n bytes in each one. This allows Cheat Engine to scan the parameters and local variables of functions in the game's call chain (the goal being to find variables used by the game's main loop). The paths found with this option can be both highly volatile and extremely useful; I use it only when I fail to find heap addresses.

Stack addresses as only static address   Takes the previous option even further by allowing only stack addresses in pointer paths.

Pointers must end with specific offsets   Can be useful if you know the offset(s) at the end of a valid path. This option will allow you to specify those offsets (starting with the last offset at the top), greatly reducing the scope of the scan.

Nr of threads scanning   Determines how many threads the scanner will use. A number equal to the number of cores in your processor often works best. A drop-down menu with options allows you to specify the priority for each thread. Idle is best if you want your scan to go very slowly, Normal is what you should use for most scans, and Time critical is useful for lengthy scans but will render your computer useless for the scan duration.

Maximum offset value   Determines the maximum value of each offset in the path. (Remember the maxAdd variable in Listing 1-1?) I typically start with a low value, increasing it only if my scan fails; 128 is a good starting value. Keep in mind that this value is mostly ignored if you're using the heap optimization options.

NOTE *What if both Only allow static and heap addresses in the path and Stack addresses as only static address are enabled? Will the scan come up empty? Seems like a fun, albeit useless, experiment.*

Once you have defined your scan options, click **OK** to start a pointer scan. When the scan completes, a results window will appear with the list of pointer chains found. This list often has thousands of results, containing both real chains and false positives.

Pointer Rescanning

The pointer scanner has a rescan feature that can help you eliminate false positives. To begin, press CTRL-R from the results window to open the Rescan pointerlist dialog, as shown in Figure 1-5.

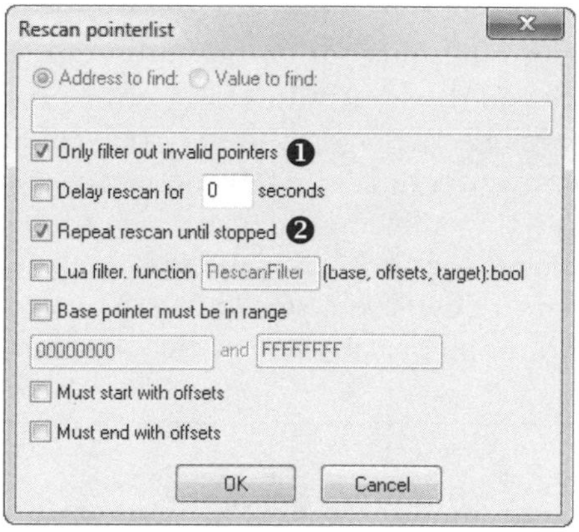

Figure 1-5: Cheat Engine Rescan pointerlist dialog

There are two main options to consider when you tell Cheat Engine to rescan:

Only filter out invalid pointers   If you check this box ❶, the rescan will discard only pointer chains that point to invalid memory, which helps if your initial result set is very large. Disable this to filter out paths that don't resolve to a specific address or value (as shown in the figure).

Repeat rescan until stopped   If you check this box ❷, the rescan will execute in a continuous loop. Ideally, you should enable this setting and let rescan run while you create a large amount of memory entropy.

For the initial rescan, enable both **Only filter out invalid pointers** and **Repeat rescan until stopped**, and then press **OK** to initiate the rescan. The rescan window will go away, and a Stop rescan loop button will appear in the results window. The result list will be constantly rescanned until you click Stop rescan loop, but spend a few minutes creating memory entropy before doing so.

In rare cases, rescanning using a rescan loop may still leave you with a large list of possible paths. When this happens, you may need to restart the game, find the address that holds your value (it may have changed!), and use the rescan feature on this address to further narrow results. In this scan, leave **Only filter out invalid pointers** unchecked and enter the *new* address in the **Address to find** field.

NOTE *If you had to close the results window, you can reopen it and load the result list by going to the main Cheat Engine window and pressing the Memory View button below the results pane. This should bring up a memory dump window. When the window appears, press CTRL-P to open the pointer scan results list. Then press CTRL-O to open the .ptr file where you saved the pointer scan.*

If your results still aren't narrow enough, try running the same scan across system restarts or even on different systems. If this still yields a large result set, each result can safely be considered static because more than one pointer chain can resolve to the same address.

Once you've narrowed down your result set, double-click on a usable pointer chain to add it to your cheat table. If you have a handful of seemingly usable chains, grab the one with the fewest offsets. If you find multiple chains with identical offsets that start with the same pointer but diverge after a certain point, your data may be stored in a dynamic data structure.

That's all there is to pointer scanning in Cheat Engine. Try it yourself!

POINTER SCANNING

Go to *https://www.nostarch.com/gamehacking/* and download *MemoryPointers .exe*. Unlike the last task, which required you to win only once, this one requires that you win 50 times in 10 seconds. Upon each win, the memory addresses for the x- and y-coordinates will change, meaning you will be able to freeze the value only if you have found a proper pointer path. Start this exercise the same way as the previous one, but once you've found the addresses, use the Pointer scan feature to locate pointer paths to them. Then, place the ball on top of the black square, freeze the value in place, and press TAB to begin the test. Just as before, the game will let you know once you've won. (Hint: Try setting the maximum level to 5 and the maximum offset value to 512. Also, play with the options to allow stack addresses, terminate the scan when a static is found, and improve the pointer scan with heap data. See which combination of options gives the best results.)

Lua Scripting Environment

Historically, bot developers rarely used Cheat Engine to update their addresses when a game released a patch because it was much easier to do so in OllyDbg. This made Cheat Engine useless to game hackers other than for initial research and development—that is, until a powerful Lua-based embedded scripting engine was implemented around Cheat Engine's robust scanning environment. While this engine was created to enable the development of simple bots within Cheat Engine, professional game hackers found they could also use it to easily write complex scripts to automatically locate addresses across different versions of a game's binary—a task that might otherwise take hours.

NOTE *You'll find more detail about the Cheat Engine Lua scripting engine on the wiki at* http://wiki.cheatengine.org/.

To start using the Lua engine, press CTRL-ALT-L from the main Cheat Engine window. Once the window opens, write your script in the text area and click **Execute script** to run it. Save a script with CTRL-S and open a saved script with CTRL-O.

The scripting engine has hundreds of functions and infinite use cases, so I'll give you just a glimpse of its abilities by breaking down two scripts. Every game is different and every game hacker writes scripts to accomplish unique goals, so these scripts are only useful for demonstrating concepts.

Searching for Assembly Patterns

This first script locates functions that compose outgoing packets and sends them to the game server. It works by searching a game's assembly code for functions that contain a certain code sequence.

```
❶ BASEADDRESS = getAddress("Game.exe")
❷ function LocatePacketCreation(packetType)
❸     for address = BASEADDRESS, (BASEADDRESS + 0x2ffffff) do
            local push = readBytes(address, 1, false)
            local type = readInteger(address + 1)
            local call = readInteger(address + 5)
❹         if (push == 0x68 and type == packetType and call == 0xE8) then
                return address
            end
        end
        return 0
    end
    FUNCTIONHEADER = { 0xCC, 0x55, 0x8B, 0xEC, 0x6A }
❺ function LocateFunctionHead(checkAddress)
        if (checkAddress == 0) then return 0 end
❻     for address = checkAddress, (checkAddress - 0x1fff), -1 do
            local match = true
            local checkheader = readBytes(address, #FUNCTIONHEADER, true)
❼         for i, v in ipairs(FUNCTIONHEADER) do
                if (v ~= checkheader[i]) then
                    match = false
                    break
                end
            end
❽         if (match) then return address + 1 end
        end
```

```
        return 0
    end
```

❾ ```
local funcAddress = LocateFunctionHead(LocatePacketCreation(0x64))
if (funcAddress ~= 0) then
    print(string.format("0x%x",funcAddress))
else
    print("Not found!")
end
```

The code begins by getting the base address of the module that Cheat Engine is attached to ❶. Once it has the base address, the function LocatePacketCreation() is defined ❷. This function loops through the first 0x2FFFFFF bytes of memory in the game ❸, searching for a sequence that represents this x86 assembler code:

```
PUSH type    ; Data is: 0x68 [4byte type]
CALL offset  ; Data is: 0xE8 [4byte offset]
```

The function checks that the type is equal to packetType, but it doesn't care what the function offset is ❹. Once this sequence is found, the function returns.

Next, the LocateFunctionHead() function is defined ❺. The function backtracks up to 0x1FFF bytes from a given address ❻, and at each address, it checks for a stub of assembler code ❼ that looks something like this:

```
INT3          ; 0xCC
PUSH EBP      ; 0x55
MOV EBP, ESP  ; 0x8B 0xEC
PUSH [-1]     ; 0x6A 0xFF
```

This stub will be present at the beginning of every function, because it's part of the function prologue that sets up the function's stack frame. Once it finds the code, the function will return the address of the stub plus 1 ❽ (the first byte, 0xCC, is padding).

To tie these steps together, the LocatePacketCreation() function is called with the packetType that I'm looking for (arbitrarily 0x64) and the resulting address is passed into the LocateFunctionHead() function ❾. This effectively locates the first function that pushes packetType into a function call and stores its address in funcAddress. This stub shows the result:

```
INT3           ; LocateFunctionHead back-tracked to here
PUSH EBP       ;    and returned this address
MOV EBP, ESP
PUSH [-1]
--snip--
PUSH [0x64]    ; LocatePacketCreation returned this address
CALL [something]
```
```

This 35-line script can automatically locate 15 different functions in under a minute.

Searching for Strings

This next Lua script scans a game's memory for text strings. It works much as the Cheat Engine's memory scanner does when you use the string value type.

```
    BASEADDRESS = getAddress("Game.exe")
❶   function findString(str)
        local len = string.len(str)
❷       local chunkSize = 4096
❸       local chunkStep = chunkSize - len
        print("Found '" .. str .. "' at:")
❹       for address = BASEADDRESS, (BASEADDRESS + 0x2ffffff), chunkStep do
            local chunk = readBytes(address, chunkSize, true)
            if (not chunk) then break end
❺           for c = 0, chunkSize-len do
❻               checkForString(address , chunk, c, str, len)
            end
        end
    end
    function checkForString(address, chunk, start, str, len)
        for i = 1, len do
            if (chunk[start+i] ~= string.byte(str, i)) then
                return false
            end
        end
❼       print(string.format("\t0x%x", address + start))
    end

❽   findString("hello")
❾   findString("world")
```

After getting the base address, the findString() function is defined ❶, which takes a string, str, as a parameter. This function loops through the game's memory ❹ in 4,096-byte-long chunks ❷. The chunks are scanned sequentially, each one starting len (the length of str) bytes before the end of the previous one ❸ to prevent missing a string that begins on one chunk and ends on another.

As findString() reads each chunk, it iterates over every byte until the overlap point in the chunk ❺, passing each subchunk into the checkForString() function ❻. If checkForString() matches the subchunk to str, it prints the address of that subchunk to the console ❼.

Lastly, to find all addresses that reference the strings "hello" and "world", the functions findString("hello") ❽ and findString("world") ❾ are called. By using this code to search for embedded debug strings and pairing it with the previous code to locate function headers, I'm able to find a large number of internal functions within a game in mere seconds.

Due to the high overhead of memory reading, optimization is extremely important when you're writing code that performs memory reads. In the previous code snippet, notice that the function findString() does not use the Lua engine's built-in readString() function. Instead, it reads big chunks of memory and searches them for the desired string. Let's break down the numbers.

A scan using readString() would try to read a string of len bytes at every possible memory address. This means it would read, at most, (0x2FFFFFF * len + len) bytes. However, findString() reads chunks of 4,096 bytes and scans them locally for matching strings. This means it would read, at most, (0x2FFFFFF + 4096 + (0x2FFFFFF / (4096 - 10)) * len) bytes. When searching for a string with a length of 10, the number of bytes that each method would read is 503,316,480 and 50,458,923, respectively.

Not only does findString() read an order of magnitude less data, it also invokes far fewer memory reads. Reading in chunks of 4,096 bytes would require a total of (0x2FFFFFF / (4096 - len)) reads. Compare that to a scan using readString(), which would need 0x2FFFFFF reads. The scan that uses findString() is a huge improvement because invoking a read is much more expensive than increasing the size of data being read. (Note that I chose 4,096 arbitrarily. I keep the chunk relatively small because reading memory can be time-consuming, and it might be wasteful to read four pages at a time just to find the string in the first.)

Closing Thoughts

By this point, you should have a basic understanding of Cheat Engine and how it works. Cheat Engine is a very important tool in your kit, and I encourage you to get some hands-on experience with it by following "Basic Memory Editing" on page 11 and "Pointer Scanning" on page 18 and playing around with it on your own.

2

DEBUGGING GAMES
WITH OLLYDBG

You can scratch the surface of what happens as a game runs with Cheat Engine, but with a good debugger, you can dig deeper until you understand the game's structure and execution flow. That makes OllyDbg essential to your game-hacking arsenal. It's packed with a myriad of powerful tools like conditional breakpoints, referenced string search, assembly pattern search, and execution tracing, making it a robust assembler-level debugger for 32-bit Windows applications.

I'll cover low-level code structure in detail in Chapter 4, but for this chapter, I assume you're at least familiar with modern code-level debuggers, such as the one packaged with Microsoft Visual Studio. OllyDbg is functionally similar to those, with one major difference: it interfaces with the assembly code of an application, working even in the absence of source code and/or debug symbols, making it ideal when you need to dig into the internals of a game. After all, game companies are rarely nice (or dumb) enough to ship their games with debug symbols!

In this chapter, I'll go over OllyDbg's user interface, show you how to use its most common debugging features, break down its expression engine, and provide some real-world examples of how you can tie it in to your game hacking endeavors. As a wrap-up, I'll teach you about some useful plug-ins and send you off with a test game designed to get you started in OllyDbg.

NOTE   *This chapter focuses on OllyDbg 1.10 and may not be entirely accurate for later versions. I use this version because, at the time of writing, the plug-in interface for OllyDbg 2 is still far less robust than the one for OllyDbg 1.*

When you feel like you have a handle on OllyDbg's interface and features, you can try it on a game yourself with "Patching an if() Statement" on page 46.

A Brief Look at OllyDbg's User Interface

Go to the OllyDbg website (*http://www.ollydbg.de/*), download and install OllyDbg, and open the program. You should see the toolbar shown in Figure 2-1 above a multiple window interface area.

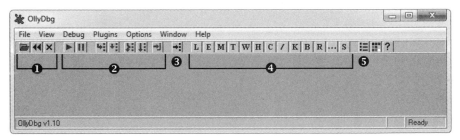

Figure 2-1: OllyDbg main window

This toolbar contains the program controls ❶, the debug buttons ❷, the Go to button ❸, the control window buttons ❹, and the Settings button ❺.

The three program controls allow you to open an executable and attach to the process it creates, restart the current process, or terminate execution of the current process, respectively. You can also complete these functions with the hotkeys F3, CTRL-F2, and ALT-F2, respectively. To attach to a process that is already running, click **File ▸ Attach**.

The debug buttons control the debugger actions. Table 2-1 describes what these buttons do, along with their hotkeys and functions. This table also lists three useful debugger actions that don't have buttons on the debug toolbar.

Table 2-1: Debug Buttons and Other Debugger Functions

Button	Hotkey	Function
Play	F9	Resumes normal execution of the process.
Pause	F12	Pauses execution of all threads within the process and brings up the CPU window at the instruction currently being executed.
Step into	F7	Single-steps to the next operation to be executed (will dive down into function calls).
Step over	F8	Steps to the next operation to be executed within current scope (will skip over function calls).
Trace into	CTRL-F11	Runs a deep trace, tracing every operation that is executed.
Trace over	CTRL-F12	Runs a passive trace that traces only operations within the current scope.
Execute until return	CTRL-F9	Executes until a return operation is hit within the current scope.
	CTRL-F7	Automatically single-steps on every operation, following execution in the disassembly window. This makes execution appear to be animated.
	CTRL-F8	Also animates execution, but steps over functions instead of stepping into them.
	ESC	Stops animation, pausing execution on the current operation.

The Go to button opens a dialog asking for a hexadecimal address. Once you enter the address, OllyDbg opens the CPU window and shows the disassembly at the specified address. When the CPU window is in focus, you can also show that information with the hotkey CTRL-G.

The control window buttons open different *control windows*, which display useful information about the process you're debugging and expose more debugging functions, like the ability to set breakpoints. OllyDbg has a total of 13 control windows, which can all be open simultaneously within the multiple window interface. Table 2-2 describes these windows, listed in the order in which they appear on the window buttons toolbar.

Table 2-2: OllyDbg's Control Windows

Window	Hotkey	Function
Log	ALT-L	Displays a list of log messages, including debug prints, thread events, debugger events, module loads, and much more.
Modules	ALT-E	Displays a list of all executable modules loaded into the process. Double-click a module to open it in the CPU window.

(continued)

Table 2-2 (continued)

Window	Hotkey	Function
Memory map	ALT-M	Displays a list of all blocks of memory allocated by the process. Double-click a block in the list to bring up a dump window of that memory block.
Threads		Displays a list of threads running in the process. For each thread in this list, the process has a structure called a *Thread Information Block (TIB)*. OllyDbg allows you to view each thread's TIB; simply right-click a thread and select Dump thread data block.
Windows		Displays a list of window handles held by the process. Right-click a window in this list to jump to or set a breakpoint on its class procedure (the function that gets called when a message is sent to the window).
Handles		Displays a list of handles held by the process. (Note that Process Explorer has a much better handle list than OllyDbg, as I will discuss in Chapter 3.)
CPU	ALT-C	Displays the main disassembler interface and controls a majority of the debugger functionality.
Patches	CTRL-P	Displays a list of any assembly code modifications you have made to modules within the process.
Call stack	ALT-K	Displays the call stack for the active thread. The window updates when the process halts.
Breakpoints	ALT-B	Displays a list of active debugger breakpoints and allows you to toggle them on and off.
References		Displays the reference list, which typically holds the search results for many different types of searches. It pops up on its own when you run a search.
Run trace		Displays a list of operations logged by a debugger trace.
Source		Displays the source code of the disassembled module if a program debug database is present.

Finally, the Settings button opens the OllyDbg settings window. Keep the default settings for now.

Now that you've had a tour of the main OllyDbg window, let's explore the CPU, Patches, and Run trace windows more closely. You'll use those windows extensively as a game hacker, and knowing your way around them is key.

OllyDbg's CPU Window

The CPU window in Figure 2-2 is where game hackers spend most of their time in OllyDbg because it is the main control window for the debugging features.

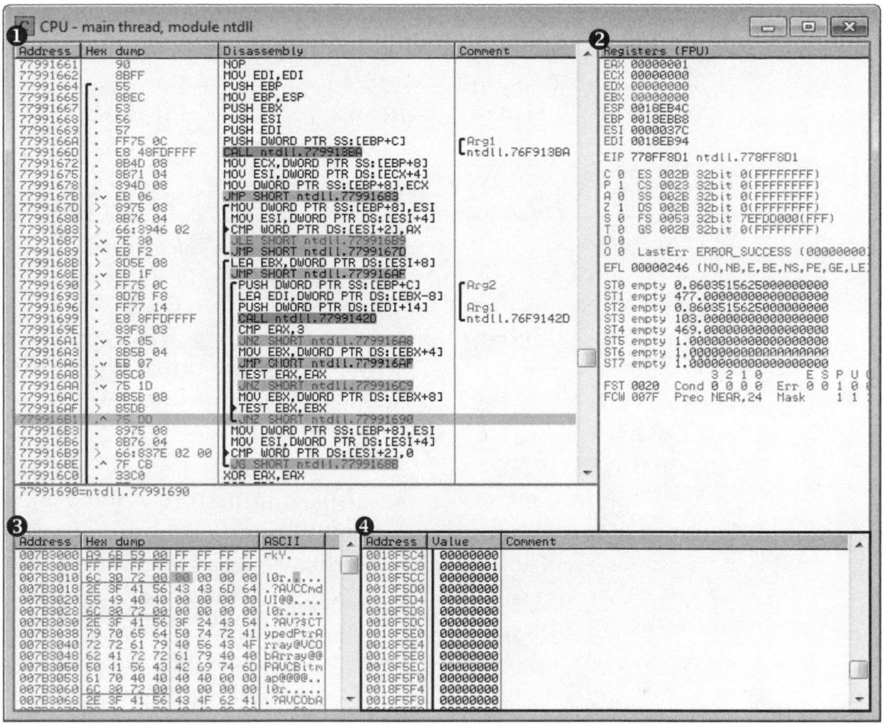

Figure 2-2: OllyDbg CPU window

This window houses four distinct control panes: the disassembler pane ❶, the registers pane ❷, the dump pane ❸, and the stack pane ❹. These four panes encapsulate OllyDbg's main debugger functions, so it's important to know them inside and out.

Viewing and Navigating a Game's Assembly Code

You'll navigate game code and control most aspects of debugging from OllyDbg's disassembler pane. This pane displays the assembly code for the current module, and its data is neatly displayed in a table composed of four distinct columns: Address, Hex dump, Disassembly, and Comment.

The Address column displays the memory addresses of each operation in the game process you're attached to. You can double-click an address in this column to toggle whether it's the *display base*. When an address is set as the display base, the Address column displays all other addresses as offsets relative to it.

The Hex dump column displays the byte code for each operation, grouping operation codes and parameters accordingly. Black braces spanning multiple lines on the left side of this column mark known function boundaries. Operations that have jumps going to them are shown with a right-facing arrow on the inside of these braces. Operations that perform jumps are shown with either up-facing or down-facing arrows, depending on the direction in which they jump, on the inside of these braces. For example, in Figure 2-2, the instruction at address 0x779916B1 (highlighted in gray) has an up-facing arrow, indicating it's an upward jump. You can think of a jump as a goto operator.

The Disassembly column displays the assembly code of each operation the game performs. So, for example, you can confirm that the instruction at 0x779916B1 in Figure 2-2 is a jump by looking at the assembly, which shows a JNZ (jump if nonzero) instruction. Black braces in this column mark the boundaries of loops. Right-facing arrows attached to these braces point to the conditional statements that control whether the loops continue or exit. The three right-facing arrows in this column in Figure 2-2 point to CMP (compare) and TEST instructions, which are used by assembly code to compare values.

The Comment column displays human-readable comments about each operation the game performs. If OllyDbg encounters known API function names, it will automatically insert a comment with the name of the function. Similarly, if it successfully detects arguments being passed to a function, it will label them (for example, Arg1, Arg2, . . . , ArgN). You can double-click in this column to add a customized comment. Black braces in this column mark the assumed boundaries of function call parameters.

NOTE   *OllyDbg infers function boundaries, jump directions, loop structures, and function parameters during code analysis, so if these columns lack boundary lines or jump arrows, just press CTRL-A to run a code analysis on the binary.*

When the disassembler pane is in focus, there are a few hotkeys you can use to quickly navigate code and control the debugger. Use F2 for Toggle breakpoint, SHIFT-F12 for Place conditional breakpoint, - (hyphen) for Go back and + (plus) for Go forward (these two work as you'd expect in a web browser), * (asterisk) for Go to EIP (which is the execution pointer in the x86 architecture), CTRL-- (hyphen) for Go to previous function, and CTRL-+ for Go to next function.

The disassembler can also populate the References window with different types of search results. When you want to change the References window's contents, right-click in the disassembler pane, mouse over the Search for menu to expand it, and select one of the following options:

All intermodular calls   Searches for all calls to functions in remote modules. This can, for example, allow you to see everywhere that a game calls Sleep(), PeekMessage(), or any other Windows API function, enabling you to inspect or set breakpoints on the calls.

All commands   Searches for all occurrences of a given operation written in assembly, where the added operators CONST and R32 will match a constant value or a register value, respectively. One use for this option might be searching for commands like MOV [0xDEADBEEF], CONST;

MOV [0xDEADBEEF], R32; and MOV [0xDEADBEEF], [R32+CONST] to list all operations that modify memory at the address 0xDEADBEEF, which could be anything, including the address of your player's health.

All sequences   Searches for all occurrences of a given sequence of
operations. This is similar to the previous options, but it allows you to
specify multiple commands.

All constants   Searches for all instances of a given hexadecimal constant. For instance, if you enter the address of your character's health,
this will list all of the commands that directly access it.

All switches   Searches for all switch-case blocks.

All referenced text strings   Searches for all strings referenced in code.
You can use this option to search through all referenced strings and see
what code accesses them, which can be useful for correlating in-game
text displays with the code that displays them. This option is also very
useful for locating any debug assertion or logging strings, which can be
a tremendous help in determining the purpose of code parts.

The disassembler can also populate the Names window with all labels
in the current module (CTRL-N) or all known labels in all modules (Search
for ▸Name in all modules). Known API functions will be automatically
labeled with their names, and you can add a label to a command by high-
lighting it, pressing SHIFT-; and entering the label when prompted. When
a labeled command is referenced in code, the label will be shown in place of
the address. One way to use this feature is to name functions that you've
analyzed (just set a label on the first command in a function) so you can
see their names when other functions call them.

Viewing and Editing Register Contents

The registers pane displays the contents of the eight processor registers, all
eight flag bits, the six segment registers, the last Windows error code, and
EIP. Underneath these values, this pane can display either *Floating-Point
Unit (FPU)* registers or debug registers; click on the pane's header to change
which registers are displayed. The values in this pane are populated only if
you freeze your process. Values that are displayed in red have been changed
since the previous pause. Double-click on values in this pane to edit them.

Viewing and Searching a Game's Memory

The dump pane displays a dump of the memory at a specific address. To
jump to an address and display the memory contents, press CTRL-G and
enter the address in the box that appears. You can also jump to the address
of an entry in the other CPU window panes by right-clicking on the Address
column and selecting Follow in dump.

While there are always three columns in the dump pane, the only one
you should always see is the Address column, which behaves much like its
cousin within the disassembler pane. The data display type you choose

determines the other two columns shown. Right-click the dump pane to change the display type; for the one shown in Figure 2-2, you'd right-click and select Hex ▸ Hex/ASCII (8 bytes).

You can set a memory breakpoint on an address shown in the dump pane by right-clicking that address and expanding the Breakpoint submenu. Select **Memory ▸ On access** from this menu to break on any code that uses the address at all, or select **Memory ▸ On write** to break only on code that writes to that space in memory. To remove a memory breakpoint, select **Remove memory breakpoint** in the same menu; this option appears only when the address you right-click has a breakpoint.

With one or more values selected in the dump, you can press CTRL-R to search the current module's code for references to addresses of the selected values; results of this search appear in the References window. You can also search for values in this pane using CTRL-B for binary strings and CTRL-N for labels. After you initiate a search, press CTRL-L to jump to the next match. CTRL-E allows you to edit any values you have selected.

NOTE *The dump windows that you can open from the Memory window work in the same way as the dump pane.*

Viewing a Game's Call Stack

The final CPU pane is the stack pane, and as the name suggests, it shows the call stack. Like the dump and disassembler panes, the stack pane has an Address column. The stack pane also has a Value column, which shows the stack as an array of 32-bit integers, and a Comment column, which shows return addresses, known function names, and other informative labels. The stack pane supports all the same hotkeys as the dump pane, with the exception of CTRL-N.

MULTICLIENT PATCHING

One type of hack, called a *multiclient patch*, overwrites the single-instance limitation code within a game's binary with no-operation code, allowing the user to run multiple game clients, even when doing so is normally forbidden. Because the code that performs instance limitation must be executed very early after a game client is launched, it can be nearly impossible for a bot to inject its patch on time. The easiest workaround for this is to make multiclient patches persist by applying them within OllyDbg and saving them directly to the game binary.

Creating Code Patches

OllyDbg's *code patches* let you make assembly code modifications for a game you want to hack, removing the need to engineer a tool tailored to that specific game. This makes prototyping *control flow hacks*—which manipulate game behavior through a mix of game design flaws, x86 assembly protocols, and common binary constructs—much easier.

Game hackers typically include perfected patches as optional features in a bot's tool suite, but in some cases, making those features persistent is actually more convenient for your end user. Luckily, OllyDbg patches provide the complete functionality you need to design, test, and permanently save code modifications to an executable binary using only OllyDbg.

To place a patch, navigate to the line of assembly code you want to patch in the CPU window, double-click the instruction you wish to modify, place a new assembly instruction in the pop-up prompt, and click **Assemble**, as shown in Figure 2-3.

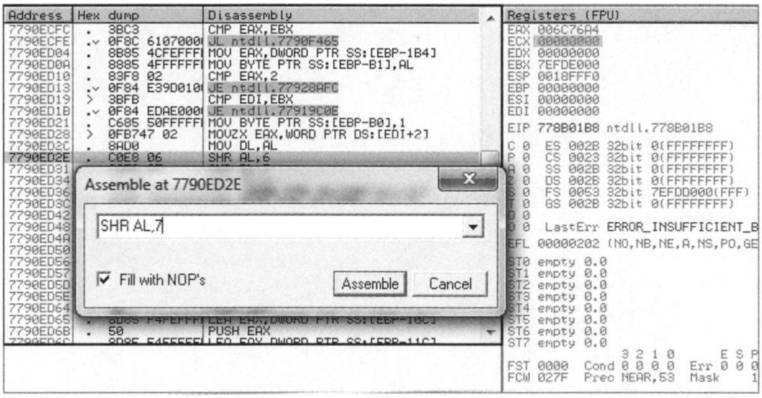

Figure 2-3: Placing a patch with OllyDbg

Always pay attention to the size of your patch—you can't just resize and move around assembled code however you'd like. Patches *larger* than the code you intend to replace will overflow into subsequent operations, potentially removing critical functionality. Patches *smaller* than the operations you intend to replace are safe, as long as Fill with NOPs is checked. This option fills any abandoned bytes with *no-operation (NOP)* commands, which are single-byte operations that do nothing when executed.

All patches you place are listed, along with the address, size, state, old code, new code, and comment, in the Patches window. Select a patch in this list to access a small but powerful set of hotkeys, shown in Table 2-3.

Table 2-3: Patches Window Hotkeys

Operator	Function
ENTER	Jumps to the patch in the disassembler.
spacebar	Toggles the patch on or off.
F2	Places a breakpoint on the patch.
SHIFT-F2	Places a conditional breakpoint on the patch.
SHIFT-F4	Places a conditional log breakpoint on the patch.
DEL	Removes the patch entry from the list only.

In OllyDbg, you can also save your patches directly to the binary. First, right-click in the disassembler and click **Copy to executable ▶ All modifications**. If you want to copy only certain patches, highlight them in the disassembly pane and press **Copy to executable ▶ Selection** instead.

DETERMINING PATCH SIZE

There are a few ways to determine whether your patch will be a different size than the original code. For example, in Figure 2-3, you can see the command at 0x7790ED2E being changed from SHR AL, 6 to SHR AL, 7. If you look at the bytes to the left of the command, you see 3 bytes that represent the memory of the command. This means our new command must either be 3 bytes or padded with NOPs if it's less than 3 bytes. Furthermore, these bytes are arranged in two columns. The first column contains 0xC0 and 0x08, which represent the command SHR and the first operand, AL. The second column contains 0x06, which represents the original operand. Because the second column shows a single byte, any replacement operand must also be 1 byte (between 0x00 and 0xFF). If this column had shown 0x00000006 instead, a replacement operand could be up to 4 bytes in length.

Typical code patches will either use all NOPs to completely remove a command (by leaving the box empty and letting it fill the entire command with NOPs) or just replace a single operand, so this method of checking patch size is almost always effective.

Tracing Through Assembly Code

When you run a trace on any program, OllyDbg single-steps over every executed operation and stores data about each one. When the trace is complete, the logged data is displayed in the Run trace window, shown in Figure 2-4.

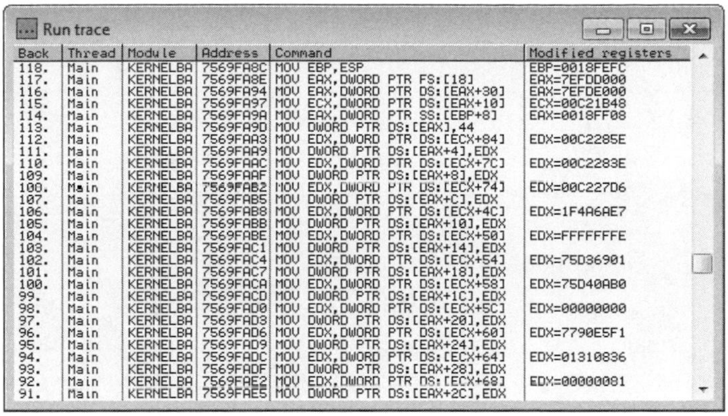

Figure 2-4: The Run trace window

The Run trace window is organized into the following six columns:

Back   The number of operations logged between an operation and the current execution state

Thread   The thread that executed the operation

Module   The module where the operation resides

Address   The address of the operation

Command   The operation that was executed

Modified registers   The registers changed by the operation and their new values

When hacking games, I find OllyDbg's trace feature very effective at helping me find pointer paths to dynamic memory when Cheat Engine scans prove inconclusive. This works because you can follow the log in the Run trace window backward from the point when the memory is used to the point where it is resolved from a static address.

This potent feature's usefulness is limited only by the creativity of the hacker using it. Though I typically use it only to find pointer paths, I've come across a few other situations where it has proven invaluable. The anecdotes in "OllyDbg Expressions in Action" on page 36 will help to illuminate the functionality and power of tracing.

OllyDbg's Expression Engine

OllyDbg is home to a custom expression engine that can compile and evaluate advanced expressions with a simple syntax. The expression engine is surprisingly powerful and, when utilized properly, can be the difference between an average OllyDbg user and an OllyDbg wizard. You can use this engine to specify expressions for many features, such as conditional breakpoints, conditional traces, and the command line plug-in. This section introduces the expression engine and the options it provides.

Parts of this section are based on the official expressions documentation (http://www.ollydbg.de/Help/i_Expressions.htm). *I have found, however, that a few of the components defined in the documentation don't seem to work, at least not in OllyDbg v1.10. Two examples are the* INT *and* ASCII *data types, which must be substituted with the aliases* LONG *and* STRING. *For this reason, here I include only components that I've personally tested and fully understand.*

Using Expressions in Breakpoints

When a *conditional breakpoint* is toggled on, OllyDbg prompts you to enter an expression for the condition; this is where most expressions are used. When that breakpoint is executed, OllyDbg silently pauses execution and evaluates the expression. If the result of the evaluation is nonzero, execution remains paused and you will see the breakpoint get triggered. But if the result of the evaluation is 0, OllyDbg silently resumes execution as if nothing happened.

With the huge number of executions that happen within a game every second, you'll often find that a piece of code is executed in far too many contexts for a breakpoint to be an effective way of getting the data you are looking for. A conditional breakpoint paired with a good understanding of the code surrounding it is a foolproof way to avoid these situations.

Using Operators in the Expression Engine

For numeric data types, OllyDbg expressions support general C-style operators, as seen in Table 2-4. While there is no clear documentation on the operator precedence, OllyDbg seems to follow C-style precedence and can use parenthesized scoping.

Table 2-4: OllyDbg Numeric Operators

Operator	Function
a == b	Returns 1 if a is equal to b, else returns 0.
a != b	Returns 1 if a is not equal to b, else returns 0.
a > b	Returns 1 if a is greater than b, else returns 0.
a < b	Returns 1 if a is less than b, else returns 0.
a >= b	Returns 1 if a is greater than or equal to b, else returns 0.
a <= b	Returns 1 if a is less than or equal to b, else returns 0.
a && b	Returns 1 if a and b are both nonzero, else returns 0.
a || b	Returns 1 if either a or b are nonzero, else returns 0.
a ^ b	Returns the result of XOR(a, b).
a % b	Returns the result of MODULUS(a, b).
a & b	Return the result of AND(a, b).
a | b	Return the result of OR(a, b).
a << b	Returns the result of a shifted b bits to the left.
a >> b	Returns the result of a shifted b bits to the right.

Operator	Function
a + b	Returns the sum of a plus b.
a - b	Returns the difference of a minus b.
a / b	Returns the quotient of a divided by b.
a * b	Returns the product of a times b.
+a	Returns the signed representation of a.
-a	Returns a*-1.
!a	Returns 1 if a is 0, else returns 0.

For strings, on the other hand, the only available operators are == and !=, which both adhere to the following set of rules:

- String comparisons are case insensitive.
- If only one of the operands is a string literal, the comparison will terminate after it reaches the length of the literal. As a result, the expression [STRING EAX]=="ABC123", where EAX is a pointer to the string ABC123XYZ, will evaluate to 1 instead of 0.
- If no type is specified for an operand in a string comparison and the other operand is a string literal (for example, "MyString"!=EAX), the comparison will first assume the nonliteral operand is an ASCII string, and, if that compare would return 0, it will try a second compare assuming the operand is a Unicode string.

Of course, operators aren't much use without operands. Let's look at some of the data you can evaluate in expressions.

Working with Basic Expression Elements

Expressions are able to evaluate many different elements, including:

CPU registers   EAX, EBX, ECX, EDX, ESP, EBP, ESI, and EDI. You can also use the 1-byte and 2-byte registers (for example, AL for the low byte and AX for the low word of EAX). EIP can also be used.

Segment registers   CS, DS, ES, SS, FS, and GS.

FPU registers   ST0, ST1, ST2, ST3, ST4, ST5, ST6, and ST7.

Simple labels   Can be API function names, such as GetModuleHandle, or user-defined labels.

Windows constants   Such as ERROR_SUCCESS.

Integers   Are written in hexadecimal format or decimal format if followed by a trailing decimal point (for example, FFFF or 65535.).

Floating-point numbers   Allow exponents in decimal format (for example, 654.123e-5).

String literals   Are wrapped in quotation marks (for example, "my string").

The expressions engine looks for these elements in the order they're listed here. For example, if you have a label that matches the name of a Windows constant, the engine uses the address of the label instead of the constant's value. But if you have a label named after a register, such as EAX, the engine uses the register value, not the label value.

Accessing Memory Contents with Expressions

OllyDbg expressions are also powerful enough to incorporate memory reading, which you can do by wrapping a memory address, or an expression that evaluates to one, in square brackets. For example, [EAX+C] and [401000] represent the contents at the addresses EAX+C and 401000. To read the memory as a type other than DWORD, you can specify the desired type either before the brackets, as in BYTE [EAX], or as the first token within them, as in [STRING ESP+C]. Supported types are listed in Table 2-5.

Table 2-5: OllyDbg Data Types

Data type	Interpretation
BYTE	8-bit integer (unsigned)
CHAR	8-bit integer (signed)
WORD	16-bit integer (unsigned)
SHORT	16-bit integer (signed)
DWORD	32-bit integer (unsigned)
LONG	32-bit integer (signed)
FLOAT	32-bit floating-point number
DOUBLE	64-bit floating-point number
STRING	Pointer to an ASCII string (null-terminated)
UNICODE	Pointer to a Unicode string (null-terminated)

Plugging memory contents directly into your OllyDbg expressions is incredibly useful in game hacking, in part because you can tell the debugger to check a character's health, name, gold, and so on in memory before breaking. You'll see an example of this in "Pausing Execution When a Specific Player's Name Is Printed" on page 37.

OllyDbg Expressions in Action

Expressions in OllyDbg use a syntax similar to that of most programming languages; you can even combine multiple expressions and nest one expression within another. Game hackers (really, all hackers) commonly use them to create conditional breakpoints, as I described in "Using Expressions in Breakpoints" on page 34, but you can use them in many different places in OllyDbg. For instance, OllyDbg's command line plug-in can evaluate expressions in place and display their results, allowing you to easily read arbitrary memory, inspect values that are being calculated by assembly code, or quickly get the results of mathematical equations. Furthermore, hackers can even create intelligent, position-agnostic breakpoints by coupling expressions with the trace feature.

In this section, I'll share some anecdotes where the expression engine has come in handy during my work. I will explain my thought process, walk through my entire debugging session, and break each expression down into its component parts so you can see some ways to use OllyDbg expressions in game hacking.

These examples contain some assembly code, but if you don't have much experience with assembly, don't worry. Just ignore the fine details and know that values like ECX, EAX, and ESP are process registers like the ones discussed in "Viewing and Editing Register Contents" on page 29. From there, I'll explain everything else.

If you get confused about an operator, element, or data type in an expression as I walk through these anecdotes, just refer to "OllyDbg's Expression Engine" on page 33.

Pausing Execution When a Specific Player's Name Is Printed

During one particular debugging session, I needed to figure out exactly what was happening when a game was drawing the names of players on screen. Specifically, I needed to invoke a breakpoint before the game drew the name "Player 1," ignoring all other names that were drawn.

Figuring Out Where to Pause

As a starting point, I used Cheat Engine to find the address of Player 1's name in memory. Once I had the address, I used OllyDbg to set a memory breakpoint on the first byte of the string. Every time this breakpoint got hit, I quickly inspected the assembly code to determine how it was using Player 1's name. Eventually, I found the name being accessed directly above a call to a function that I had previously given the name printText(). I had found the code that was drawing the name.

I removed my memory breakpoint and replaced it with a code breakpoint on the call to printText(). There was a problem, however: because the call to printText() was inside a loop that iterated over every player in the game, my new breakpoint was getting hit every time a name was drawn—and that was much too often. I needed to fix it to hit only on a specific player.

Inspecting the assembly code at my previous memory breakpoint told me that each player's name was accessed using the following assembly code:

```
PUSH DWORD PTR DS:[EAX+ECX*90+50]
```

The EAX register contained the address of an array of player data; I'll call it playerStruct. The size of playerStruct was 0x90 bytes, the ECX register contained the iteration index (the famous variable i), and each player's name was stored 0x50 bytes after the start of its respective playerStruct. This meant that this PUSH instruction essentially put EAX[ECX].name (the name of the player at index i) on the stack to be passed as an argument to the printText() function call. The loop, then, broke down to something like the following psuedocode:

```
playerStruct EAX[MAX_PLAYERS]; // this is filled elsewhere
for (int ❶ECX = 0; ECX < MAX_PLAYERS; ECX++) {
    char* name = ❷EAX[ECX].name;
    breakpoint(); // my code breakpoint was basically right here
    printText(name);
}
```

Purely through analysis, I determined that the playerStruct() function contained data for all players, and the loop iterated over the total number of players (counting up with ECX ❶), fetched the character name ❷ for each index, and printed the name.

Crafting the Conditional Breakpoint

Knowing that, to pause execution only when printing "Player 1" all I had to do was check the current player name before executing my breakpoint. In pseudocode, the new breakpoint would look like this:

```
if (EAX[ECX].name == "Player 1") breakpoint();
```

Once I figured out the form of my new breakpoint, I needed to access EAX[ECX].name from within the loop. That's where OllyDbg's expression engine came in: I could achieve my goal by making slight modifications to the expression that the assembly code used, leaving me with this expression:

```
[STRING EAX + ECX*0x90 + 0x50] == "Player 1"
```

I removed the code breakpoint on printText() and replaced it with a conditional breakpoint that used this expression, which told OllyDbg to break only if the string value stored at EAX + ECX*0x90 + 0x50 matched Player 1's name. This breakpoint hit only when "Player 1" was being drawn, allowing me to continue my analysis.

The amount of work it took to engineer this breakpoint might seem extensive, but with practice, the entire process becomes as intuitive as writing code. Experienced hackers can do this in a matter of seconds.

In practice, this breakpoint enabled me to inspect certain values in the playerStruct() function for "Player 1" as soon as he appeared on screen. Doing it this way was important, as the states of these values were relevant to my analysis only in the first few frames after the player entered the screen. Creatively using breakpoints like this can enable you to analyze all sorts of complex game behavior.

Pausing Execution When Your Character's Health Drops

During another debugging session, I needed to find the first function called after my character's health dropped below the maximum. I knew two ways to approach this problem:

- Find every piece of code that accesses the health value and place a conditional breakpoint that checks the health on each one. Then, once one of these breakpoints is hit, single-step through the code until the next function call.
- Use OllyDbg's trace function to create a dynamic breakpoint that can stop exactly where I need.

The first method required more setup and was not easily repeatable, mostly due to the sheer number of breakpoints needed and the fact that I'd have to single-step by hand. In contrast, the latter method had a quick setup, and since it did everything automatically, it was easily repeatable. Though using the trace function would slow the game down considerably (every single operation was captured by the trace), I chose the latter method.

Writing an Expression to Check Health

Once again, I started by using Cheat Engine to find the address that stored my health. Using the method described in "Cheat Engine's Memory Scanner" on page 5, I determined the address to be 0x40A000.

Next, I needed an expression that told OllyDbg to return 1 when my health was below maximum and return 0 otherwise. Knowing that my health was stored at 0x40A000 and that the maximum value was 500, I initially devised this expression:

```
[0x40A000] < 500.
```

This expression would invoke a break when my health was below 500 (remember, decimal numbers must be suffixed with a period in the expression engine), but instead of waiting for a function to be called, the break would happen immediately. To ensure that it waited until a function was called, I appended another expression with the && operator:

```
[0x40A000] < 500. && [❶BYTE EIP] == 0xE8
```

On x86 processors, the EIP register stores the address of the operation being executed, so I decided to check the first byte at EIP ❶ to see if it was equal to 0xE8. This value tells the processor to execute a *near function call*, which is the type of call I was looking for.

Before starting my trace, I had to do one last thing. Because the trace feature repeatedly single-steps (Trace into uses step into and Trace over uses step over, as described in "A Brief Look at OllyDbg's User Interface" on page 24), I needed to start the trace at a location scoped at or above the level of any code that could possibly update the health value.

Figuring Out Where to Start the Trace

To find a good location, I opened the game's main module in OllyDbg's CPU window, right-clicked in the disassembler pane, and selected Search for ▸All intermodular calls. The References window popped up and displayed a list of external API functions that were called by the game. Nearly all gaming software polls for new messages using the Windows USER32.PeekMessage() function, so I sorted the list using the Destination column and typed PEEK (you can search the list by simply typing a name with the window in focus) to locate the first call to USER32.PeekMessage().

Thanks to the Destination sorting, every call to this function was listed in a contiguous chunk following the first, as shown in Figure 2-5. I set a breakpoint on each by selecting it and pressing F2.

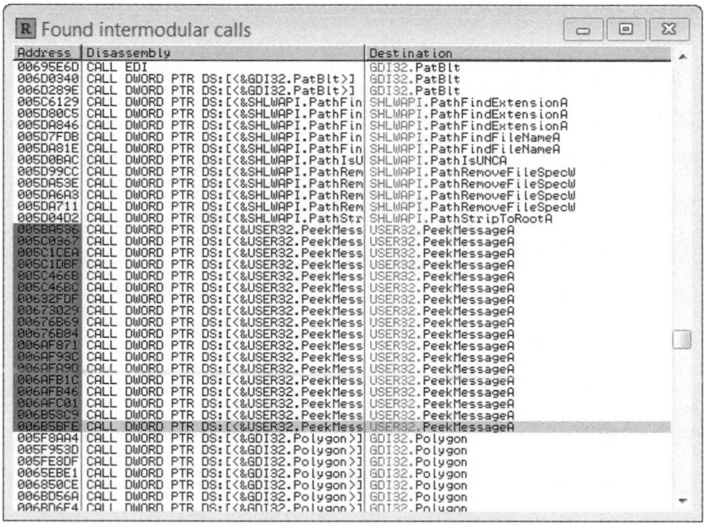

Figure 2-5: OllyDbg's Found intermodular calls window

Though there were around a dozen calls to USER32.PeekMessage(), only two of them were setting off my breakpoints. Even better, the active calls were beside one another in an unconditional loop. At the bottom of this loop were a number of internal function calls. This looked exactly like a main game loop.

Activating the Trace

To finally set my trace, I removed all of my previous breakpoints and placed one at the top of the suspected main loop. I removed the breakpoint as soon as it was hit. I then pressed CTRL-T from the CPU window, which brought up a dialog called Condition to pause run trace, shown in Figure 2-6. Within this new dialog, I enabled the Condition is TRUE option, placed my expression in the box beside it, and pressed OK. Then, I went back to the CPU window and pressed CTRL-F11 to begin a Trace Into session.

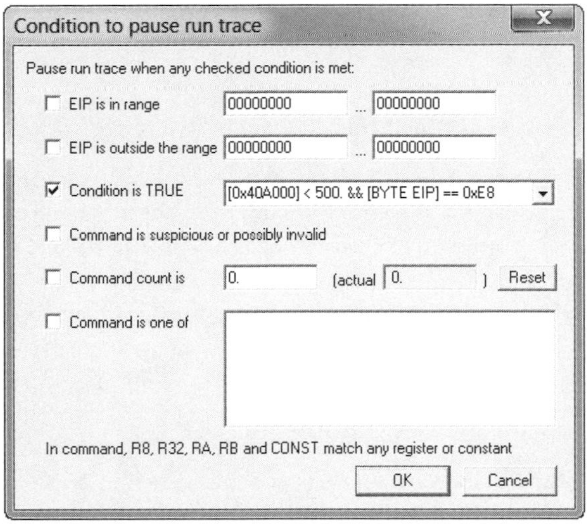

Figure 2-6: Condition to pause run trace dialog

Once the trace began, the game ran so slowly it was nearly unplayable. To decrease my test character's health, I opened a second instance of the game, logged into a different character, and attacked my test character. When the execution of the trace caught up to real time, OllyDbg saw my health change and triggered the breakpoint on the following function call—just as expected.

In this game, the main pieces of code that would modify the health value were directly invoked from the network code. Using this trace, I was able to find the function that the network module called directly after a network packet told the game to change the player's health. Here's the psuedocode of what the game was doing:

```
void network::check() {
    while (this->hasPacket()) {
        packet = this->getPacket();
        if (packet.type == UPDATE_HEALTH) {
            oldHealth = player->health;
            player->health = packet.getInteger();
❶           observe(HEALTH_CHANGE, oldHealth, player->health);
        }
    }
}
```

I knew the game had code that needed to execute only when the player's health was changed, and I needed to add code that could also respond to such changes. Without knowing the overall code structure, I guessed that the health-dependent code would be executed from some function call directly after health was updated. My trace conditional breakpoint confirmed this hunch, as it broke directly on the observe() function ❶. From there, I was able to place a *hook* on the function (*hooking*, a way to intercept function calls, is described in "Hooking to Redirect Game Execution" on page 153) and execute my own code when the player's health changed.

OllyDbg Plug-ins for Game Hackers

OllyDbg's highly versatile plug-in system is perhaps one of its most powerful features. Experienced game hackers often configure their OllyDbg environments with dozens of useful plug-ins, both publicly available and custom-made.

You can download popular plug-ins from the OpenRCE (*http://www.openrce.org/downloads/browse/OllyDbg_Plugins*) and tuts4you (*http://www.tuts4you.com/download.php?list.9/*) plug-in repositories. Installing them is easy: just unzip the plug-in files and place them inside OllyDbg's installation folder.

Once installed, some plug-ins can be accessed from the OllyDbg's Plugin menu item. Other plug-ins, however, might be found only in specific places throughout the OllyDbg interface.

You can find hundreds of potent plug-ins using these online repositories, but you should be careful when constructing your arsenal. Working in an environment bloated by unused plug-ins can actually impede productivity. In this section, I've carefully selected four plug-ins that I believe are not only integral to a game hacker's toolkit but also noninvasive to the environment.

Copying Assembly Code with Asm2Clipboard

Asm2Clipboard is a minimalistic plug-in from the OpenRCE repository that allows you to copy chunks of assembly code from the disassembler pane to the clipboard. This can be useful for updating address offsets and devising code caves, two game-hacking essentials I cover deeply in Chapters 5 and 7.

With Asm2Clipboard installed, you can highlight a block of assembly code in the disassembler, right-click the highlighted code, expand the Asm2Clipboard submenu, and select either Copy fixed Asm code to clipboard or Copy Asm code to clipboard. The latter prepends the code address of each instruction as a comment, while the former copies only the pure code.

Adding Cheat Engine to OllyDbg with Cheat Utility

The Cheat Utility plug-in from tuts4you provides a highly slimmed-down version of Cheat Engine within OllyDbg. While Cheat Utility only allows you to do exact-value scans with a very limited number of data types, it can make simple scans much easier when you don't need the full functionality of Cheat Engine to find what you're looking for. After installing Cheat Utility, to open its interface (shown in Figure 2-7), select **Plugins ▸ Cheat utility ▸ Start**.

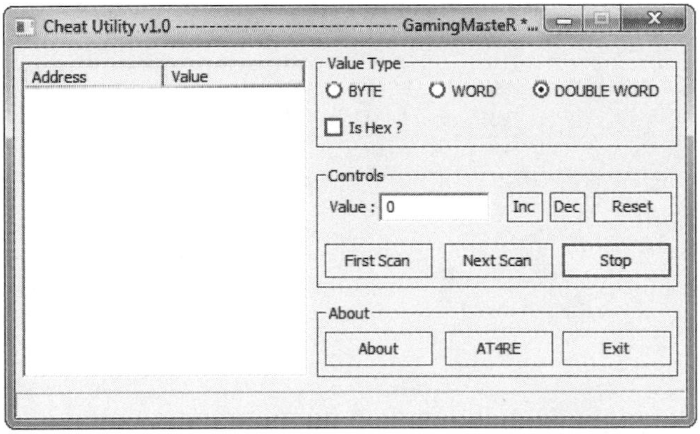

Figure 2-7: Cheat Utility interface

Cheat Utility's user interface and operation mimic Cheat Engine closely, so review Chapter 1 if you need a refresher.

NOTE *Games Invader, an updated version of Cheat Utility also from tuts4you, was created to provide more functionality. I've found it buggy, however, and I prefer Cheat Utility since I can always use Cheat Engine for advanced scans.*

Controlling OllyDbg Through the Command Line

The command line plug-in enables you to control OllyDbg through a small command line interface. To access the plug-in, either press ALT-F1 or select Plugins ▸ Command line ▸ Command line. You should then see a window, shown in Figure 2-8, which acts as the command line interface.

Figure 2-8: Command line interface

To execute a command, type it into the input box ❶ and press ENTER. You will see a session-level command history in the center list ❷, and the bottom label displays the command's return value ❸ (if any).

Though there are many commands available, I find a majority of them useless. I primarily use this tool as a way to test that expressions are parsing as expected and as a handy calculator, but there are a few additional use cases that are also worth mentioning. I've described these in Table 2-6.

Table 2-6: Command Line Plug-in Commands

Command	Function
BC identifier	Removes any breakpoints present on identifier, which can be a code address or API function name.
BP identifier [,condition]	Places a debugger breakpoint on identifier, which can be a code address or API function name. When identifier is an API function name, the breakpoint will be placed on the function entry point. The condition parameter is an optional expression that, if present, will be set as the breakpoint condition.
BPX label	Places a debugger breakpoint on every instance of label within the module currently being disassembled. This label will typically be an API function name.
CALC expression ? expression	Evaluates expression and displays the result.
HD address	Removes any hardware breakpoints present on address.
HE address	Places a hardware on-execute breakpoint on address.
HR address	Places a hardware on-access breakpoint on address. Only four hardware breakpoints can exist at a time.
HW address	Places a hardware on-write breakpoint on address.
MD	Removes any existing memory breakpoint, if present.
MR address1, address2	Places a memory on-access breakpoint starting at address1 and spanning until address2. Will replace any existing memory breakpoint.
MW address1, address2	Places a memory on-write breakpoint starting at address1 and spanning until address2. Will replace any existing memory breakpoint.
WATCH expression W expression	Opens the Watches window and adds expression to the watch list. Expressions in this list will be reevaluated every time the process receives a message and the evaluation results will be displayed beside them.

The command line plug-in was made by the OllyDbg developer and should come preinstalled with OllyDbg.

Visualizing Control Flow with OllyFlow

OllyFlow, which can be found in the OpenRCE plug-in directory, is a purely visual plug-in that can generate code graphs like the one in Figure 2-9 and display them using Wingraph32.

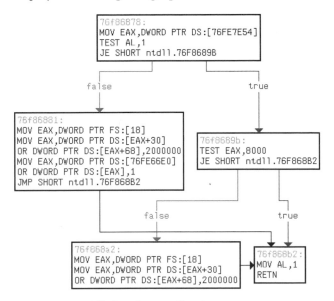

Figure 2-9: An OllyFlow function flowchart

Wingraph32 is not provided with OllyFlow, but it is available with the free version of IDA here: https://www.hex-rays.com/products/ida/. *Download it and drop the .exe in your OllyDbg installation folder.*

Though not interactive, these graphs allow you to easily identify constructs such as loops and nested if() statements in game code, which can be paramount in control flow analysis. With OllyFlow installed, you can generate a graph by going to Plugins ▶ OllyFlow (alternatively, right-click in the disassembler pane and expand the OllyFlow graph submenu) and selecting one of the following options:

Generate function flowchart Generates a graph of the function currently in scope, breaking apart different code blocks and showing jump paths. Figure 2-9 shows a function flowchart. Without a doubt, this is OllyFlow's most useful feature.

Generate xrefs from graph Generates a graph of all functions called by the function that is currently in scope.

Generate xrefs to graph Generates a graph of all functions that call the function currently in scope.

Generate call stack graph   Generates a graph of the assumed call path from the process entry point to the function currently in scope.

Generate module graph   Theoretically generates a complete graph of all function calls in the entire module, but rarely actually works.

To get an idea of the usefulness of OllyFlow, take a look at the graph in Figure 2-9 and compare it to the relatively simple assembly function that generated it:

```
76f86878:
❶    MOV EAX,DWORD PTR DS:[76FE7E54]
     TEST AL,1
     JE ntdll.76F8689B
76f86881:
❷    MOV EAX,DWORD PTR FS:[18]
     MOV EAX,DWORD PTR DS:[EAX+30]
     OR DWORD PTR DS:[EAX+68],2000000
     MOV EAX,DWORD PTR DS:[76FE66E0]
     OR DWORD PTR DS:[EAX],1
     JMP ntdll.76F868B2
76f8689b:
❸    TEST EAX,8000
     JE ntdll.76F868B2
76f868a2:
❹    MOV EAX,DWORD PTR FS:[18]
     MOV EAX,DWORD PTR DS:[EAX+30]
     OR DWORD PTR DS:[EAX+68],2000000
76f868b2:
❺    MOV AL,1
     RETN
```

There are five boxes in Figure 2-9, and they map to the five pieces of this function. The function starts with ❶, and it falls through to ❷ if the branch fails or jumps to ❸ if it succeeds. After ❷ executes, it jumps directly to piece ❺, which then returns out of the function. After ❸ executes, it either falls through to ❹ or branches to ❺ to return directly. After ❹ executes, it unconditionally falls through to ❺. What this function does is irrelevant to understanding OllyFlow; for now, just focus on seeing how the code maps to the graph.

PATCHING AN IF() STATEMENT

If you think you're ready to get your hands dirty with OllyDbg, keep reading. Go to *https://www.nostarch.com/gamehacking/*, download the book's resource files, grab *BasicDebugging.exe*, and execute it. At first glance, you'll see that it looks like the classic game Pong. In this version of Pong, the ball is invisible to you when it is on your opponent's screen. Your task is to disable this feature so that you can always see the ball. To make it easier for you, I've made the game autonomous. You don't have to play, only hack.

To start, attach OllyDbg to the game. Then focus the CPU window on the main module (find the .exe in the module list and double-click it) and use the Referenced text strings feature to locate the string that is displayed when the ball is hidden. Next, double-click the string to bring it up in the code and analyze the surrounding code until you find the if() statement that determines whether to hide the ball. Lastly, using the code-patching feature, patch the if() statement so the ball is always drawn. As an added bonus, you might try using OllyFlow to graph this function so you can get a better understanding of what exactly it is doing. (Hint: The if() statement checks whether the ball's x-coordinate is less than 0x140. If so, it jumps to code that draws the ball. If not, it draws the scene without the ball. If you can change 0x140 to, say, 0xFFFF, the ball will never get hidden.)

Closing Thoughts

OllyDbg is a much more complex beast than Cheat Engine, but you'll learn best by using it, so dive in and get your hands dirty! You can start by pairing the controls taught in this chapter with your debugging skills and going to work on some real games. If you are not yet ready to tamper with your virtual fate, however, try tackling the example in "Patching an if() Statement" for a practice environment. When you're done, read on to Chapter 3, where I'll introduce you to Process Monitor and Process Explorer, two tools you'll find invaluable in game-hacking reconnaissance.

3

RECONNAISSANCE WITH PROCESS MONITOR AND PROCESS EXPLORER

 Cheat Engine and OllyDbg can help you tear apart a game's memory and code, but you also need to understand how the game interacts with files, registry values, network connections, and other processes. To learn how those interactions work, you must use two tools that excel at monitoring the external actions of processes: Process Monitor and Process Explorer. With these tools, you can track down the complete game map, locate save files, identify registry keys used to store settings, and enumerate the Internet Protocol (IP) addresses of remote game servers.

In this chapter, I'll teach you how to use both Process Monitor and Process Explorer to log system events and inspect them to see how a game was involved. Useful mainly for initial reconnaissance, these tools are amazing at giving a clear, verbose picture of exactly how a game interacts with your system. You can download both programs from the Windows Sysinternals website (*https://technet.microsoft.com/en-us/sysinternals/*).

Process Monitor

You can learn a lot about a game simply by exploring how it interacts with the registry, filesystem, and network. Process Monitor is a powerful system-monitoring tool that logs such events in real time and lets you seamlessly integrate the data into a debugging session. This tool provides extensive amounts of useful data regarding a game's interaction with the external environment. With calculated review (and sometimes, spontaneous intuition) on your part, this data can reveal details about data files, network connections, and registry events that are helpful to your ability to see and manipulate how the game functions.

In this section, I'll show you how to use Process Monitor to log data, navigate it, and make educated guesses about the files a game interacts with. After this interface tour, you'll have a chance to try out Process Monitor for yourself in "Finding a High Score File" on page 55.

Logging In-Game Events

Process Monitor's logs can hold all sorts of potentially useful information, but their most practical use is to help you figure out where data files, such as in-game item definitions, might be stored. When you start Process Monitor, the first dialog you see is the Process Monitor Filter, shown in Figure 3-1.

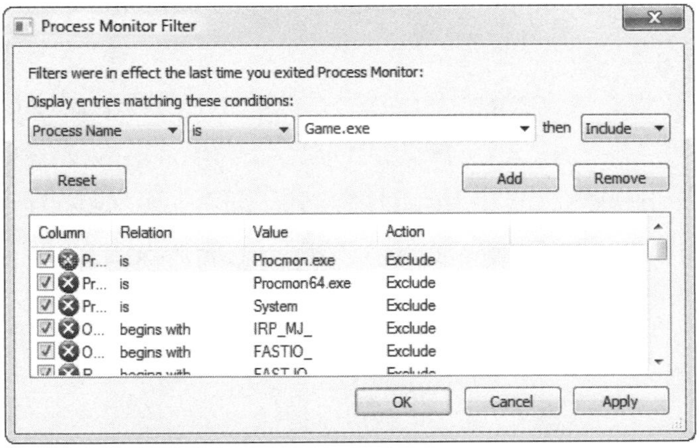

Figure 3-1: Process Monitor Filter dialog

This dialog allows you to show or suppress events based on a number of dynamic properties they possess. To start monitoring processes, select **Process Name ▶ Is ▶ *YourGameFilename.exe* ▶ Include** and then press **Add**,

Apply, and **OK**. This tells Process Monitor to show events invoked by *YourGameFilename.exe*. With the proper filters set, you will be taken to the main window shown in Figure 3-2.

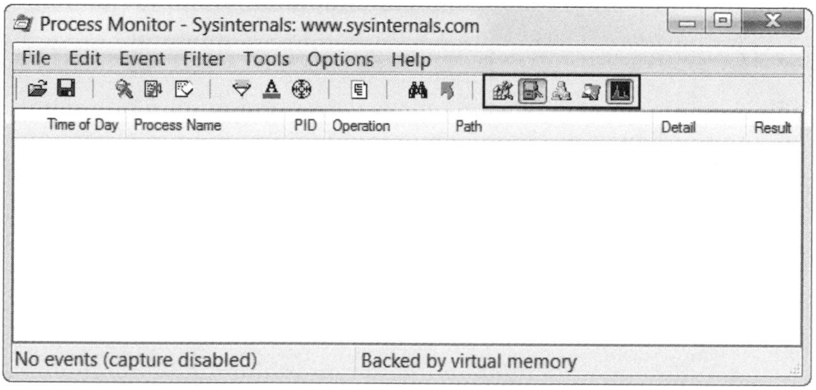

Figure 3-2: Process Monitor main window

To configure the columns displayed in Process Monitor's log area, right-click on the header and choose **Select Columns**. There's an impressive number of options, but I recommend seven.

Time of Day Lets you see when actions are happening.

Process Name Is useful if you're monitoring multiple processes, but with the single-process filter that is typically used for games; disabling this option can save precious space.

Process ID Is like Process Name, but it shows the ID rather than the name.

Operation Shows what action was performed; thus, this option is compulsory.

Path Shows the path of the action's target; also compulsory.

Detail Is useful only in some cases, but enabling it won't hurt.

Result Shows when actions, such as loading files, fail.

As you show more columns, the log can get very crowded, but sticking with these options should help keep the output succinct.

Once the monitor is running and you've defined the columns you wish to see, there are five event class filters, outlined in black in Figure 3-2, that you can toggle to clean up your logs even further. Event class filters let you choose which events to show in the log, based on type. From left to right, these filters are as follows:

Registry Shows all registry activity. There will be a lot of white noise in the registry upon process creation, as games rarely use the registry and Windows libraries always use it. Leaving this filter disabled can save a lot of space in the log.

Filesystem Shows all filesystem activity. This is the most important event class filter, since knowing where data files are stored and how they are accessed is integral to writing an effective bot.

Network Shows all network activity. The call stack on network events can be useful in finding network-related code within a game.

Process and thread activity Shows all process and thread actions. The call stack on these events can give you insight into how a game's code handles threads.

Process profiling Periodically shows information about the memory and CPU usage of each running process; a game hacker will rarely use it.

If class-level event filtering is still not precise enough to filter out unwanted pollution in your logs, right-click on specific events for event-level filtering options. Once you have your event filtering configured to log only what you need, you can begin navigating the log. Table 3-1 lists some useful hotkeys for controlling the log's behavior.

Table 3-1: Process Monitor Hotkeys

Hotkey	Action
CTRL-E	Toggles logging.
CTRL-A	Toggles automatic scrolling of the log.
CTRL-X	Clears the log.
CTRL-L	Displays the Filter dialog.
CTRL-H	Displays the Highlight dialog. This dialog looks very similar to the Filter dialog, but it is used to indicate which events should be highlighted.
CTRL-F	Displays the Search dialog.
CTRL-P	Displays the Event Properties dialog for the selected event.

As you navigate the log, you can examine the operations recorded to see the fine-grained details of an event.

Inspecting Events in the Process Monitor Log

Process Monitor logs every data point it possibly can about an event, enabling you to learn more about these events than just the files they act upon. Carefully inspecting data-rich columns, such as Result and Detail, can yield some very interesting information.

For example, I've found that games sometimes read data structures, element by element, directly from files. This behavior is apparent when a log contains a large number of reads to the same file, where each read has sequential offsets but differing lengths. Consider the hypothetical event log shown in Table 3-2.

Table 3-2: Example Event Log

Operation	Path	Detail
Create File	C:\file.dat	Desired Access: Read
Read File	C:\file.dat	Offset: 0 Size: 4
Read File	C:\file.dat	Offset: 4 Size: 2
Read File	C:\file.dat	Offset: 6 Size: 2
Read File	C:\file.dat	Offset: 8 Size: 4
Read File	C:\file.dat	Offset: 12 Size: 4
...	...	...Continues to read chunks of 4 bytes for a while

This log reveals that the game is reading a structure from the file piece by piece, disclosing some hints about what the structure looks like. For example, let's say that these reads reflect the following data file:

```
struct myDataFile
{
    int header;        // 4 bytes (offset 0)
    short effectCount; // 2 bytes (offset 4)
    short itemCount;   // 2 bytes (offset 6)
    int* effects;
    int* items;
};
```

Compare the log in Table 3-2 with this structure. First, the game reads the 4 header bytes. Then, it reads two 2-byte values: effectCount and itemCount. It then creates two integer arrays, effects and items, of respective lengths effectCount and itemCount. The game then fills these arrays with data from the file, reading 4 bytes effectCount + itemCount times.

NOTE *Developers definitely shouldn't use a process like this to read data from a file, but you'd be amazed at how often it happens. Fortunately for you, naïveté like this just makes your analysis easier.*

In this case, the event log can identify small pieces of information within a file. But keep in mind that, while correlating the reads with the known structure is easy, it's much harder to reverse engineer an unknown structure from nothing but an event log. Typically, game hackers will use a debugger to get more context about each interesting event, and the data from Process Monitor can be seamlessly integrated into a debugging session, effectively tying together the two powerful reverse engineering paradigms.

Debugging a Game to Collect More Data

Let's step away from this hypothetical file read and look at how Process Monitor lets you transition from event logging to debugging. Process Monitor stores a complete stack trace for each event, showing the full execution chain that led to the event being triggered. You can view these stack traces in the Stack tab of the Event Properties window (double-click the event or press CTRL-P), as shown in Figure 3-3.

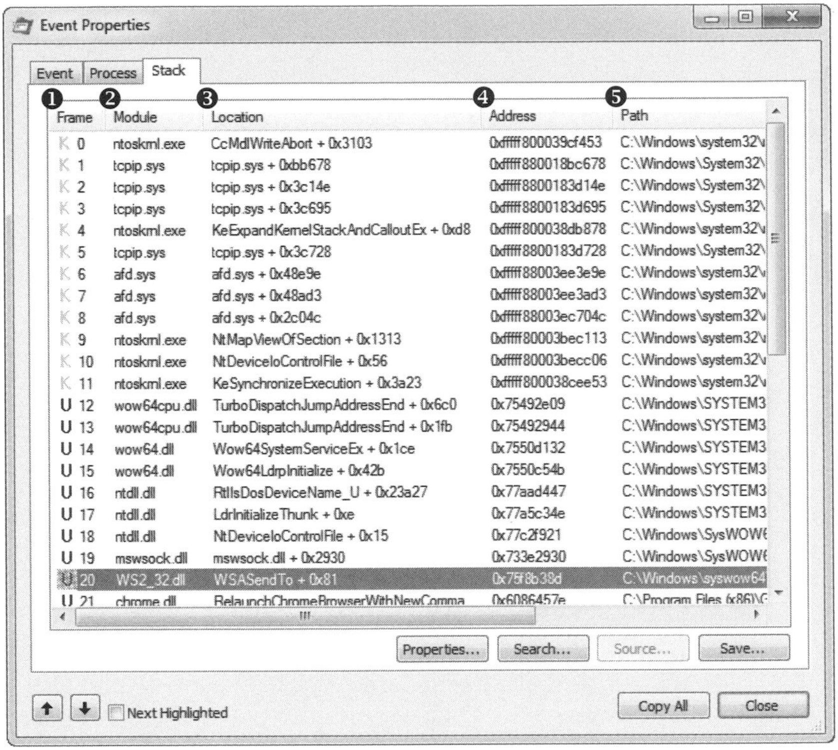

Figure 3-3: Process Monitor event call stack

The stack trace is displayed in a table starting with a Frame column ❶, which shows the execution mode and stack frame index. A pink *K* in this column means the call happened in kernel mode, while a blue *U* means it happened in user mode. Since game hackers typically work in user mode, kernel mode operations are usually meaningless.

The Module column ❷ shows the executable module where the calling code was located. Each module is just the name of the binary that made the call; this makes it easy to identify which calls were actually made from within a game binary.

The Location column ❸ shows the name of the function that made each call, as well as the call offset. These function names are deduced from the export table of the module and will generally not be present for the functions within a game binary. When no function names are present, the Location column instead shows the module name and the call's *offset* (how many bytes past the origin address the call is in memory) from the module's base address.

NOTE   *In the context of code, the offset is how many bytes of assembly code are between an item and its origin.*

The Address column ❹ shows the code address of the call, which is very useful because you can jump to the address in the OllyDbg disassembler. Finally, the Path column ❺ shows the path to the module that made the call.

In my opinion, the stack trace is, by far, the most powerful feature in Process Monitor. It reveals the entire context that led to an event, which can be immensely useful when you are debugging a game. You can use it to find the exact code that triggered an event, crawl up the call chain to see how it got there, and even determine exactly what libraries were used to complete each action.

Process Monitor's sister application, Process Explorer, doesn't have many capabilities beyond those in Process Monitor or OllyDbg. But it does expose some of those capabilities much more effectively, making it an ideal pick in certain situations.

FINDING A HIGH SCORE FILE

If you're ready to test your Process Monitor skills, you've come to the right place. Open the *GameHackingExamples/Chapter3_FindingFiles* directory and execute *FindingFiles.exe*. You'll see that it is a game of Pong, like the one in "Patching an if() Statement" on page 46. Unlike in Chapter 2, though, now the game is actually playable. It also displays your current score and your all-time-high score.

Now restart the game, firing up Process Monitor before executing it for the second time. Filtering for filesystem activity and creating any other filters you see fit, try to locate where the game stores the high-score file. For bonus points, try to modify this file to make the game show the highest possible score.

Process Explorer

Process Explorer is an advanced task manager (it even has a button you can press to make it your default task manager), and it's very handy when you're starting to understand how a game operates. It provides complex data about running processes, such as parent and child processes, CPU usage, memory usage, loaded modules, open handles, and command line arguments, and it can manipulate those processes. It exceeds at showing you high-level information, such as process trees, memory consumption, file access, and process IDs, all of which can be very useful.

Of course, none of this data is specifically useful in isolation. But with a keen eye, you can make correlations and draw some useful conclusions about what global objects—including files, mutexes, and shared memory segments—a game has access to. Additionally, the data shown in Process Explorer can be even more valuable when cross-referenced with data gathered in a debugging session.

This section introduces the Process Explorer interface, discusses the properties it shows, and describes how you can use this tool to manipulate *handles* (references to system resources). After this introduction, use "Finding and Closing a Mutex" on page 60 to hone your skills.

Process Explorer's User Interface and Controls

When you open Process Explorer, you see a window that is split into three distinct sections, as in Figure 3-4.

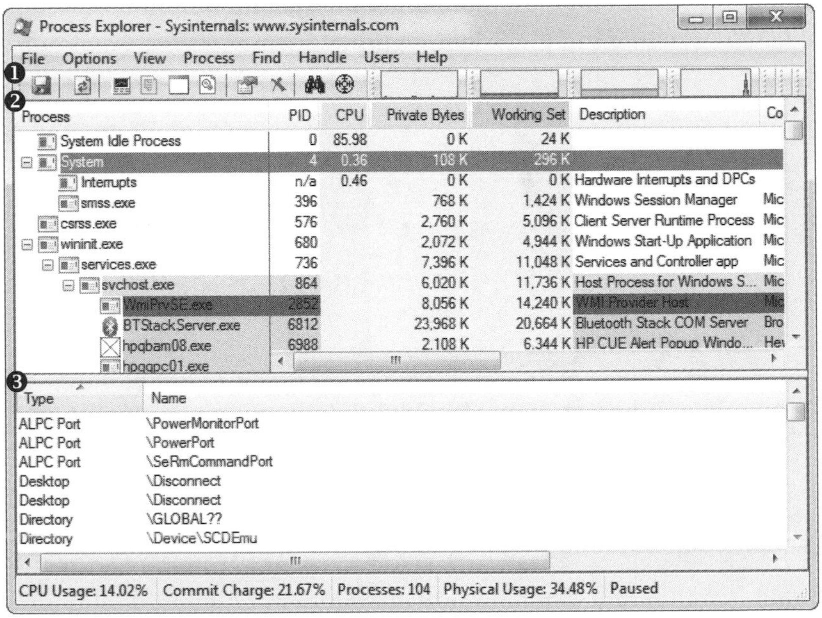

Figure 3-4: Process Explorer main window

Those three sections are the toolbar ❶, an upper pane ❷, and a lower pane ❸. The upper pane shows a list of processes, utilizing a tree structure to display their parent/child relationships. Different processes are highlighted with different colors; if you don't like the current colors, click **Options ▸ Configure Colors** to display a dialog that allows you to view and change them.

Just as in Process Monitor, the display for this table is highly versatile, and you can customize it by right-clicking on the table header and choosing Select Columns. There are probably more than 100 customization options, but I find that the defaults with the addition of the ASLR Enabled column work just fine.

NOTE   Address Space Layout Randomization (ASLR) *is a Windows security feature that allocates executable images at unpredictable locations, and knowing whether it's on is invaluable when you're trying to alter game state values in memory.*

The lower pane has three possible states: Hidden, DLLs, and Handles. The Hidden option hides the pane from view, DLLs displays a list of Dynamic Link Libraries loaded within the current process, and Handles shows a list of handles held by the process (visible in Figure 3-4). You can hide or unhide the entire lower pane by toggling View ▶ Show Lower Pane. When it is visible, you can change the information display by selecting either View ▶ Lower Pane View ▶ DLLs or View ▶ Lower Pane View ▶ Handles.

You can also use hotkeys to quickly change between lower pane modes without affecting processes in the upper pane. These hotkeys are listed in Table 3-3.

Table 3-3: Process Explorer Hotkeys

Hotkey	Action
CTRL-F	Search through lower pane data sets for a value.
CTRL-L	Toggle the lower pane between hidden and visible.
CTRL-D	Toggle the lower pane to display DLLs.
CTRL-H	Toggle the lower pane to display handles.
spacebar	Toggle process list autorefresh.
ENTER	Display the Properties dialog for the selected process.
DEL	Kill the selected process.
SHIFT-DEL	Kill the selected process and all child processes.

Use the GUI or hotkeys to practice changing modes. When you're acquainted with the main window, we'll look at another important Process Explorer dialog, called Properties.

Examining Process Properties

Much like Process Monitor, Process Explorer has a very kinetic approach to data gathering; the end result is a broad and verbose spectrum of information. In fact, if you open the Properties dialog (shown in Figure 3-5) for a process, you'll see a massive tab bar containing 10 tabs.

The Image tab, selected by default and shown in Figure 3-5, displays the executable name, version, build date, and complete path. It also displays the current working directory and the Address Space Layout Randomization status of the executable. ASLR status is the most important piece of information here, because it has a direct effect on how a bot can read the memory from a game. I'll talk about this more in Chapter 6.

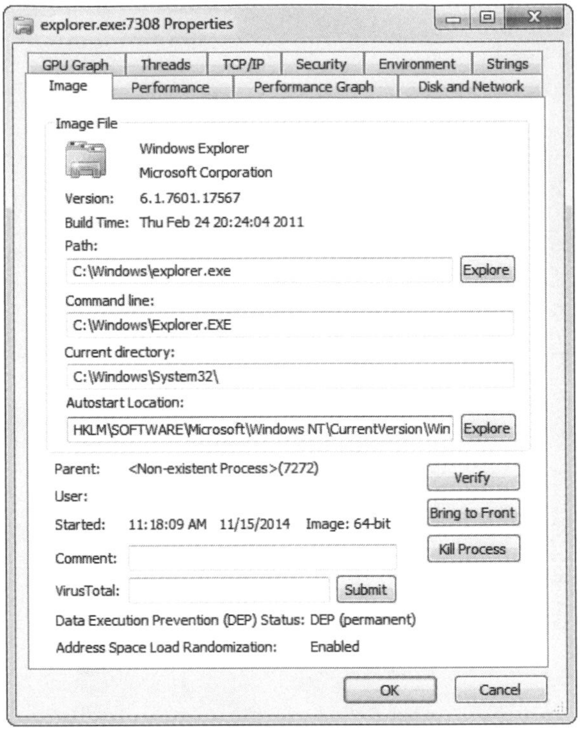

Figure 3-5: Process Explorer Properties dialog

The Performance, Performance Graph, Disk and Network, and GPU Graph tabs display a myriad of metrics about the CPU, memory, disk, network, and GPU usage of the process. If you create a bot that injects into a game, this information can be very useful to determine how much of a performance impact your bot has on the game.

The TCP/IP tab displays a list of active TCP connections, which you can use to find any game server IP addresses that a game connects to. If you're trying to test connection speed, terminate connections, or research a game's network protocol, this information is critical.

The Strings tab displays a list of strings found in either the binary or the memory of the process. Unlike the string list in OllyDbg, which shows only strings referenced by assembly code, the list includes any occurrences of three or more consecutive readable characters, followed by a null terminator. When a game binary is updated, you can use a diffing tool on this list from each game version to determine whether there are any new strings that you want to investigate.

The Threads tab shows you a list of threads running within the process and allows you to pause, resume, or kill each thread; the Security tab displays the security privileges of the process; and the Environment tab displays any environment variables known to or set by the process.

If you open the Properties dialog for a .NET process, you'll notice two additional tabs: .NET Assemblies and .NET Performance. The data in these tabs is pretty self-explanatory. Please keep in mind that a majority of the techniques in this book won't work with games written in .NET.

Handle Manipulation Options

As you've seen, Process Explorer can provide you with a wealth of information about a process. That's not all it's good for, though: it can also manipulate certain parts of a process. For example, you can view and manipulate open handles from the comfort of Process Explorer's lower pane (see Figure 3-4). This alone makes a strong argument for adding Process Explorer to your toolbox. Closing a handle is as simple as right-clicking on it and selecting Close Handle. This can come in handy when you want, for instance, to close mutexes, which is essential to certain types of hacks.

You can right-click on the lower pane header and click Select Columns to customize the display. One column you might find particularly useful is Handle Value, which can help when you see a handle being passed around in OllyDbg and want to know what it does.

Closing Mutexes

Games often allow only one client to run at a time; this is called *single-instance limitation.* You can implement single-instance limitation in a number of ways, but using a system mutex is common because mutexes are sessionwide and can be accessed by a simple name. It's trivial to limit instances with mutexes, and thanks to Process Explorer, it's just as trivial to remove that limit, allowing you to run multiple instances of a game at the same time.

First, here's how a game might tackle single-instance limitation with a mutex:

```
int main(int argc, char *argv[]) {
    // create the mutex
    HANDLE mutex = CreateMutex(NULL, FALSE, "onlyoneplease");
    if (GetLastError() == ERROR_ALREADY_EXISTS) {
        // the mutex already exists, so exit
        ErrorBox("An instance is already running.");
        return 0;
    }
    // the mutex didn't exist; it was just created, so
    // let the game run
    RunGame();
    // the game is over; close the mutex to free it up
    // for future instances
    if (mutex)
        CloseHandle(mutex);
    return 0;
}
```

This example code creates a mutex named onlyoneplease. Next, the function checks GetLastError() to see whether the mutex was already created, and if so, it closes the game. If the mutex doesn't already exist, the game creates the first instance, thereby blocking any future game clients from running. In this example, the game runs normally, and once it finishes, CloseHandle() is called to close the mutex and allow future game instances to run.

You can use Process Explorer to close instance-limiting mutexes and run many game instances simultaneously. To do so, choose the Handles view of the lower pane, look for all handles with a type of Mutant, determine which one is limiting instances of the game, and close that mutex.

WARNING *Mutexes are also used to synchronize data across threads and processes. Close one only if you're sure that its sole purpose is the one you're trying to subvert!*

Multiclient hacks are generally in high demand, so being able to quickly develop them for emerging games is crucial to your overall success as a bot developer within that market. Since mutexes are one of the most common ways to achieve single-instance limitation, Process Explorer is an integral tool for prototyping these kinds of hacks.

Inspecting File Accesses

Unlike Process Monitor, Process Explorer can't show a list of filesystem calls. On the other hand, the Handles view of Process Explorer's lower pane can show all file handles that a game currently has open, revealing exactly what files are in continuous use without the need to set up advanced filtering criteria in Process Monitor. Just look for handles with a type of File to see all files the game is currently using.

This functionality can come in handy if you're trying to locate logfiles or save files. Moreover, you can locate named pipes that are used for interprocess communication (IPC); these are files prefixed with *\Device\ NamedPipe*. Seeing one of these pipes is often a hint that the game is talking to another process.

FINDING AND CLOSING A MUTEX

To put your Process Explorer skills to use, go to the *GameHackingExamples/ Chapter3_CloseMutex* directory and execute *CloseMutex.exe*. This game plays exactly like the one in "Finding a High Score File" on page 55, but it prevents you from simultaneously running multiple instances. As you might have guessed, it does this using a single-instance-limitation mutex. Using Process Explorer's Handles view in the lower pane, find the mutex responsible for this limitation and close it. If you succeed, you'll be able to open a second instance of the game.

Closing Thoughts

To be effective when using Process Monitor and Process Explorer, you need, above all else, a deep familiarity with the data that these applications display as well as the interfaces they use to display it. While this chapter's overview is a good baseline, the intricacies of these applications can be learned only through experience, so I encourage you to play around with them on your system.

You won't use these tools on a regular basis, but at some point, they'll save the day: as you struggle to figure out how some code works, you'll recall an obscure piece of information that caught your eye during a previous Process Explorer or Process Monitor session. That's why I consider them useful reconnaissance tools.

PART 2

GAME DISSECTION

4

FROM CODE TO MEMORY: A GENERAL PRIMER

 At the lowest level, a game's code, data, input, and output are complex abstractions of erratically changing bytes. Many of these bytes represent variables or machine code generated by a compiler that was fed the game's source code. Some represent images, models, and sounds. Others exist only for an instant, posted by the computer's hardware as input and destroyed when the game finishes processing them. The bytes that remain inform the player of the game's internal state. But humans can't think in bytes, so the computer must translate them in a way we can understand.

There's a huge disconnect in the opposite direction as well. A computer doesn't actually understand high-level code and visceral game content, so these must be translated from the abstract into bytes. Some content—such as images, sounds, and text—is stored losslessly, ready to be presented to the player at a microsecond's notice. A game's code, logic, and variables, on the other hand, are stripped of all human readability and compiled down to machine data.

By manipulating a game's data, game hackers obtain humanly improbable advantages within the game. To do this, however, they must understand how a developer's code manifests once it has been compiled and executed. Essentially, they must think like computers.

To get you thinking like a computer, this chapter will begin by teaching you how numbers, text, simple structures, and unions are represented in memory at the byte level. Then you'll dive deeper to explore how class instances are stored in memory and how abstract instances know which virtual functions to call at runtime. In the last half of the chapter, you'll take an x86 assembly language crash course that covers syntax, registers, operands, the call stack, arithmetic operations, branching operations, function calls, and calling conventions.

This chapter focuses very heavily on general technical details. There isn't a lot of juicy information that immediately relates to hacking games, but the knowledge you gain here will be central in the coming chapters, when we talk about topics like programmatically reading and writing memory, injecting code, and manipulating control flow.

Since C++ is the de facto standard for both game and bot development, this chapter explains the relationships between C++ code and the memory that represents it. Most native languages have very similar (sometimes identical) low-level structure and behavior, however, so you should be able to apply what you learn here to just about any piece of software.

All of the example code in this chapter is in the *GameHackingExamples/ Chapter4_CodeToMemory* directory of this book's source files. The included projects can be compiled with Visual Studio 2010 but should also work with any other C++ compiler. Download them at *https://www.nostarch.com/ gamehacking/* and compile them if you want to follow along.

How Variables and Other Data Manifest in Memory

Properly manipulating a game's state can be very hard, and finding the data that controls it is not always as easy as clicking Next Scan and hoping Cheat Engine won't fail you. In fact, many hacks must manipulate dozens of related values at once. Finding these values and their relationships often requires you to analytically identify structures and patterns. Moreover, developing game hacks typically means re-creating the original structures within your bot's code.

To do these things, you need an in-depth understanding of exactly how variables and data are laid out in the game's memory. Through example code, OllyDbg memory dumps, and some tables to tie everything together, this section will teach you everything there is to know about how different types of data manifest in memory.

Numeric Data

Most of the values game hackers need (like the player's health, mana, location, and level) are represented by numeric data types. Because numeric data types are also a building block for all other data types, understanding them is extremely important. Luckily, they have relatively straightforward representations in memory: they are predictably aligned and have a fixed bit width. Table 4-1 shows the five main numeric data types you'll find in Windows games, along with their sizes and ranges.

Table 4-1: Numeric Data Types

Type name(s)	Size	Signed range	Unsigned range
char, BYTE	8 bits	−128 to 127	0 to 255
short, WORD, wchar_t	16 bits	−32,768 to −32,767	0 to 65535
int, long, DWORD	32 bits	−2,147,483,648 to 2,147,483,647	0 to 4,294,967,295
long long	64 bits	−9,223,372,036,854,775,808 to 9,223,372,036,854,775,807	0 to 18,446,744,073,709,551,615
float	32 bits	$+/-1.17549*10^{-38}$ to $+/-3.40282*10^{38}$	N/A

The sizes of numeric data types can differ between architectures and even compilers. Since this book focuses on hacking x86 games on Windows, I'm using type names and sizes made standard by Microsoft. With the exception of float, the data types in Table 4-1 are stored with *little-endian ordering*, meaning the least significant bytes of an integer are stored in the lowest addresses occupied by that integer. For example, Figure 4-1 shows that DWORD 0x0A0B0C0D is represented by the bytes 0x0D 0x0C 0x0B 0x0A.

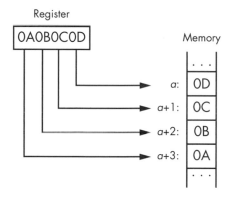

Figure 4-1: Little-endian ordering diagram

The float data type can hold mixed numbers, so its representation in memory isn't as simple as that of other data types. For example, if you see

0x0D 0x0C 0x0B 0x0A in memory and that value is a float, you can't simply convert it to 0x0A0B0C0D. Instead, float values have three components: the *sign* (bit 0), *exponent* (bits 1–8), and *mantissa* (bits 9–31).

The sign determines whether the number is negative or positive, the exponent determines how many places to move the decimal point (starting before the mantissa), and the mantissa holds an approximation of the value. You can retrieve the stored value by evaluating the expression *mantissa* $\times 10^n$ (where n is the exponent) and multiplying the result by –1 if the sign is set.

Now let's look at some numeric data types in memory. Listing 4-1 initializes nine variables.

```
unsigned char ubyteValue = 0xFF;
char byteValue = 0xFE;
unsigned short uwordValue = 0x4142;
short wordValue = 0x4344;
unsigned int udwordValue = 0xDEADBEEF;
int dwordValue = 0xDEADBEEF;
unsigned long long ulongLongValue = 0xEFCDAB8967452301;
long long longLongValue = 0xEFCDAB8967452301;
float floatValue = 1337.7331;
```

Listing 4-1: Creating variables of numeric data types in C++

Starting from the top, this example includes variables of types char, short, int, long long, and float. Four of these are unsigned, and five are signed. (In C++, a float can't be unsigned.) Taking into account what you've learned so far, carefully study the relationship between the code in Listing 4-1 and the memory dump in Figure 4-2. Assume that the variables are declared in global scope.

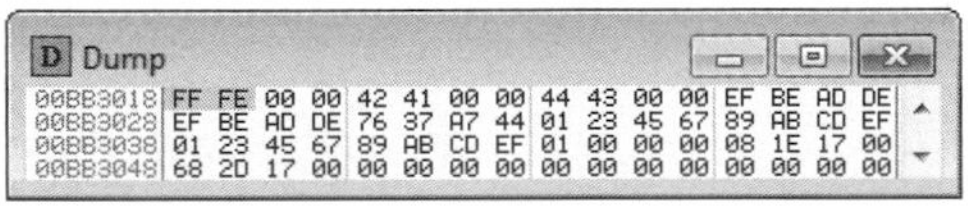

Figure 4-2: OllyDbg memory dump of our numeric data

You might notice that some values seem arbitrarily spaced out. Since it's much faster for processors to access values residing at addresses that are multiples of the address size (which is 32 bits in x86), compilers *pad* values with zeros in order to align them on such addresses—hence, padding is also called *alignment*. Single-byte values are not padded, since operations that access them perform the same regardless of alignment.

Keeping this in mind, take a look at Table 4-2, which provides a sort of memory-to-code crosswalk between the memory dump in Figure 4-2 and the variables declared in Listing 4-1.

Table 4-2: Memory-to-Code Crosswalk for Listing 4-1 and Figure 4-2

Address	Size	Data	Object
0x00BB3018	1 byte	0xFF	ubyteValue
0x00BB3019	1 byte	0xFE	byteValue
0x00BB301A	2 bytes	0x00 0x00	Padding before uwordValue
0x00BB301C	2 bytes	0x42 0x41	uwordValue
0x00BB301E	2 bytes	0x00 0x00	Padding before wordValue
0x00BB3020	2 bytes	0x44 0x43	wordValue
0x00BB3022	2 bytes	0x00 0x00	Padding before udwordValue
0x00BB3024	4 bytes	0xEF 0xBE 0xAD 0xDE	udwordValue
0x00BB3028	4 bytes	0xEF 0xBE 0xAD 0xDE	dwordValue
0x00BB302C	4 bytes	0x76 0x37 0xA7 0x44	floatValue
0x00BB3030	8 bytes	0x01 0x23 0x45 0x67 0x89 0xAB 0xCD 0xEF	ulongLongValue
0x00BB3038	8 bytes	0x01 0x23 0x45 0x67 0x89 0xAB 0xCD 0xEF	LongLongValue

The Address column lists locations in memory, and the Data column tells you exactly what's stored there. The Object column tells you which variable from Listing 4-1 each piece of data relates to. Notice that floatValue is placed before ulongLongValue in memory, even though it's the last variable declared in Listing 4-1. Because these variables are declared in global scope, the compiler can place them wherever it wants. This particular move is likely a result of either alignment or optimization.

String Data

Most developers use the term *string* as if it's synonymous with *text*, but text is only the most common use for strings. At a low level, strings are just arrays of arbitrary numeric objects that appear linear and unaligned in memory. Listing 4-2 shows four text string declarations.

```
// char will be 1 byte per character
char* thinStringP = "my_thin_terminated_value_pointer";
char thinStringA[40] = "my_thin_terminated_value_array";

// wchar_t will be 2 bytes per character
wchar_t* wideStringP = L"my_wide_terminated_value_pointer";
wchar_t wideStringA[40] = L"my_wide_terminated_value_array";
```

Listing 4-2: Declaring several strings in C++

In the context of text, strings hold character objects (char for 8-bit encoding or wchar_t for 16-bit encoding), and the end of each string is specified by a *null terminator*, a character equal to 0x0. Let's look at the memory where these variables are stored, as shown in the two memory dumps in Figure 4-3.

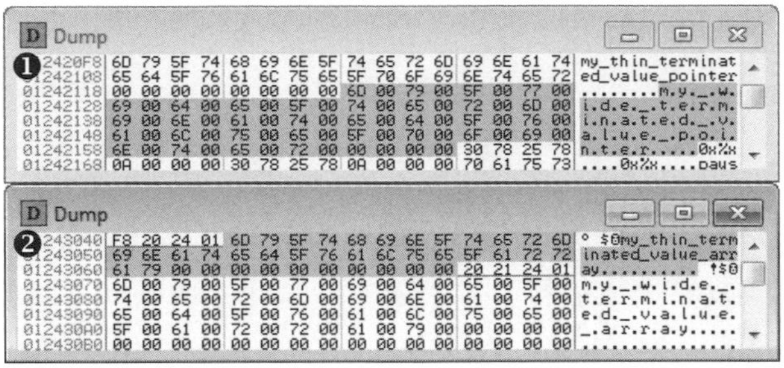

Figure 4-3: In this OllyDbg memory dump of string data, the human-readable text in the ASCII column is the text we stored in Listing 4-2.

If you're not used to reading memory, the OllyDbg dump might be a bit difficult to follow at this point. Table 4-3 shows a deeper look at the correlation between the code in Listing 4-2 and the memory in Figure 4-3.

Table 4-3: Memory-to-Code Crosswalk for Listing 4-2 and Figure 4-3

Address	Size	Data	Object
		Pane 1	
0x012420F8	32 bytes	0x6D 0x79 0x5F {...} 0x74 0x65 0x72	thinStringP characters
0x01242118	4 bytes	0x00 0x00 0x00 0x00	thinStringP terminator and padding
0x0124211C	4 bytes	0x00 0x00 0x00 0x00	Unrelated data
0x01242120	64 bytes	0x6D 0x00 0x79 {...} 0x00 0x72 0x00	wideStringP characters
0x01242160	4 bytes	0x00 0x00 0x00 0x00	wideStringP terminator and padding
{...}			Unrelated data
		Pane 2	
0x01243040	4 bytes	0xF8 0x20 0x24 0x01	Pointer to thinStringP at 0x012420F8
0x01243044	30 bytes	0x6D 0x79 0x5F {...} 0x72 0x61 0x79	thinStringA characters
0x01243062	10 bytes	0x00 repeated 10 times	thinStringA terminator and array fill
0x0124306C	4 bytes	0x20 0x21 0x24 0x01	Pointer to wideStringP at 0x01242120
0x01243070	60 bytes	0x6D 0x00 0x79 {...} 0x00 0x79 0x00	wideStringA characters
0x012430AC	20 bytes	0x00 repeated 10 times	wideStringA terminator and array fill

In Figure 4-3, pane 1 shows that the values stored where thinStringP (address 0x01243040) and wideStringP (address 0x0124306C) belong in memory are only 4 bytes long and contain no string data. That's because these variables are actually pointers to the first characters of their respective arrays. For example, thinStringP contains 0x012420F8, and in pane 2 in Figure 4-3, you can see "my_thin_terminated_value_pointer" located at address 0x012420F8.

Look at the data between these pointers in pane 1, and you can see the text being stored by thinStringA and wideStringA. Furthermore, notice that thinStringA and wideStringA are padded beyond their null terminators; this is because these variables were declared as arrays with length 40, so they are filled up to 40 characters.

Data Structures

Unlike the data types we have previously discussed, *structures* are containers that hold multiple pieces of simple, related data. Game hackers who know how to identify structures in memory can mimic those structures in their own code. This can greatly reduce the number of addresses they must find, as they need to find only the address to the start of the structure, not the address of every individual item.

NOTE   *This section talks about structures as simple containers that lack member functions and contain only simple data. Objects that exceed these limitations will be discussed in "Classes and VF Tables" on page 74.*

Structure Element Order and Alignment

Since structures simply represent an assortment of objects, they don't visibly manifest in memory dumps. Instead, a memory dump of a structure shows the objects that are contained within that structure. The dump would look much like the others I've shown in this chapter, but with important differences in both order and alignment.

To see these differences, start by taking a look at Listing 4-3.

```
struct MyStruct {
    unsigned char ubyteValue;
    char byteValue;
    unsigned short uwordValue;
    short wordValue;
    unsigned int udwordValue;
    int dwordValue;
    unsigned long long ulongLongValue;
    long long longLongValue;
    float floatValue;
};
MyStruct& m = 0;
```

```
printf("Offsets: %d,%d,%d,%d,%d,%d,%d,%d,%d\n",
        &m->ubyteValue, &m->byteValue,
        &m->uwordValue, &m->wordValue,
        &m->udwordValue, &m->dwordValue,
        &m->ulongLongValue, &m->longLongValue,
        &m->floatValue);
```

Listing 4-3: A C++ structure and some code that uses it

This code declares a structure named MyStruct and creates a variable named m that supposedly points to an instance of the structure at address 0. There's not actually an instance of the structure at address 0, but this trick lets me use the ampersand operator (&) in the printf() call to get the address of each member of the structure. Since the structure is located at address 0, the address printed for each member is equivalent to its offset from the start of the structure.

The ultimate purpose of this example is to see exactly how each member is laid out in memory, relative to the start of the structure. If you were to run the code, you'd see the following output:

```
Offsets: 0,1,2,4,8,12,16,24,32
```

As you can see, the variables in MyStruct are ordered exactly as they were defined in code. This sequential member layout is a mandatory property of structures. Compare this to the example from Listing 4-1, when we declared an identical set of variables; in the memory dump from Figure 4-2, the compiler clearly placed some values out of order in memory.

Furthermore, you may have noticed that the members are not aligned like the globally scoped variables in Listing 4-1; if they were, for example, there would be 2 padding bytes before uwordValue. This is because structure members are aligned on addresses divisible by either the *struct member alignment* (a compiler option that accepts 1, 2, 4, 8, or 16 bytes; in this example, it's set to 4) or the size of the member—whichever is smaller. I arranged the members of MyStruct so that the compiler didn't need to pad the values.

If, however, we put a char immediately after ulongLongValue, the printf() call would give the following output:

```
Offsets: 0,1,2,4,8,12,16,28,36
```

Now, take a look at the original and the modified outputs together:

```
Original: Offsets: 0,1,2,4,8,12,16,24,32
Modified: Offsets: 0,1,2,4,8,12,16,28,36
```

In the modified version, the last two values, which are the offsets for longLongValue and floatValue from the start of the structure, have changed. Thanks to the struct member alignment, the variable longLongValue moves by 4 bytes (1 for the char value and 3 following it) to ensure it gets placed on an address divisible by 4.

How Structures Work

Understanding structures—how they are aligned and how to mimic them—can be very useful. For instance, if you replicate a game's structures in your own code, you can read or write those entire structures from memory in a single operation. Consider a game that declares the player's current and max health like so:

```
struct {
    int current;
    int max;
} vital;
vital health;
```

If an inexperienced game hacker wants to read this information from memory, they might write something like this to fetch the health values:

```
int currentHealth = readIntegerFromMemory(currentHealthAddress);
int maxHealth =  readIntegerFromMemory(maxHealthAddress);
```

This game hacker doesn't realize that seeing these values right next to each other in memory could be more than a lucky happenstance, so they've used two separate variables. But if you came along with your knowledge of structures, you might conclude that, since these values are closely related and are adjacent in memory, our hacker could have used a structure instead:

```
  struct {
      int current;
      int max;
  } _vital;
❶ _vital health = readTypeFromMemory<_vital>(healthStructureAddress);
```

Since this code assumes a structure is being used and correctly mimics it, it can fetch both health and max health in just one line ❶. We'll dive deeper into how to write your own code to read memory from in Chapter 6.

Unions

Unlike structures, which encapsulate multiple pieces of related data, *unions* contain a single piece of data that is exposed through multiple variables. Unions follow three rules:

- The size of a union in memory is equal to that of its largest member.
- Members of a union all reference the same memory.
- A union inherits the alignment of its largest member.

The printf() call in the following code helps illustrate the first two rules:

```
union {
    BYTE byteValue;
    struct {
```

```
        WORD first;
        WORD second;
    } words;
    DWORD value;
} dwValue;
dwValue.value = 0xDEADBEEF;
printf("Size %d\nAddresses 0x%x,0x%x\nValues 0x%x,0x%x\n",
    sizeof(dwValue), &dwValue.value, &dwValue.words,
    dwValue.words.first, dwValue.words.second);
```

This call to printf() outputs the following:

```
Size 4
Addresses 0x2efda8,0x2efda8
Values 0xbeef,0xdead
```

The first rule is illustrated by the Size value, which is printed first. Even though dwValue has three members that occupy a total of 9 bytes, it has a size of only 4 bytes. The size result validates the second rule as well, because dwValue.value and dwValue.words both point to address 0x2efda8, as shown by the values printed after the word Addresses. The second rule is also validated by the fact that dwValue.words.first and dwValue.words.second contain 0xbeef and 0xdead, printed after Values, which makes sense considering that dwValue.value is 0xdeadbeef. The third rule isn't demonstrated in this example because we don't have enough memory context, but if you were to put this union inside a structure and surround it with whatever types you like, it would in fact always align like a DWORD.

Classes and VF Tables

Much like structures, *classes* are containers that hold and isolate multiple pieces of data, but classes can also contain function definitions.

A Simple Class

Classes with normal functions, such as bar in Listing 4-4, conform to the same memory layouts as structures.

```
class bar {
public:
    bar() : bar1(0x898989), bar2(0x10203040) {}
    void myfunction() { bar1++; }
    int bar1, bar2;
};

bar _bar = bar();
printf("Size %d; Address 0x%x : _bar\n", sizeof(_bar), &_bar);
```

Listing 4-4: A C++ class

The printf() call in Listing 4-4 would output the following:

```
Size 8; Address 0x2efd80 : _bar
```

Even though bar has two member functions, this output shows that it spans only the 8 bytes needed to hold bar1 and bar2. This is because the bar class doesn't include abstractions of those member functions, so the program can call them directly.

NOTE *Access levels such as public, private, and protected do not manifest in memory. Regardless of these modifiers, members of classes are still ordered as they are defined.*

A Class with Virtual Functions

In classes that do include abstract functions (often called *virtual* functions), the program must know which function to call. Consider the class definitions in Listing 4-5:

```
class foo {
public:
foo() : myValue1(0xDEADBEEF), myValue2(0xBABABABA) {}
    int myValue1;
    static int myStaticValue;
    virtual void bar() { printf("call foo::bar()\n"); }
    virtual void baz() { printf("call foo::baz()\n"); }
    virtual void barbaz() {}
    int myValue2;
};

int foo::myStaticValue = 0x12121212;

class fooa : public foo {
public:
    fooa() : foo() {}
    virtual void bar() { printf("call fooa::bar()\n"); }
    virtual void baz() { printf("call fooa::baz()\n"); }
};

class foob : public foo {
public:
    foob() : foo() {}
    virtual void bar() { printf("call foob::bar()\n"); }
    virtual void baz() { printf("call foob::baz()\n"); }
};
```

Listing 4-5: The foo, fooa, and foob classes

The class foo has three virtual functions: bar, baz, and barbaz. Classes fooa and foob inherit from class foo and overload both bar and baz. Since fooa and foob have a public base class of foo, a foo pointer can point to them, but the program must still call the correct versions of bar and baz. You can see this by executing the following code:

```
foo* _testfoo = (foo*)new fooa();
_testfoo->bar(); // calls fooa::bar()
```

And here is the output:

```
call fooa::bar()
```

The output shows that _testfoo->bar() invoked fooa::bar() even though _testfoo is a foo pointer. The program knew which version of the function to call, because the compiler included a *VF (virtual function) table* in the memory of _testfoo. VF tables are arrays of function addresses that abstract class instances use to tell a program where their overloaded functions are located.

Class Instances and Virtual Function Tables

To understand the relationship between class instances and VF tables, let's inspect a memory dump of the three objects declared in this listing:

```
foo _foo = foo();
fooa _fooa = fooa();
foob _foob = foob();
```

These objects are of the types defined in Listing 4-5. You can see them in memory in Figure 4-4.

Figure 4-4: OllyDbg memory dump of class data

Pane 1 shows that each class instance stores its members just like a structure, but it precedes them with a DWORD value that points to the class instance's VF table. Pane 2 shows the VF tables for each of our three class instances. The memory-to-code crosswalk in Table 4-4 shows how these panes and the code tie together.

Table 4-4: Memory-to-Code Crosswalk for Listing 4-5 and Figure 4-4

Address	Size	Data	Object
		Pane 1	
0x0018FF20	4 bytes	0x004022B0	Start of _foo and pointer to foo VF table
0x0018FF24	8 bytes	0xDEADBEEF 0xBABABABA	_foo.myValue1 and _foo.myValue2
0x0018FF2C	4 bytes	0x004022C0	Start of _fooa and pointer to fooa VF table
0x0018FF30	8 bytes	0xDEADBEEF 0xBABABABA	_fooa.myValue1 and _fooa.myValue2
0x0018FF38	4 bytes	0x004022D0	Start of _foob and pointer to foob VF table
0x0018FF3C	8 bytes	0xDEADBEEF 0xBABABABA	_foob.myValue1 and _foob.myValue2
{...}			Unrelated data
		Pane 2	
0x004022B0	4 bytes	0x00401060	Start of foo VF table; address of foo::bar
0x004022B4	4 bytes	0x00401080	Address of foo::baz
0x004022B8	4 bytes	0x004010A0	Address of foo::barbaz
0x004022BC	4 bytes	0x0040243C	Unrelated data
0x004022C0	4 bytes	0x004010D0	Start of fooa VF table; address of fooa::bar
0x004022C4	4 bytes	0x004010F0	Address of fooa::baz
0x004022C8	4 bytes	0x004010A0	Address of foo::barbaz
0x004022CC	4 bytes	0x004023F0	Unrelated data
0x004022D0	4 bytes	0x00401130	Start of foob VF table; address of foob::bar
0x004022D4	4 bytes	0x00401150	Address of foob::baz
0x004022D8	4 bytes	0x004010A0	Address of foo::barbaz

This crosswalk shows how the VF tables for the code in Listing 4-5 are laid out in memory. Each VF table is generated by the compiler when the binary is made, and the tables remain constant. To save space, instances of the same class all point to the same VF table, which is why the VF tables aren't placed inline with the class.

Since we have three VF tables, you might wonder how a class instance knows which VF table to use. The compiler places code similar to the following bit of assembly in each virtual class constructor:

```
MOV DWORD PTR DS:[EAX], VFADDR
```

This example takes the static address of a VF table (VFADDR) and places it in memory as the first member of the class.

Now look at addresses 0x004022B0, 0x004022C0, and 0x004022D0 in Table 4-4. These addresses contain the beginning of the foo, fooa, and foob VF tables. Notice that foo::barbaz exists in all three VF tables; this is because the function is not overloaded by either subclass, meaning instances of each subclass will call the original implementation directly.

Notice, too, that foo::myStaticValue does not appear in this crosswalk. Since the value is static, it doesn't actually need to exist as a part of the foo class; it's placed inside this class only for better code organization. In reality, it gets treated like a global variable and is placed elsewhere.

VF TABLES AND CHEAT ENGINE

Remember Cheat Engine's First element of pointerstruct must point to module option for pointer scans from Figure 1-4 on page 14? Now that you've read a bit about VF tables, that knowledge should help you understand how this option works: it makes Cheat Engine ignore all heap chunks where the first member is not a pointer to a valid VF table. It speeds up scans, but it works only if every step in a pointer path is part of an abstract class instance.

The memory tour ends here, but if you have trouble identifying a chunk of data in the future, come back to this section for reference. Next, we'll look at how a computer can understand a game's high-level source code in the first place.

x86 Assembly Crash Course

When a program's source code is compiled into a binary, it is stripped of all unnecessary artifacts and translated into *machine code*. This machine code, made up of only bytes (command bytes are called *opcodes*, but there are also bytes representing operands), gets fed directly to the processor and tells it exactly how to behave. Those 1s and 0s flip transistors to control computation, and they can be extremely difficult to understand. To make computers a little easier to talk to, engineers working with such code use *assembly language*, a shorthand that represents raw machine opcodes with abbreviated names (called mnemonics) and a simplistic syntax.

Assembly language is important for game hackers to know because many powerful hacks can be achieved only through direct manipulation of a game's assembly code, via methods such as NOPing or hooking. In this section, you'll learn the basics of *x86 assembly language*, a specific flavor of assembly made for speaking to 32-bit processors. Assembly language is very extensive, so for the sake of brevity this section talks only about the small subset of assembly concepts that are most useful to game hackers.[1]

NOTE *Throughout this section, many small snippets of assembly code include comments set off by a semicolon (;) to describe each instruction in greater detail.*

Command Syntax

Assembly language is used to describe machine code, so its syntax is pretty simplistic. While this syntax makes it very easy for someone to understand individual commands (also called *operations*), it also makes understanding complex blocks of code very hard. Even algorithms that are easily readable in high-level code seem obfuscated when written in assembly. For example, the following snippet of pseudocode:

```
if (EBX > EAX)
    ECX = EDX
else
    ECX = 0
```

would look like Listing 4-6 in x86 assembly.

```
    CMP EBX, EAX
    JG label1
    MOV ECX, 0
    JMP label2
label1:
    MOV ECX, EDX
label2:
```

Listing 4-6: Some x86 assembly commands

Therefore, it takes extensive practice to understand even the most trivial functions in assembly. Understanding individual commands, however, is very simple, and by the end of this section, you'll know how to parse the commands I just showed you.

Instructions

The first part of an assembly command is called an *instruction*. If you equate an assembly command to a terminal command, the instruction is the program to run. At the machine code level, instructions are typically the first byte of a command;[2] there are also some 2-byte instructions, where the first byte is 0x0F. Regardless, an instruction tells the processor exactly what to do. In Listing 4-6, CMP, JG, MOV, and JMP are all instructions.

---

1. Randall Hyde's *The Art of Assembly Language, 2nd edition* (No Starch Press, 2010) is a wonderful book that can teach you everything there is to know about assembly.

2. Each command must fit within 15 bytes. Most commands are 6 or fewer.

Operand Syntax

While some instructions are complete commands, the vast majority are incomplete unless followed by *operands*, or parameters. Every command in Listing 4-6 has at least one operand, like EBX, EAX, and label1.

Assembly operands come in three forms:

Immediate value   An integer value that is declared inline (hexadecimal values have a trailing h).

Register   A name that refers to a processor register.

Memory offset   An expression, placed in brackets, that represents the memory location of a value. The expression can be an immediate value or a register. Alternatively, it can be either the sum or difference of a register and immediate value (something like [REG+Ah] or [REG-10h]).

Each instruction in x86 assembly can have between zero and three operands, and commas are used to separate multiple operands. In most cases, instructions that require two operands have a *source operand* and a *destination operand*. The ordering of these operands is dependent on the assembly syntax. For example, Listing 4-7 shows a group of pseudocommands written in the Intel syntax, which is used by Windows (and, thus, by Windows game hackers):

```
  MOV R1, 1          ; set R1 (register) to 1 (immediate)
❶ MOV R1, [BADF00Dh] ; set R1 to value at [BADF00Dh] (memory offset)
  MOV R1, [R2+10h]   ; set R1 to value at [R2+10h] (memory offset)
  MOV R1, [R2-20h]   ; set R1 to value at [R2+20h] (memory offset)
```

Listing 4-7: Demonstrating Intel syntax

In the Intel syntax, the destination operand comes first, followed by the source, so at ❶, R1 is the destination and [BADF00Dh] is the source. On the other hand, compilers like GCC (which can be used to write bots on Windows) use a syntax known as AT&T, or UNIX, syntax. This syntax does things a little differently, as you can see in the following example:

```
MOV $1, %R1          ; set R1 (register) to 1 (immediate)
MOV 0xBADF00D, %R1   ; set R1 to value at 0xBADF00D (memory offset)
MOV 0x10(%R2), %R1   ; set R1 to value at 0x10(%R2) (memory offset)
MOV -0x20(%R2), %R1  ; set R1 to value at -0x20(%R2) (memory offset)
```

This code is the AT&T version of Listing 4-7. AT&T syntax not only reverses the operand order but also requires operand prefixing and has a different format for memory offset operands.

Assembly Commands

Once you understand assembly instructions and how to format their operands, you can start writing commands. The following code shows an assembly function, consisting of some very basic commands, that essentially does nothing.

```
PUSH EBP        ; put EBP (register) on the stack
MOV EBP, ESP    ; set EBP to value of ESP (register, top of stack)
PUSH -1         ; put -1 (immediate) on the stack
ADD ESP, 4      ; negate the 'PUSH -1' to put ESP back where it was (a PUSH
                ; subtracts 4 from ESP, since it grows the stack)
MOV ESP, EBP    ; set ESP to the value of EBP (they will be the same anyway,
                ; since we have kept ESP in the same place)
POP EBP         ; set EBP to the value on top of the stack (it will be what
                ; EBP started with, put on the stack by PUSH EBP)
XOR EAX, EAX    ; exclusive-or EAX (register) with itself (same effect as
                ; 'MOV EAX, 0' but much faster)
RETN            ; return from the function with a value of 0 (EAX typically
                ; holds the return value)
```

The first two lines, a PUSH command and a MOV command, set up a stack frame. The next line pushes −1 to the stack, which is undone when the stack is set back to its original position by the ADD ESP, 4 command. Following that, the stack frame is removed, the return value (stored in EAX) is set to 0 with an XOR instruction, and the function returns.

You'll learn more about stack frames and functions in "The Call Stack" on page 86 and "Function Calls" on page 94. For now, turn your attention to the constants in the code—namely EBP, ESP, and EAX, which are used frequently in the code as operands. These values, among others, are called *processor registers*, and understanding them is essential to understanding the stack, function calls, and other low-level aspects of assembly code.

Processor Registers

Unlike high-level programming languages, assembly language does not have user-defined variable names. Instead, it accesses data by referencing its memory address. During intensive computation, however, it can be extremely costly for the processor to constantly deal with the overhead of reading and writing data to RAM. To mitigate this high cost, x86 processors provide a small set of temporary variables, called processor registers, which are small storage spaces within the processor itself. Since accessing these registers requires far less overhead than accessing RAM, assembly uses them to describe its internal state, pass volatile data around, and store context-sensitive variables.

General Registers

When assembly code needs to store or operate on arbitrary data, it uses a subset of process registers called *general registers*. These registers are used exclusively to store process-specific data, such as a function's local variables. Each general register is 32 bits and thus can be thought of as a DWORD variable. General registers are also optimized for specific purposes:

EAX, the accumulator   This register is optimized for mathematical computations. Some operations, such as multiplication and division, can only occur in EAX.

EBX, the base register   This register is used arbitrarily for extra storage. Since its 16-bit predecessor, BX, was the only register that operations could use to reference memory addresses, EBX was used as a reference to RAM. In x86 assembly, however, all registers can be address references, leaving EBX without a true purpose.

ECX, the counter   This register is optimized to act as the counter variable (often called i in high-level code) in a loop.

EDX, the data register   This register is optimized to act as a helper to EAX. In 64-bit computations, for instance, EAX acts as bits 0–31 and EDX acts as bits 32–63.

These registers also have a set of 8- and 16-bit subregisters that you can use to access partial data. Think of every general register as a union, where a register name describes the 32-bit member and the subregisters are alternate members that allow access to smaller pieces of the register. The following code shows what this union might look like for EAX:

```
union {
    DWORD EAX;
    WORD AX;
    struct {
        BYTE L;
        BYTE H;
    } A;
} EAX;
```

In this example, AX allows access to the lower WORD of EAX, while AL allows access to the lower BYTE of AX and AH to its higher BYTE. Every general register has this structure, and I outline the other registers' subregisters in Figure 4-5.

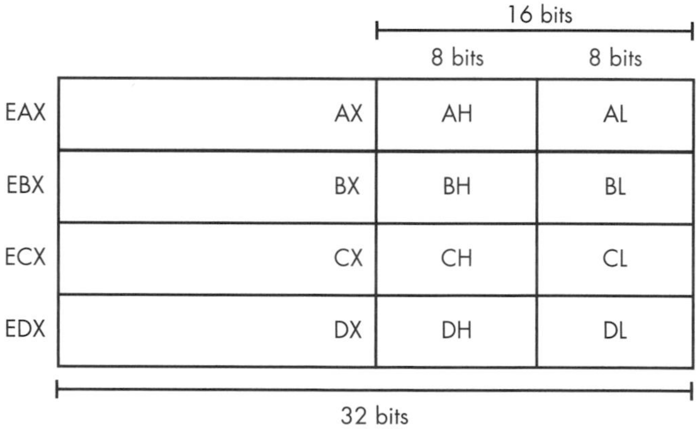

| | | 16 bits | |
		8 bits	8 bits
EAX	AX	AH	AL
EBX	BX	BH	BL
ECX	CX	CH	CL
EDX	DX	DH	DL
		32 bits	

Figure 4-5: x86 registers and subregisters

EAX, EBC, ECX, and EDX have higher words, too, but the compiler will almost never access them on its own, as it can just use the lower word when it needs word-only storage.

Index Registers

x86 assembly also has four *index registers*, which are used to access data streams, reference the call stack, and keep track of local information. Like the general registers, index registers are 32 bits, but index registers have more strictly defined purposes:

EDI, the destination index   This register is used to index memory targeted by write operations. If there are no write operations in a piece of code, the compiler can use EDI for arbitrary storage if needed.

ESI, the source index   This register is used to index memory targeted by read operations. It can also be used arbitrarily.

ESP, the stack pointer   This register is used to reference the top of the call stack. All stack operations directly access this register. You must use ESP only when working with the stack, and it must always point to the top of the stack.

EBP, the stack base pointer   This register marks the bottom of the stack frame. Functions use it as a reference to their parameters and local variables. Some code may be compiled with an option to omit this behavior, in which case EBP can be used arbitrarily.

Like the general registers, each index register has a 16-bit counterpart: DI, SI, SP, and BP, respectively. However, the index registers have no 8-bit subregisters.

WHY DO SOME X86 REGISTERS HAVE SUBREGISTERS?

There is a historical reason why both general and index registers have 16-bit counterparts. The x86 architecture was based on a 16-bit architecture, from which it *extended* the registers AX, BX, CX, DX, DI, SI, SP, and BP. Appropriately, the extensions retain the same names but are prefixed with an *E*, for "extended." The 16-bit versions remain for backward compatibility. This also explains why index registers have no 8-bit abstractions: they are intended to be used as memory-address offsets, and there is no practical need to know partial bytes of such values.

The Execution Index Register

The Execution Index register, referred to as *EIP*, has a very concrete purpose: it points to the address of the code currently being executed by the processor. Because it controls the flow of execution, it is directly incremented by the processor and is off-limits to assembly code. To modify EIP, assembly code must indirectly access it using operations such as CALL, JMP, and RETN.

The EFLAGS Register

Unlike high-level code, assembly language doesn't have binary comparison operators like ==, >, and <. Instead, it uses the CMP command to compare two values, storing the resulting information in the EFLAGS register. Then, the code changes its control flow using special operations that depend on the value stored in ELFAGS.

While comparison commands are the only user-mode operations that can access EFLAGS, they use only this register's *status* bits: 0, 2, 4, 6, 7, and 11. Bits 8–10 act as control flags, bits 12–14 and 16–21 act as system flags, and the remaining bits are reserved for the processor. Table 4-5 shows the type, name, and description of each EFLAGS bit.

Table 4-5: EFLAGS bits

Bit(s)	Type	Name	Description
0	Status	Carry	Set if a carry or borrow was generated from the most significant bit during the previous instruction.
2	Status	Parity	Set if the least significant byte resulting from the previous instruction has an even number of bits set.
4	Status	Adjust	Same as the carry flag, but considers the 4 least significant bits.
6	Status	Zero	Set if the resulting value from the previous instruction is equal to 0.
7	Status	Sign	Set if the resulting value from the previous instruction has its sign bit (most significant bit) set.
8	Control	Trap	When set, the processor sends an interrupt to the operating system kernel after executing the next operation.
9	Control	Interrupt	When not set, the system ignores maskable interrupts.
10	Control	Direction	When set, ESI and EDI are decremented by operations that automatically modify them. When not set, they are incremented.
11	Status	Overflow	Set when a value is overflowed by the previous instruction, such as when ADD is performed on a positive value and the result is a negative value.

The EFLAGS register also contains a system bit and a reserved bit, but those are irrelevant in user-mode assembly and game hacking, so I've omitted them from this table. Keep EFLAGS in mind when you're debugging game code to figure out how it works. For example, if you set a breakpoint on a JE (jump if equal) instruction, you can look at the EFLAGS 0 bit to see whether the jump will be taken.

Segment Registers

Finally, assembly language has a set of 16-bit registers called *segment registers*. Unlike other registers, segment registers are not used to store data; they are used to locate it. In theory, they point to isolated segments of memory, allowing different types of data to be stored in completely separate memory segments. The implementation of such segmentation is left up to the operating system. These are the x86 segment registers and their intended purposes:

CS, the code segment   This register points to the memory that holds an application's code.

DS, the data segment   This register points to the memory that holds an application's data.

ES, FS, and GS, the extra segments   These registers point to any proprietary memory segments used by the operating system.

SS, the stack segment   This register points to memory that acts as a dedicated call stack.

In assembly code, segment registers are used as prefixes to memory offset operands. When a segment register isn't specified, DS is used by default. This means that the command PUSH [EBP] is effectively the same as PUSH DS:[EBP]. But the command PUSH FS:[EBP] is different: it reads memory from the FS segment, not the DS segment.

If you look closely at the Windows x86 implementation of memory segmentation, you might notice that these segment registers were not exactly used as intended. To see this in action, you can run the following commands with the OllyDbg command line plug-in while OllyDbg is attached to a paused process:

```
? CALC (DS==SS && SS==GS && GS==ES)
? 1
? CALC DS-CS
? 8
? CALC FS-DS
; returns nonzero (and changes between threads)
```

This output tells us three distinct things. First, it shows that there are only three segments being used by Windows: FS, CS, and everything else. This is demonstrated by DS, SS, GS, and ES being equal. For the same reason, this output shows that DS, SS, GS, and ES can all be used interchangeably, as they all point to the same memory segments. Lastly, since FS changes depending on the thread, this output shows that it is thread dependent. FS is an interesting segment register, and it points to certain thread-specific data. In "Bypassing ASLR in Production" on page 128, we'll explore how the data in FS can be used to bypass ASLR—something most bots will need to do.

In fact, in assembly code generated for Windows by a compiler, you'd only ever see three segments used: DS, FS, and SS. Interestingly enough, even though CS seems to show a constant offset from DS, it has no real purpose in user-mode code. Knowing all of these things, you can further conclude that there are only two segments being used by Windows: FS and everything else.

These two segments actually point to different locations in the same memory (there's no simple way to verify this, but it is true), which shows that Windows actually doesn't use memory segments at all. Instead, it uses a flat memory model in which segment registers are nearly irrelevant. While all segment registers point to the same memory, only FS and CS point to different locations, and CS is not used.

In conclusion, there are only three things you need to know about segment registers when working with x86 assembly in Windows. First, DS, SS, GS, and ES are interchangeable, but for clarity DS should be used to access data and SS should be used to access the call stack. Second, CS can be safely forgotten. Third, FS is the only segment register with a special purpose; it should be left alone for now.

The Call Stack

Registers are powerful, but unfortunately they come in very limited supply. In order for assembly code to effectively store all of its local data, it must also use the *call stack*. The stack is used to store many different values, including function parameters, return addresses, and some local variables.

Understanding the ins and outs of the call stack will come in handy when you're reverse engineering a game. Moreover, you'll rely on this knowledge heavily when we jump into control flow manipulation in Chapter 8.

Structure

You can think of the call stack as a *FILO (first-in-last-out)* list of DWORD values that can be directly accessed and manipulated by assembly code. The term *stack* is used because the structure resembles a stack of paper: objects are both added to and removed from the top. Data is added to the stack through the PUSH *operand* command, and it is removed (and placed in a register) through the POP *register* command. Figure 4-6 shows how this process might look.

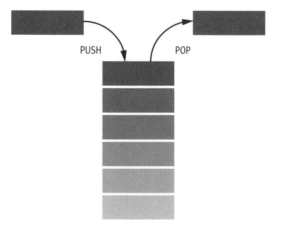

Figure 4-6: The structure of a stack

In Windows, the stack grows from higher memory addresses to lower ones. It occupies a finite block of memory, piling up to address 0x00000000 (the absolute top) from address *n* (the absolute bottom). This means that ESP (the pointer to the top of the stack) decreases as items are added and increases as items are removed.

The Stack Frame

When an assembly function uses the stack to store data, it references the data by creating a *stack frame*. It does so by storing ESP in EBP and then subtracting *n* bytes from ESP, effectively opening an *n*-byte gap that is *framed* between the registers EBP and ESP. To better understand this, first imagine that the stack in Figure 4-7 is passed to a function that requires 0x0C bytes of local storage space.

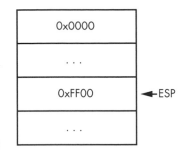

In this example, address 0x0000 is the absolute top of the stack. We have unused memory from addresses 0x0000 to 0xFF00

Figure 4-7: Initial example stack (read from bottom to top)

– 4, and at the time of the function call, 0xFF00 is the top of the stack. ESP points to this address. The stack memory after 0xFF00 is used by preceding functions in the call chain (from 0xFF04 to 0xFFFF). When the function is called, the first thing it does is execute the following assembly code, which creates a stack frame of 0x0C (12 in decimal) bytes:

```
PUSH EBP      ; saves the bottom of the lower stack frame
MOV EBP, ESP  ; stores the bottom of the current stack frame, in EBP
              ; (also 4 bytes above the lower stack frame)
SUB ESP, 0x0C ; subtracts 0x0C bytes from ESP, moving it up the stack
              ; to mark the top of the stack frame
```

After this code executes, the stack looks more like the one shown in Figure 4-8. After creating this stack, the function can work with the 0x0C bytes it allocated on the stack.

0x0000 is still the absolute top of the stack. We have unused stack memory from addresses 0x0000 to 0xFF00 – 20, and the memory at address 0xFF00 – 16 contains the final 4 bytes of local storage (referenced by [EBP-Ch]). This is also the top of the current stack frame, so ESP points here. 0xFF00 – 12 contains the middle 4 bytes of local storage (referenced by [EBP-8h]), and 0xFF00 – 8 contains the first 4 bytes of local storage (referenced by [EBP-4h]). EBP points to 0xFF00 – 4, which is the bottom of the current stack frame; this address holds the original value of EBP. 0xFF00 is the top of the lower stack frame, and the original ESP in Figure 4-7 pointed here. Finally, you can still see the stack memory from preceding functions in the call chain from 0xFF04 to 0xFFFF.

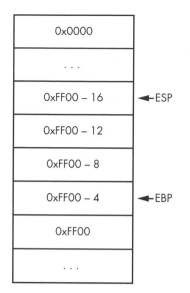

0x0000
. . .
0xFF00 – 16	◄—ESP
0xFF00 – 12
0xFF00 – 8
0xFF00 – 4	◄—EBP
0xFF00
. . .

Figure 4-8: Example stack with stack frame set up (read from bottom to top)

With the stack in this state, the function is free to use its local data as it pleases. If this function called another function, the new function would build its own stack frame using the same technique (the stack frames really stack up). Once a function finishes using a stack frame, however, it must restore the stack to its previous state. In our case, that means making the stack look like it did in Figure 4-7. When the second function finishes, our first function cleans the stack using the following two commands:

```
MOV ESP, EBP   ; demolishes the stack frame, bringing ESP to 4 bytes above
               ; its original value (0xFF00-4)
POP EBP        ; restores the bottom of the old stack frame that was saved by
               ; 'PUSH EBP'. Also adds 4 bytes to ESP, putting it back at
               ; its original value
```

But if you want to change the parameters passed to a function in a game, don't look for them in that function's stack frame. A function's parameters are stored in the stack frame of the function that called it, and they're referenced through [EBP+8h], [EBP+Ch], and so on. They start at [EBP+8h] because [EBP+4h] stores the function's return address. ("Function Calls" on page 94 explains this topic further.)

NOTE   *Code can be compiled with stack frames disabled. When this is the case, you'll notice that functions don't open with PUSH EBP and instead reference everything relative to ESP. More often than not, though, stack frames are enabled in compiled game code.*

Now that you have a grasp on the fundamentals of assembly code, let's explore some specifics that will come in handy when hacking games.

Important x86 Instructions for Game Hacking

While assembly language has hundreds of instructions, many well-equipped game hackers understand only a small subset of them, which I cover in detail here. This subset typically encapsulates all instructions that are used to modify data, call functions, compare values, or jump around within code.

Data Modification

Data modification often happens over several assembly operations, but the end result has to be stored either in memory or in a register, typically with the MOV instruction. The MOV operation takes two operands: a destination and a source. Table 4-6 shows all possible sets of MOV operands and the results you can expect from those calls.

Table 4-6: Operands to the MOV Instruction

Instruction syntax	Result
MOV R1, R2	Copies R2's value to R1.
MOV R1, [R2]	Copies the value from the memory referenced by R2 to R1.
MOV R1, [R2+Ah]	Copies the value from the memory referenced by R2+0xA to R1.
MOV R1, [DEADBEEFh]	Copies the value from the memory at 0xDEADBEEF to R1.
MOV R1, BADF00Dh	Copies the value 0xBADF00D to R1.
MOV [R1], R2	Copies R2's value to the memory referenced by R1.
MOV [R1], BADF00Dh	Copies the value 0xBADF00D to the memory referenced by R1.
MOV [R1+4h], R2	Copies R2's value to the memory referenced by R1+0x4.
MOV [R1+4h], BADF00Dh	Copies the value 0xBADF00D to the memory referenced by R1+0x4.
MOV [DEADBEEFh], R1	Copies R1's value to the memory at 0xDEADBEEF.
MOV [DEADBEEFh], BADF00Dh	Copies the value 0xBADF00D to the memory at 0xDEADBEEF.

The MOV instruction can take a lot of operand combinations, but some aren't allowed. First, the destination operand can't be an immediate value; it must be a register or memory address, because immediate values can't be modified. Second, values can't be directly copied from one memory address to another. Copying a value requires two separate operations, like so:

```
MOV EAX, [EBP+10h]   ; copy memory from EBP+0x10 to EAX
MOV [DEADBEEFh], EAX ; MOV the copied memory to memory at 0xDEADBEEF
```

These instructions copy whatever is stored at EBP+0x10 to the memory at 0xDEADBEEF.

Arithmetic

Like many high-level languages, assembly language has two types of arithmetic: unary and binary. Unary instructions take a single operand that acts as both a destination and a source. This operand can be a register or a memory address. Table 4-7 shows the common unary arithmetic instructions in x86.

Table 4-7: Unary Arithmetic Instructions

Instruction syntax	Result
INC *operand*	Adds 1 to the operand value.
DEC *operand*	Subtracts 1 from the operand value.
NOT *operand*	Logically negates the operand value (flips all bits).
NEG *operand*	Performs two's-complement negation (flips all bits and adds 1; essentially multiplies by −1).

Binary instructions (which make up the majority of x86 arithmetic), on the other hand, are syntactically similar to the MOV instruction. They require two operands and have similar operand limitations. Unlike MOV, however, their destination operand serves a second purpose: it is also the left-hand value in the calculation. For example, the assembly operation ADD EAX,EBX equates to EAX = EAX + EBX or EAX += EBX in C++. Table 4-8 shows the common x86 binary arithmetic instructions.

Table 4-8: Binary Arithmetic Instructions

Instruction syntax	Function	Operand notes
ADD *destination, source*	*destination* += *source*	
SUB *destination, source*	*destination* -= *source*	
AND *destination, source*	*destination* &= *source*	
OR *destination, source*	*destination* |= *source*	
XOR *destination, source*	*destination* ^= *source*	
SHL *destination, source*	*destination* = *destination* << *source*	*source* must be CL or an 8-bit immediate value.
SHR *destination, source*	*destination* = *destination* >> *source*	*source* must be CL or an 8-bit immediate value.
IMUL *destination, source*	*destination* *= *source*	*destination* must be a register; source cannot be an immediate value.

Of these arithmetic instructions, IMUL is special because you can pass it a third operand, in the form of an immediate value. With this prototype, the destination operand is no longer involved in the calculation, which instead takes place between the remaining operands. For example, the assembly command IMUL EAX,EBX,4h equates to EAX = EBX * 0x4 in C++.

You can also pass a single operand to IMUL.[3] In this case, the operand acts as the source and can be either a memory address or a register. Depending on the size of the source operand, the instruction will use different parts of the EAX register for inputs and output, as shown in Table 4-9.

Table 4-9: Possible IMUL Register Operands

Source size	Input	Output
8 bits	AL	16 bit, stored in AH:AL (which is AX)
16 bits	AX	32 bit, stored in DX:AX (bits 0–15 in AX and bits 16–31 in DX)
32 bits	EAX	64 bit, stored in EDX:EAX (bits 0–31 in EAX and bits 32–64 in EDX)

Notice that even though the input is only one register, each output uses two registers. That's because in multiplication, the result generally is larger than the inputs.

Let's look at an example calculation using IMUL with a single 32-bit operand:

```
IMUL [BADF00Dh] ; 32-bit operand is at address 0xBADF00D
```

This command behaves like the following pseudocode:

```
EDX:EAX = EAX * [BADF00Dh]
```

Similarly, here's an operation that uses IMUL with a single 16-bit operand:

```
IMUL CX ; 16-bit operand is stored in CX
```

And its corresponding pseudocode:

```
DX:AX = AX * CX
```

Finally, this is an IMUL command with a single 8-bit operand:

```
IMUL CL ; 8-bit operand is stored in CL
```

And its corresponding pseudocode:

```
AX = AL * CL
```

---

3. There is also an unsigned multiplication instruction, MUL, which only works with a single operand.

x86 assembly language has division as well, through the IDIV instruction.[4] The IDIV instruction accepts a single source operand and follows register rules similar to those for IMUL. As Table 4-10 shows, IDIV operations require two inputs and two outputs.

Table 4-10: Possible IDIV Register Operands

Source size	Input	Output
8 bit	16 bit, stored in AH:AL (which is AX)	Remainder in AH; quotient in AL
16 bit	32 bit, stored in DX:AX	Remainder in DX; quotient in AX
32 bit	64 bit, stored in EDX:EAX	Remainder in EDX; quotient in EAX

In division, the inputs are generally larger than the output, so here the inputs take two registers. Moreover, division operations must store a remainder, which gets stored in the first input register. For example, here's how a 32-bit IDIV calculation would look:

```
MOV EDX, 0       ; there's no high-order DWORD in the input, so EDX is 0
MOV EAX, inputValue ; 32-bit input value
IDIV ECX         ; divide EDX:EAX by ECX
```

And here's some pseudocode that expresses what happens under the hood:

```
EAX = EDX:EAX / ECX ; quotient
EDX = EDX:EAX % ECX ; remainder
```

These details of IDIV and IMUL are important to remember, as the behavior can otherwise be quite obfuscated when you're simply looking at the commands.

Branching

After evaluating an expression, programs can decide what to execute next based on the result, typically using constructs such as if() statements or switch() statements. These control flow statements don't exist at the assembly level, however. Instead, assembly code uses the EFLAGS register to make decisions and jump operations to execute different blocks; this process is called *branching*.

To get the proper value in EFLAGS, assembly code uses one of two instructions: TEST or CMP. Both compare two operands, set the status bits of EFLAGS, and then discard any results. TEST compares the operands using a logical AND, while CMP uses signed subtraction to subtract the latter operand from the former.

---

4. Just as MUL is to IMUL, DIV is the unsigned counterpart to IDIV.

In order to branch properly, the code has a jump command immediately following the comparison. Each type of jump instruction accepts a single operand that specifies the address of the code to jump to. How a particular jump instruction behaves depends on the status bits of EFLAGS. Table 4-11 describes some x86 jump instructions.

Table 4-11: Common x86 Jump Instructions

Instruction	Name	Behavior
JMP dest	Unconditional jump	Jumps to dest (sets EIP to dest).
JE dest	Jump if equal	Jumps if ZF (zero flag) is 1.
JNE dest	Jump if not equal	Jumps if ZF is 0.
JG dest	Jump if greater	Jumps if ZF is 0 and SF (sign flag) is equal to OF (overflow flag).
JGE dest	Jump if greater or equal	Jumps if SF is equal to OF.
JA dest	Unsigned JG	Jumps if CF (carry flag) is 0 and ZF is 0.
JAE dest	Unsigned JGE	Jumps if CF is 0.
JL dest	Jump if less	Jumps if SF is not equal to OF.
JLE dest	Jump if less or equal	Jumps if ZF is 1 or SF is not equal to OF.
JB dest	Unsigned JL	Jumps if CF is 1.
JBE dest	Unsigned JLE	Jumps if CF is 1 or ZF is 1.
JO dest	Jump if overflow	Jumps if OF is 1.
JNO dest	Jump if not overflow	Jumps if OF is 0.
JZ dest	Jump if zero	Jumps if ZF is 1 (identical to JE).
JNZ dest	Jump if not zero	Jumps if ZF is 0 (identical to JNE).

Remembering which flags control which jump instructions can be a pain, but their purpose is clearly expressed in their name. A good rule of thumb is that a jump preceded by a CMP is the same as its corresponding operator. For example, Table 4-11 lists JE as "jump if equal," so when JE follows a CMP operation, it's the same as the == operator. Similarly, JGE would be >=, JLE would be >=, and so on.

As an example, consider the high-level code shown in Listing 4-8.

```
--snip--
if (EBX > EAX)
    ECX = EDX;
else
    ECX = 0;
--snip--
```

Listing 4-8: A simple conditional statement

This if() statement just checks whether EBX is greater than EAX and sets ECX based on the result. In assembly, the same statement may look something like this:

```
    --snip--
    CMP EBX, EAX  ; if (EBX > EAX)
    JG label1     ; jump to label1 if EBX > EAX
    MOV ECX, 0    ; ECX = 0 (else block)
    JMP label2    ; jump over the if block
label1:
❶   MOV ECX, EDX  ; ECX = EDX (if block)
label2:
    --snip--
```

The assembly for the if() statement in Listing 4-8 begins with a CMP instruction and branches if EBX is greater than EAX. If the branch is taken, EIP is set to the if block at ❶ courtesy of the JG instruction. If the branch is not taken, the code continues executing linearly and hits the else block immediately after the JG instruction. When the else block finishes executing, an unconditional JMP sets EIP to 0x7, skipping over the if block.

Function Calls

In assembly code, functions are isolated blocks of commands executed through the CALL instruction. The CALL instruction, which takes a function address as the only operand, pushes a return address onto the stack and sets EIP to its operand value. The following pseudocode shows a CALL in action, with memory addresses on the left in hex:

```
0x1: CALL EAX
0x2: ...
```

When CALL EAX is executed, the next address is pushed to the stack and EIP is set to EAX, showing that CALL is essentially a PUSH and JMP. The following pseudocode underscores this point:

```
0x1: PUSH 3h
0x2: JMP EAX
0x3: ...
```

While there's an extra address between the PUSH instruction and the code to execute, the result is the same: before the block of code at EAX is executed, the address of the code that follows the branch is pushed to the stack. This happens so the *callee* (the function being called) knows where to jump to in the *caller* (the function doing the call) when it returns.

If a function without parameters is called, a CALL command is all that's necessary. If the callee takes parameters, however, the parameters must first be pushed onto the stack in reverse order. The following pseudocode shows how a function call with three parameters might look:

```
PUSH 300h    ; arg3
PUSH 200h    ; arg2
PUSH 100h    ; arg1
CALL ECX     ; call
```

When the callee is executed, the top of the stack contains a return address that points to the code after the call. The first parameter, 0x100, is below the return address on the stack. The second parameter, 0x200, is below that, followed by the third parameter, 0x300. The callee sets up its stack frame, using memory offsets from EBP to reference each parameter. Once the callee has finished executing, it restores the caller's stack frame and executes the RET instruction, which pops the return address off the stack and jumps to it.

Since the parameters are not a part of the callee's stack frame, they remain on the stack after RET is executed. If the caller is responsible for cleaning the stack, it adds 12 (3 parameters, at 4 bytes each) to ESP immediately after CALL ECX completes. If the callee is responsible, it cleans up by executing RET 12 instead of RET. This responsibility is determined by the callee's *calling convention.*

A function's calling convention tells the compiler how the assembly code should pass parameters, store instance pointers, communicate the return value, and clean the stack. Different compilers have different calling conventions, but the ones listed in Table 4-12 are the only four that a game hacker is likely to encounter.

Table 4-12: Calling Conventions to Know for Game Hacking

Directive	Cleaner	Notes
cdecl	caller	Default convention in Visual Studio.
__stdcall	callee	Convention used by Win32 API functions.
__fastcall	callee	First two DWORD (or smaller) parameters are passed in ECX and EDX.
__thiscall	callee	Used for member functions. The pointer to the class instance is passed in ECX.

The Directive column in Table 4-12 gives the name of the calling convention, and the Cleaner column tells you whether the caller or callee is responsible for cleaning the stack given that directive. In the case of these four calling conventions, parameters are always pushed right to left, and return values are always stored in EAX. This is a standard, but not a rule; it can differ across other calling conventions.

Closing Thoughts

My goal in writing this chapter was to help you understand memory and assembly in a general sense, before we dig into game-hacking specifics. With your newfound ability to think like a computer, you should be adequately armed to start tackling more advanced memory forensics tasks. If you're itching for a peek at how you'll apply all of this to something real, flip to "Applying Call Hooks to Adobe AIR" on page 169 or "Applying Jump Hooks and VF Hooks to Direct3D" on page 175.

If you want some hands-on time with memory, compile this chapter's example code and use Cheat Engine or OllyDbg to inspect, tweak, and poke at the memory until you've got the hang of it. This is important, as the next chapter will build on these skills by teaching you advanced memory forensic techniques.

5

ADVANCED MEMORY FORENSICS

Whether you hack games as a hobby or a business, you'll eventually find yourself between a rock and . . . an unintelligible memory dump. Be it a race with a rival bot developer to release a highly requested feature, a battle against a game company's constant barrage of updates, or a struggle to locate some complex data structure in memory, you'll need top-notch memory forensics skills to prevail.

Successful bot development is precariously balanced atop speed and skill, and tenacious hackers must rise to the challenge by swiftly releasing ingenious features, promptly responding to game updates, and readily searching for even the most elusive pieces of data. Doing this, however, requires a comprehensive understanding of common memory patterns, advanced data structures, and the purpose of different pieces of data.

Those three aspects of memory forensics are perhaps the most effective weapons in your arsenal, and this chapter will teach you how to use them. First, I'll discuss advanced memory-scanning techniques that focus on searching for data by understanding its purpose and usage. Next, I'll teach you how to use memory patterns to tackle game updates and tweak your bots without having to relocate all of your addresses from scratch. To wrap up, I'll dissect the four most common complex data structures in the C++ standard library (std::string, std::vector, std::list, and std::map) so you can recognize them in memory and enumerate their contents. By the end of the chapter, my hope is that you'll have a deep understanding of memory forensics and be able to take on any challenge related to memory scanning.

Advanced Memory Scanning

Within a game's source code, each piece of data has a cold, calculated definition. When the game is being played, however, all of that data comes together to create something new. Players only experience the beautiful scenery, visceral sounds, and intense adventures; the data that drives these experiences is irrelevant.

With that in mind, imagine Hacker A has just started tearing into his favorite game, wanting to automate some of the boring bits with a bot. He doesn't have a complete understanding of memory yet, and to him, the data is nothing but assumptions. He thinks, "I have 500 health, so I can find the health address by telling Cheat Engine to look for a 4-byte integer with a value of 500." Hacker A has an accurate understanding of data: it's just information (values) stored at particular locations (addresses) using defined structures (types).

Now imagine Hacker B, who already understands the game both inside and out; she knows how playing the game alters its state in memory, and the data no longer has any secrets. She knows that every defined property of the data can be determined given its purpose. Unlike Hacker A, Hacker B has an understanding of data that transcends the confines of a single variable declaration: she considers the data's *purpose* and *usage*. In this section, we'll discuss both.

Each piece of data in a game has a purpose, and the assembly code of the game must, at some point, reference the data to fulfill that purpose. Finding the unique code that uses a piece of data means finding a version-agnostic marker that persists across game updates until the data is either removed or its purpose is changed. Let me show you why this is important.

Deducing Purpose

So far, I've only shown you how to blindly search memory for a given piece of data without considering how it's being used. This method can be effective, but it is not always efficient. In many cases, it's much quicker to deduce the purpose of data, determine what code might use that data, and then locate that code to ultimately find the address of the data.

This might not sound easy, but neither does "scan the game's memory for a specific value of a specific data type, and then continuously filter the result list based on changing criteria," which is what you've learned to do thus far. So let's look at how we might locate the address for health given its purpose. Consider the code in Listing 5-1.

```
struct PlayerVital {
    int current, maximum;
};
PlayerVital health;
--snip--
printString("Health: %d of %d\n", health.current, health.maximum);
```

Listing 5-1: A structure containing the player's vitals, and a function that displays them

If you pretend that printString() is a fancy function to draw text on an in-game interface, then this code is pretty close to what you might find in a game. The PlayerVital structure has two properties: the current value and a maximum value. The value health is a PlayerVital structure, so it has these properties, too. Based on the name alone, you can deduce that health exists to display information about the player's health, and you can see this purpose fulfilled when printString() uses the data.

Even without the code, you can intuitively draw similar conclusions by just looking at the health text displayed in the game's interface; a computer can't do anything without code, after all. Aside from the actual health variable, there are a few code elements that need to exist to show a player this text. First, there needs to be some function to display text. Second, the strings Health and of must be nearby.

NOTE *Why do I assume the text is split into two separate strings instead of one? The game interface shows that the current health value is between these two strings, but there are many ways that could happen, including format strings, strcat(), or text aligned with multiple display text calls. When you're analyzing data, it's best to keep your assumptions broad to account for all possibilities.*

To find health without using a memory scanner, we could utilize these two distinct strings. We probably wouldn't have a clue what the function to display text looks like, where it is, or how many times it's called, though. Realistically, the strings are all we would know to look for, and that's enough. Let's walk through it.

Finding the Player's Health with OllyDbg

I'll walk you through how to track down the health structure in this section, but I've also included the binary I analyze in the book's resource files. To follow along and get some hands-on practice, use the file *Chapter5_AdvancedMemoryForensics_Scanning.exe.*

First, open OllyDbg and attach it to the executable. Then, open OllyDbg's Executable modules window and double-click the main module; in my example, the main module is the only *.exe* in the module's window.

The CPU window should pop up. Now, right-click in the Disassembler pane and select **Search for ▸ All referenced text strings**. This should open the References window, shown in Figure 5-1.

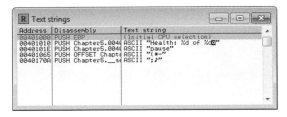

Figure 5-1: OllyDbg's References window, showing only a list of strings. There would be a lot more than four in a real game.

From this window, right-click and select **Search for text**. A search dialog appears. Enter the string you're looking for, as shown in Figure 5-2, and make the search as broad as possible by disabling **Case sensitive** and enabling **Entire scope**.

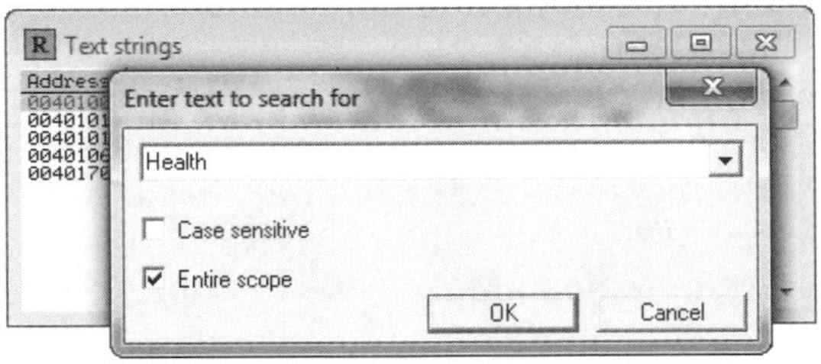

Figure 5-2: Searching for strings in OllyDbg

Click **OK** to execute the search. The References window comes back into focus with the first match highlighted. Double-click the match to see the assembly code that uses the string inside the CPU window. The Disassembler pane focuses on the line of code at 0x401030, which pushes the format string parameter to printString(). You can see this line in Figure 5-3, where I've highlighted the entire function call block.

Figure 5-3: Viewing the printString() call in the CPU window's Disassembler pane

By reading the assembly code, you can get a very accurate understanding of exactly what the game is doing. The black bracket on the left shows that the string Health is inside a function call. Notice the arguments to that function. In order, these are EAX ❶, ECX ❷, and the format string at 0x4020D0 ❸. EAX is the value at 0x40301C, ECX is the value at 0x403018, and the format string contains Health. Since the string contains two format placeholders, you can assume that the remaining two parameters are the arguments for those placeholders.

Knowing what the arguments are and that they are pushed in reverse order, you can work backward and conclude that the original code looked something like Listing 5-2.

```
int currentHealth; // value at 0x403018
int maxHealth;     // value at 0x40301C
--snip--
someFunction("Health: %d of %d\n",
    currentHealth, maxHealth);
```

Listing 5-2: How a game hacker might interpret the assembly that Figure 5-3 compiles to

The values stored in EAX and ECX are adjacent in memory, which means they may be part of a structure. To keep it simple, though, this example just shows them as variable definitions. Either way, these are the two numbers used to display the player's health. Because both of these important values were displayed in the game's UI, it was easy to make assumptions about the underlying code that displays them. When you know the purpose of a piece of data, you can quickly find the code responsible for fulfilling it; in this case, that knowledge helped us quickly find both addresses.

In many cases, finding addresses can be this easy, but some pieces of data have such complex purposes that it's harder to guess what to look for. Figuring out how to search for map data or character locations in OllyDbg, for instance, can be pretty tricky.

Strings are far from the only markers that you can use to find the data you want to change in a game, but they are definitely the easiest to teach without giving contrived examples. Moreover, some games have logging or error strings embedded in their code, and poking around in the Referenced text strings window of OllyDbg can be a quick way to determine whether these strings are present. If you become familiar with a game's logging practices, you'll be able to find values even more easily.

Determining New Addresses After Game Updates

When application code is modified and recompiled, a brand-new binary that reflects the changes is produced. This binary might be very similar to the previous one, or the binaries might be nothing alike; the difference between the two versions has a direct correlation to the complexity of the high-level changes. Small changes, like modified strings or updated constants, can leave binaries nearly identical and often have no effect on the addresses of code or data. But more complex changes—like added features, a new user interface, refactored internals, or new in-game content—often cause shifts in the location of crucial memory.

AUTOMATICALLY FIND CURRENTHEALTH AND MAXHEALTH

In "Searching for Assembly Patterns" on page 19 and "Searching for Strings" on page 21, I showed a few Cheat Engine Lua scripts and explained how they worked. Using the findString() function in these examples, you can make Cheat Engine automatically locate the address of the format string that we just found manually in OllyDbg. Next, you can write a small function to scan for this address following byte 0x68 (the byte for the PUSH command, as you can see beside it at 0x401030 in Figure 5-3) to locate the address of the code that pushes it to the stack. Then, you can read 4 bytes from pushAddress - 5 and pushAddress - 12 to locate currentHealth and maxHealth, respectively.

This may not seem useful since we've already found the addresses, but if this were a real game, these addresses would change when an update is released. Using this knowledge to automate finding them can be very helpful. If you're up to the challenge, give it a whirl!

Due to constant bug fixes, content improvements, and feature additions, online games are among the most rapidly evolving types of software. Some games release updates as often as once a week, and game hackers often spend a majority of their time reverse engineering the new binaries in order to accordingly update their bots.

If you create advanced bots, they will become increasingly supported by a foundation of memory addresses. When an update comes, determining the new addresses for a large number of values and functions is the most time-consuming inevitability you will face. Relying on the "Tips for Winning the Update Race" can be very beneficial, but the tips won't help you locate the updated addresses. You can automatically locate some addresses using Cheat Engine scripts, but that won't always work either. Sometimes you'll have to do the dirty work by hand.

If you try to reinvent the wheel and find these addresses the same way you did initially, you'll be wasting your time. You actually have a big advantage, though: the old binary and the addresses themselves. Using these two things, it is possible to find every single address you need to update in a fraction of the time.

Figure 5-4 shows two different disassemblies: a new game binary on the left and the previous version on the right. I have taken this image from an actual game (which will remain nameless) in order to give you a realistic example.

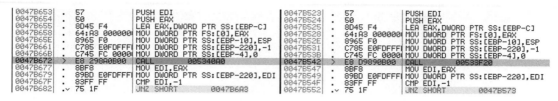

Figure 5-4: Side-by-side disassemblies of two versions of one game

My bot modified the code at 0x047B542 (right), and I needed to find the corresponding code in the new version, which I discovered at 0x047B672 (left). This function call invokes a packet-parsing function when a packet has been received. In order to find this address originally (and by "originally," I mean about 100 updates previous), I figured out how the game's network protocol worked, set breakpoints on many network-related API calls, stepped through execution, and inspected data on the stack until I found something that looked similar to what I expected given my knowledge of the protocol.

TIPS FOR WINNING THE UPDATE RACE

In saturated markets, being the first bot developer to release a stable update is critical to success. The race starts the second the game updates, and hackers determined to be the fastest will spend hundreds of hours preparing. These are the most common ways to stay on top:

Create update alarms By writing software that alerts you as soon as the game patches, you can begin working on your updates as soon as possible.

Automate bot installs Games often schedule expected updates at times when the fewest players are online. Botters hate waking up and downloading new software before they bot, but they love waking up to find it silently installed while the game is patching.

Use fewer addresses The less there is to update, the better. Consolidating related data into structures and eliminating unnecessary memory address usage can save a bunch of time.

Have great test cases Data changes, and hackers make mistakes. Having ways to quickly test every feature can be the difference between a stable bot and one that randomly crashes, gets users killed, or even leads to their characters being banned from the game.

Attacking updates with these practices will give you a sizable head start, but they might not always be enough to lead you to victory. Above all else, strive to understand reverse engineering as much as possible and use that understanding to your advantage.

I could have followed the same steps for each of the 100+ updates since then, but that would have been unnecessary. The code stayed relatively the same throughout the years, which let me use patterns from the old code to find that function call's address in the new code.

Now, consider this chunk of assembly code:

```
PUSH EDI
PUSH EAX
LEA EAX,DWORD PTR SS:[EBP-C]
MOV DWORD PTR FS:[0],EAX
MOV DWORD PTR SS:[EBP-10],ESP
MOV DWORD PTR SS:[EBP-220],-1
MOV DWORD PTR SS:[EBP-4],0
```

Does it look familiar? Compare it to Figure 5-4, and you'll see that this exact code exists right above the highlighted function call in both versions of the game. Regardless of what it does, the combination of operations looks pretty distinctive; because of the number of different offsets the code is using relative to EBP, it's unlikely that an identical chunk of code exists in any other part of the binary.

Every time I have to update this address, I open the old binary in OllyDbg, highlight this chunk of operations, right-click, and select Asm2Clipboard ▶ Copy fixed asm to clipboard. Then, I open the new binary in OllyDbg, navigate to the CPU Window, press CTRL-S, paste the assembly code, and hit Find. In 9.5 cases out of 10, this places me directly above the function call I need to find in the new version.

When an update comes, you can use the same method to find nearly all of your known addresses. It should work for every address you can find easily in assembly code. There are a few caveats, though:

- OllyDbg limits search to eight operations, so you must find code markers of that size or smaller.

- The operations you use cannot contain any other addresses, as those addresses have likely changed.

- If parts of the game have changed that use the address you're looking for, the code might be different.

- If the game changes compilers or switches optimization settings, almost all code will be entirely different.

As discussed in "Automatically Find currentHealth and maxHealth" on page 102, you can benefit from writing scripts that carry out these tasks for you. Serious game hackers work very hard to automatically locate as many addresses as possible, and some of the best bots are engineered to automatically detect their addresses at runtime, every time. It can be a lot of work initially, but the investment can definitely pay off.

Identifying Complex Structures in Game Data

Chapter 4 described how a game might store data in static structures. This knowledge will suffice when you're trying to find simple data, but it falls short for data that is stored through dynamic structures. This is because dynamic structures might be scattered across different memory locations, follow long pointer chains, or require complex algorithms to actually extract the data from them.

This section explores common dynamic structures you'll find in video game code, and how to read data from them once they're found. To begin, I'll talk about the underlying composition of each dynamic structure. Next, I'll outline the algorithms needed to read the data from these structures. (For simplicity, each algorithm discussion assumes you have a pointer to an instance of the structure as well as some way to read from memory.) Lastly, I'll cover tips and tricks that can help you determine when a value you're searching for in memory is actually encapsulated in one of these structures, so you'll know when to apply this knowledge. I'll focus on C++, as its object-oriented nature and heavily used standard library are typically responsible for such structures.

NOTE *Some of these structures might differ slightly from machine to machine based on compilers, optimization settings, or standard library implementations, but the basic concepts will remain the same. Also, in the interest of brevity, I will be omitting irrelevant parts of these structures, such as custom allocators or comparison functions. Working example code can be found at* https://www.nostarch.com/gamehacking/ *in the resource files for Chapter 5.*

The std::string Class

Instances of std::string are among the most common culprits of dynamic storage. This class from the C++ Standard Template Library (STL) abstracts string operations away from the developer while preserving efficiency, making it widely used in all types of software. A video game might use std::string structure for any string data, such as creature names.

Examining the Structure of a std::string

When you strip away the member functions and other nondata components of the std::string class, this is the structure that remains:

```
class string {
    union {
        char* dataP;
        char dataA[16];
    };
    int length;
};

// point to a string in memory
string* _str = (string*)stringAddress;
```

The class reserves 16 characters that are presumably used to store the string in place. It also, however, declares that the first 4 bytes can be a pointer to a character. This might seem odd, but it's a result of optimization. At some point, the developers of this class decided that 15 characters (plus a null terminator) was a suitable length for many strings, and they chose to save on memory allocations and de-allocations by reserving 16 bytes of memory in advance. To accommodate longer strings, they allowed the first 4 bytes of this reserved memory to be used as a pointer to the characters of these longer strings.

NOTE *If the code were compiled to 64 bits, then it would actually be the first 8 (not 4) bytes that point to a character. Throughout this example, however, you can assume 32-bit addresses and that* int *is the size of an address.*

Accessing string data this way takes some overhead. The function to locate the right buffer looks something like this:

```
const char* c_str() {
    if (_str->length <= 15)
        return (const char*)&_str->dataA[0];
    else
        return (const char*)_str->dataP;
}
```

The fact that a std::string can be either a complete string or a pointer to a longer string makes this particular structure quite tricky from a game-hacking perspective. Some games may use std::string to store strings that only rarely exceed 15 characters. When this is the case, you might implement bots that rely on these strings, never knowing that the underlying structure is in fact more complicated than a simple string.

Overlooking a std::string Can Ruin Your Fun

Not knowing the true nature of the structure containing the data you need can lead you to write a bot that works only some of the time and fails when it counts. Imagine, for example, that you're trying to figure out how a game stores creature data. In your hypothetical search, you find that all the creatures in the game are stored in an array of structures that look something like Listing 5-3.

```
struct creatureInfo {
    int uniqueID;
    char name[16];
    int nameLength;
    int healthPercent;
    int xPosition;
    int yPosition;
    int modelID;
```

```
    int creatureType;
};
```

Listing 5-3: How you might interpret creature data found in memory

After scanning the creature data in memory, say you notice that the first 4 bytes of each structure are unique for each creature, so you call those bytes the uniqueID and assume they form a single int property. Looking further in the memory, you find that the creature's name is stored right after uniqueID, and after some deduction, you figure out the name is 16 bytes long. The next value you see in memory turns out to be the nameLength; it's a bit strange that a null-terminated string has an associated length, but you ignore that oddity and continue analyzing the data in memory. After further analysis, you determine what the remaining values are for, define the structure shown in Listing 5-3, and write a bot that automatically attacks creatures with certain names.

After weeks of testing your bot while hunting creatures with names like *Dragon, Cyclops, Giant,* and *Hound,* you decide it's time to give your bot to your friends. For the inaugural use, you gather everyone together to kill a boss named *Super Bossman Supreme.* The entire team sets the bot to attack the boss first and target lesser creatures like a *Demon* or *Grim Reaper* when the boss goes out of range.

Once your team arrives at the boss's dungeon . . . you're all slowly obliterated.

What went wrong in this scenario? Your game must be storing creature names with std::string, not just a simple character array. The name and nameLength fields in creatureInfo are, in fact, part of a std::string field, and the name character array is a union of dataA and dataP members. *Super Bossman Supreme* is longer than 15 characters, and because the bot was not aware of the std::string implementation, it didn't recognize the boss. Instead, it constantly retargeted summoned *Demon* creatures, effectively keeping you from targeting the boss while he slowly drained your health and supplies.

Determining Whether Data Is Stored in a std::string

Without knowing how the std::string class is structured, you'd have trouble tracking down bugs like the hypothetical one I just described. But pair what you've learned here with experience, and you can avoid these kinds of bugs entirely. When you find a string like name in memory, don't just assume it's stored in a simple array. To figure out whether a string is in fact a std::string, ask yourself these questions:

- Why is the string length present for a null-terminated string? If you can't think of a good reason, then you may have a std::string on your hands.

- Do some creatures (or other game elements, depending on what you're looking for) have names longer than 16 letters, but you find room for only 16 characters in memory? If so, the data is almost definitely stored in a std::string.

- Is the name stored in place, requiring the developer to use strcpy() to modify it? It's probably a std::string, because working with raw C strings in this way is considered bad practice.

Finally, keep in mind that there is also a class called std::wstring that is used to store wide strings. The implementation is very similar, but wchar_t is used in place of every char.

The std::vector Class

Games must keep track of many dynamic arrays of data, but managing dynamically sized arrays can be very tricky. For speed and flexibility, game developers often store such data using a templated STL class called std::vector instead of a simple array.

Examining the Structure of a std::vector

A declaration of this class looks something like Listing 5-4.

```
template<typename T>
class vector {
    T* begin;
    T* end;
    T* reservationEnd;
};
```

Listing 5-4: An abstracted std::vector object

This template adds an extra layer of abstraction, so I'll continue this description using a std::vector declared with the DWORD type. Here's how a game might declare that vector:

```
std::vector<DWORD> _vec;
```

Now, let's dissect what a std::vector of DWORD objects would look like in memory. If you had the address of _vec and shared the same memory space, you could re-create the underlying structure of the class and access _vec as shown in Listing 5-5.

```
class vector {
    DWORD* begin;
    DWORD* end;
    DWORD* tail;
};
// point to a vector in memory
vector* _vec = (vector*)vectorAddress;
```

Listing 5-5: A DWORD std::vector object

You can treat the member begin like a raw array, as it points to the first element in the std::vector object. There is no array length member, though, so you must calculate the vector's length based on begin and end, which is an empty object following the final object in the array. The length calculation code looks like this:

```
int length() {
    return ((DWORD)_vec->end - (DWORD)_vec->begin) / sizeof(DWORD);
}
```

This function simply subtracts the address stored in begin from the address stored in end to find the number of bytes between them. Then, to calculate the number of objects, it divides the number of bytes by the number of bytes per object.

Using begin and this length() function, you can safely access elements in _vec. That code would look something like this:

```
DWORD at(int index) {
    if (index >= _vec->length())
        throw new std::out_of_range();
    return _vec->begin[index];
}
```

Given an index, this code will fetch an item from the vector. But if the index is greater than the vector's length, a std::out_of_range exception will be thrown. Adding values to a std::vector would be very expensive if the class couldn't reserve or reuse memory, though. To remedy this, the class implements a function called reserve() that tells the vector how many objects to leave room for.

The absolute size of a std::vector (its *capacity*) is determined through an additional pointer, which is called tail in the vector class we've re-created. The calculation for the capacity resembles the length calculation:

```
int capacity() {
    return ((DWORD)_vec->tail - (DWORD)_vec->begin) / sizeof(DWORD);
}
```

To find the capacity of a std::vector, instead of subtracting the begin address from the end address, as you would to calculate length, this function subtracts the begin address from tail. Additionally, you can use this calculation a third time to determine the number of free elements in the vector by using tail and end instead:

```
int freeSpace() {
    return ((DWORD)_vec->tail - (DWORD)_vec->end) / sizeof(DWORD);
}
```

Given proper memory reading and writing functions, you can use the declaration in Listing 5-4 and the calculations that follow to access and manipulate vectors in the memory of a game. Chapter 6 discusses reading memory in detail, but for now, let's look at ways you can determine whether data you're interested in is stored in a std::vector.

Determining Whether Data Is Stored in a std::vector

Once you've found an array of data in a game's memory, there are a few steps you can follow to determine whether it is stored in a std::vector. First, you can be sure that the array is not stored in a std::vector if it has a static address, because std::vector objects require pointer paths to access the underlying array. If the array *does* require a pointer path, having a final offset of 0 would indicate a std::vector. To confirm, you can change the final offset to 4 and check if it points to the final object in the array instead of the first one. If so, you're almost definitely looking at a vector, as you've just confirmed the begin and end pointers.

The std::list Class

Similar to std::vector, std::list is a class that you can use to store a collection of items in a linked list. The main differences are that std::list doesn't require a contiguous storage space for elements, cannot directly access elements by their index, and can grow in size without affecting any previous elements. Due to the overhead required to access items, it is rare to see this class used in games, but it shows up in some special cases, which I'll discuss in this section.

Examining the Structure of a std::list

The std::list class looks something like Listing 5-6.

```
template<typename T>
class listItem {
    listItem<T>* next;
    listItem<T>* prev;
    T value;
};

template<typename T>
class list {
    listItem<T>* root;
    int size;
};
```

Listing 5-6: An abstracted std::list object

There are two classes here: listItem and list. To avoid extra abstraction while explaining how std::list works, I'll describe this object as it would look when the type is DWORD. Here's how a game would declare a std::list of the DWORD type:

```
std::list<DWORD> _lst;
```

Given that declaration, the std::list is structured like the code in Listing 5-7.

```
class listItem {
    listItem* next;
    listItem* prev;
    DWORD value;
};
class list {
    listItem* root;
    int size;
};
// point to a list
list* _lst = (list*)listAddress;
```

Listing 5-7: A DWORD std::list object

The class list represents the list header, while listItem represents a value stored in the list. Instead of being stored contiguously, the items in the list are stored independently. Each item contains a pointer to the item that comes after it (next) and the one that comes before it (prev), and these pointers are used to locate items in the list. The root item acts as a marker for the end of the list; the next pointer of the last item points to root, as does the prev pointer of the first item. The root item's next and prev pointers also point to the first item and the last item, respectively. Figure 5-5 shows what this looks like.

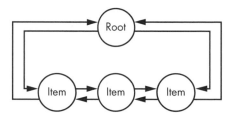

Figure 5-5: A std::list flowchart

Given this structure, you can use the following code to iterate over a std::list object:

```
// iterate forward
listItem* it - _lst->root->next;
for (; it != _lst->root; it = it->next)
    printf("Value is %d\n", it->value);

// iterate backward
listItem* it = _lst->root->prev;
for (; it != _lst->root; it = it->prev)
    printf("Value is %d\n", it->value);
```

The first loop starts at the first item (root->next) and iterates forward (it = it->next) until it hits the end marker (root). The second loop starts at the last item (root->pres) and iterates backward (it = it->prev) until it hits the end marker (root). This iteration relies on next and prev because unlike objects in an array, objects in a std::list are not contiguous. Since the memory of each object in a std::list is not contiguous, there's no quick-and-dirty way to calculate the size. Instead, the class just defines a size member. Additionally, the concept of reserving space for new objects is irrelevant for lists, so there's no variable or calculation to determine a list's capacity.

Determining Whether Game Data Is Stored in a std::list

Identifying objects stored in the std::list class can be tricky, but there are a few hints you can watch for. First, items in a std::list cannot have static addresses, so if the data you seek has a static address, then you're in the clear. Items that are obviously part of a collection may, however, be part of a std::list if they're not contiguous in memory.

Also consider that objects in a std::list can have infinitely long pointer chains (think it->prev->next->prev->next->prev . . .), and pointer scanning for them in Cheat Engine will show many more results when No Looping Pointers is turned off.

You can also use a script to detect when a value is stored in a linked list. Listing 5-8 shows a Cheat Engine script that does just this.

```
function _verifyLinkedList(address)
    local nextItem = readInteger(address) or 0
    local previousItem = readInteger(address + 4) or 0
    local nextItemBack = readInteger(nextItem + 4)
    local previousItemForward = readInteger(previousItem)

    return (address == nextItemBack
            and address == previousItemForward)
end

function isValueInLinkedList(valueAddress)
    for address = valueAddress - 8, valueAddress - 48, -4 do
        if (_verifyLinkedList(address)) then
            return address
        end
    end
    return 0
end

local node = isValueInLinkedList(addressOfSomeValue)
if (node > 0) then
    print(string.format("Value in LL, top of node at 0x0%x", node))
end
```

Listing 5-8: Determining whether data is in a std::list using a Cheat Engine Lua script

There's quite a bit of code here, but what it's doing is actually pretty simple. The isValueInLinkedList() function takes an address of some value and then looks backward for up to 40 bytes (10 integer objects, in case the value is in some larger structure), starting 8 bytes above the address (two pointers must be present, and they are 4 bytes each). Because of memory alignment, this loop iterates in steps of 4 bytes.

On each iteration, the address is passed to the _verifyLinkedList() function, which is where the magic happens. If we look at it in terms of linked list structure as defined in this chapter, the function simply does this:

```
return (node->next->prev == node && node->prev->next == node)
```

That is, the function basically assumes the memory address it's given points to a linked list, and it makes sure the supposed node has valid next and previous nodes. If the nodes are valid, the assumption was correct and the address is that of a linked list node. If the nodes don't exist or don't point to the right locations, the assumption was wrong and the address is not part of a linked list.

Keep in mind that this script won't give you the address of the list's root node but simply the address of the node containing the value you've given it. To properly traverse a linked list, you'll need to scan for a valid pointer path to the root node, so you'll need its address.

Finding that address can require some searching of memory dumps, a lot of trial and error, and a ton of head scratching, but it's definitely possible. The best way to start is to follow the chain of prev and next nodes until you find a node with data that is either blank, nonsensical, or filled with the value 0xBAADF00D (some, but not all, standard library implementations use this value to mark root nodes).

This investigation can also be made easier if you know exactly how many nodes are in the list. Even without the list header, you can determine the amount of nodes by continuously following the next pointer until you end up back at your starting node, as in Listing 5-9.

```
function countLinkedListNodes(nodeAddress)
    local counter = 0
    local next = readInteger(nodeAddress)
    while (next ~= nodeAddress) do
        counter = counter + 1
        next = readInteger(next)
    end
    return counter
end
```

Listing 5-9: Determining the size of an arbitrary std::list using a Cheat Engine Lua script

First, this function creates a counter to store the number of nodes and a variable to store the next node's address. The while loop then iterates over the nodes until it ends up back at the initial node. Finally, it returns the counter variable, which was incremented on every iteration of the loop.

The std::map Class

Like a std::list, a std::map uses links between elements to form its structure. Unique to std::map, however, is the fact that each element stores two pieces of data (a key and a value), and sorting the elements is an inherent property of the underlying data structure: a red-black tree. The following code shows the structures that compose a std::map.

```
template<typename keyT, typename valT>
struct mapItem {
    mapItem<keyT, valT>* left;
    mapItem<keyT, valT>* parent;
    mapItem<keyT, valT>* right;
    keyT key;
    valT value;
};

template<typename keyT, typename valT>
struct map {
    DWORD irrelevant;
    mapItem<keyT, valT>* rootNode;
    int size;
}
```

A red-black tree is a self-balancing binary search tree, so a std::map is, too. In the STL's std::map implementation, each element (or node) in the tree has three pointers: left, parent, and right. In addition to the pointers, each node also has a key and a value. The nodes are arranged in the tree based on a comparison between their keys. The left pointer of a node points to a node with a smaller key, and the right pointer points to a node with a larger key. The parent points to the upper node. The first node in the tree is called the rootNode, and nodes that lack children point to it.

Visualizing a std::map

Figure 5-6 shows a std::map that has the keys 1, 6, 8, 11, 13, 15, 17, 22, 25, and 27.

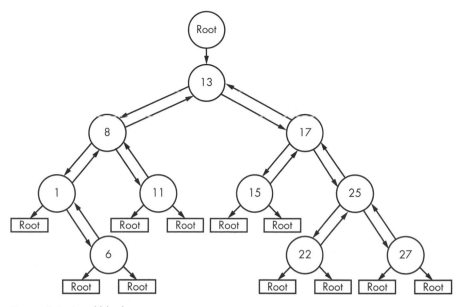

Figure 5-6: A red-black tree

The top node (holding the value 13) is pointed to by the parent of rootNode. Everything to the left of it has a smaller key, and everything to the right has a greater key. This is true for any node in the tree, and this truth enables efficient key-based search. While not represented in the image, the left pointer of the root node will point to the leftmost node (1), and the right pointer will point to the rightmost node (27).

Accessing Data in a std::map

Once again, I'll use a static std::map definition when discussing how to extract data from the structure. Since the template takes two types, I'll also use some pseudotypes to keep things obvious. Here's the declaration for the std::map object I'll reference for the rest of the section:

```
typedef int keyInt;
typedef int valInt;
std::map<keyInt, valInt> myMap;
```

With this declaration, the structure of myMap becomes:

```
struct mapItem {
    mapItem* left;
    mapItem* parent;
    mapItem* right;
    keyInt key;
    valInt value;
};
struct map {
    DWORD irrelevant;
    mapItem* rootNode;
```

```
    int size;
}
map* _map = (map*)mapAddress;
```

There are some important algorithms that you might need to access the data in a std::map structure in a game. First, blindly iterating over every item in the map can be useful if you just want to see all of the data. To do this sequentially, you could write an iteration function like this:

```
void iterateMap(mapItem* node) {
    if (node == _map->rootNode) return;
    iterateMap(node->left);
    printNode(node);
    iterateMap(node->right);
}
```

A function to iterate over an entire map would first read the current node and check whether it's the rootNode. If not, it would recurse left, print the node, and recurse right.

To call this function, you'd have to pass a pointer to the rootNode as follows:

```
iterateMap(_map->rootNode->parent);
```

The purpose of a std::map, however, is to store keyed data in a quickly searchable way. When you need to locate a node given a specific key, mimicking the internal search algorithm is preferable to scanning the entire tree. The code for searching a std::map looks something like this:

```
mapItem* findItem(keyInt key, mapItem* node) {
    if (node != _map->rootNode) {
        if (key == node->key)
            return node;
        else if (key < node->key)
            return findItem(key, node->left);
        else
            return findItem(key, node->right);
    } else return NULL;
}
```

Starting at the top of the tree, you simply recurse left if the current key is greater than the search key and recurse right if it is smaller. If the keys are equal, you return the current node. If you reach the bottom of the tree and don't find the key, you return NULL because the key isn't stored in the map.

Here's one way you might use this findItem() function:

```
mapItem* ret = findItem(someKey, _map->rootNode->parent);
if (ret)
    printNode(ret);
```

As long as findItem() doesn't return NULL, this code should print a node from _map.

Determining Whether Game Data Is Stored in a std::map

Typically, I don't even consider whether data could be in a std::map until I know the collection is not an array, a std::vector, or a std::list. If you rule out all three options, then as with a std::list, you can look at the three integer values before the value and check if they point to memory that could possibly be other map nodes.

Once again, this can be done with a Lua script in Cheat Engine. The script is similar to the one I showed for lists, looping backward over memory to see if a valid node structure is found before the value. Unlike the list code, though, the function that verifies a node is much trickier. Take a look at the code in Listing 5-10, and then I'll dissect it.

```
function _verifyMap(address)
    local parentItem = readInteger(address + 4) or 0

    local parentLeftItem = readInteger(parentItem + 0) or 0
    local parentRightItem = readInteger(parentItem + 8) or 0

❶   local validParent =
        parentLeftItem == address
        or parentRightItem == address
    if (not validParent) then return false end

    local tries = 0
    local lastChecked = parentItem
    local parentsParent = readInteger(parentItem + 4) or 0
❷   while (readInteger(parentsParent + 4) ~= lastChecked and tries < 200) do
        tries = tries + 1
        lastChecked = parentsParent
        parentsParent = readInteger(parentsParent + 4) or 0
    end

    return readInteger(parentsParent + 4) == lastChecked
end
```

Listing 5-10: Determining whether data is in a std::map using a Cheat Engine Lua script

Given address, this function checks if address is in a map structure. It first checks if there's a valid parent node and, if so, checks whether that parent node points to address on either side ❶. But this check isn't enough. If the check passes, the function will also climb up the line of parent nodes until it reaches a node that is the parent of its own parent ❷, trying 200 times before calling it quits. If the climb succeeds in finding a node that is its own grandparent, then address definitely points to a map node. This works because, as I outlined in "Visualizing a std::map" on page 114, at the top of every map is a root node whose parent points to the first node in the tree, and that node's parent points back to the root node.

I bet you didn't expect to run into the grandfather paradox from time travel when reading a game-hacking book!

Using this function and a slightly modified backtracking loop from Listing 5-8, you can automatically detect when a value is inside a map:

```
function isValueInMap(valueAddress)
    for address = valueAddress - 12, valueAddress - 52, -4 do
        if (_verifyMap(address)) then
            return address
        end
    end
    return 0
end

local node = isValueInMap(addressOfSomeValue)
if (node > 0) then
    print(string.format("Value in map, top of node at 0x0%x", node))
end
```

Aside from function names, the only change in this code from Listing 5-8 is that it starts looping 12 bytes before the value instead of 8, because a map has three pointers instead of the two in a list. One good consequence of a map's structure is that it's easy to obtain the root node. When the _verifyMap function returns true, the parentsParent variable will contain the address of the root node. With some simple modifications, you could return this to the main call and have everything you need to read the data from a std::map in one place.

Closing Thoughts

Memory forensics is the most time-consuming part of hacking games, and its obstacles can appear in all shapes and sizes. Using purpose, patterns, and a deep understanding of complex data structures, however, you can quickly overcome these obstacles. If you're still a bit confused about what's going on, make sure to download and play with the example code provided, as it contains proofs of concept for all of the algorithms covered in this chapter.

In Chapter 6, we'll start diving in to the code you need to read from and write to a game's memory from your own programs so you can take the first step in putting to work all of this information about memory structures, addresses, and data.

6

READING FROM AND
WRITING TO GAME MEMORY

Earlier chapters discussed how memory is structured as well as how to scan and modify memory using Cheat Engine and OllyDbg. Working with memory will be essential when you begin to write bots, and your code will need to know how to do so.

This chapter digs into the code-level details of memory manipulation. First, you'll learn how to use code to locate and obtain handles to game processes. Next, you'll learn how to use those handles to read from and write to memory both from remote processes and from injected code. To wrap up, you'll learn bypasses for a certain memory protection technique, complete with a small example of code injection. You'll find the example code for this chapter in the *GameHackingExamples/Chapter6_AccessingMemory* directory in this book's source files.

NOTE   *When I talk about API functions in this chapter (and in later ones), I'm referring to the Windows API unless otherwise specified. If I don't mention a header file for the library, you can assume it is* Windows.h.

Obtaining the Game's Process Identifier

To read from or write to a game's memory, you need its *process identifier (PID)*, a number that uniquely identifies an active process. If the game has a visible window, you can obtain the PID of the process that created that window by calling `GetWindowThreadProcessId()`. This function takes the window's handle as the first parameter and outputs the PID to the second parameter. You can find the window's handle by passing its title (the text on the taskbar) as the second parameter to `FindWindow()`, as shown in Listing 6-1.

```
HWND myWindow =
    FindWindow(NULL, "Title of the game window here");
DWORD PID;
GetWindowThreadProcessId(myWindow, &PID);
```

Listing 6-1: Fetching a window's handle to obtain a PID

With the window handle secured, all you have to do is create a place to store the PID and call `GetWindowThreadProcessId()`, as shown in this example.

If a game isn't windowed or the window name isn't predictable, you can find the game's PID by enumerating all processes and looking for the name of the game binary. Listing 6-2 does this using the API functions `CreateToolhelp32Snapshot()`, `Process32First()`, and `Process32Next()` from *tlhelp32.h*.

```
#include <tlhelp32.h>

PROCESSENTRY32 entry;
entry.dwSize = sizeof(PROCESSENTRY32);
HANDLE snapshot =
    CreateToolhelp32Snapshot(TH32CS_SNAPPROCESS, NULL);
if (Process32First(snapshot, &entry) == TRUE) {
    while (Process32Next(snapshot, &entry) == TRUE) {
        wstring binPath = entry.szExeFile;
        if (binPath.find(L"game.exe") != wstring::npos) {
            printf("game pid is %d\n", entry.th32ProcessID);
            break;
        }
    }
}
CloseHandle(snapshot);
```

Listing 6-2: Fetching a game's PID without the window name

Listing 6-2 might look a bit more complex than Listing 6-1, but underneath all that code, the function is actually like a canonical for (*iterator; comparator; increment*) loop. The `CreateToolhelp32Snapshot()` function obtains a list of processes named snapshot, and entry is an *iterator* over that list. The value returned by `Process32First()` initializes the iterator, while `Process32Next()` *increments* it. Finally, the Boolean return value of

`Process32Next()` is the *comparator*. This code just iterates over a snapshot of every running process, looks for one whose binary path contains the text *game.exe*, and prints its PID.

Obtaining Process Handles

Once you know a game's PID, you can obtain a handle to the process itself using an API function called `OpenProcess()`. This function allows you to fetch handles with the access levels you need to read from and write to memory. This is crucial to game hacking, as any function that operates on a process will require a handle with proper access.

Let's take a look at the prototype of `OpenProcess()`:

```
HANDLE OpenProcess(DWORD DesiredAccess, BOOL InheritHandle, DWORD ProcessId);
```

The first parameter, `DesiredAccess`, expects one or a mixture of process access flags to set on the handle that `OpenProcess()` returns. There are many flags you can use, but these are the most common in game hacking:

PROCESS_VM_OPERATION The returned handle can be used with `VirtualAllocEx()`, `VirtualFreeEx()`, and `VirtualProtectEx()` to allocate, free, and protect chunks of memory, respectively.

PROCESS_VM_READ The returned handle can be used with `ReadProcessMemory()`.

PROCESS_VM_WRITE The returned handle can be used with `WriteProcessMemory()`, but it must also have `PROCESS_VM_OPERATION` rights. You can set both flags by passing `PROCESS_VM_OPERATION | PROCESS_VM_WRITE` as the `DesiredAccess` parameter.

PROCESS_CREATE_THREAD The returned handle can be used with `CreateRemoteThread()`.

PROCESS_ALL_ACCESS The returned handle can be used to do anything. Avoid using this flag, as it can only be used by processes with debug privileges enabled and has compatibility issues with older versions of Windows.

When fetching a handle to a game, you can typically just set the `OpenProcess()` function's second parameter, `InheritHandle`, to `false`. The third parameter, `ProcessId`, expects the PID of the process to be opened.

Working with OpenProcess()

Now let's walk through an example call to `OpenProcess()` that uses a handle with access permissions allowing it to read from and write to memory:

```
DWORD PID = getGamePID();
HANDLE process = OpenProcess(
    PROCESS_VM_OPERATION |
        PROCESS_VM_READ |
        PROCESS_VM_WRITE,
```

```
        FALSE,
        PID
);
❶ if (process == INVALID_HANDLE_VALUE) {
        printf("Failed to open PID %d, error code %d",
                PID, GetLastError());
}
```

First, the call to getGamePID() fetches the PID you're looking for. (The function is something you'll have to write yourself, though it could just be one of the snippets I showed in Listings 6-1 and 6-2, fleshed out into a full-blown function.) Then, the code calls OpenProcess() with three flags: the PROCESS_VM_OPERATION flag gives this handle memory access permissions, and the other two combined give it read and write permissions. This example also contains an error-handling case ❶, but as long as you have the correct PID, you have valid access flags, and your code is running under the same or higher permissions as the game (for example, if you start your bot using Run As Admin), the call should never fail.

Once you're done using a handle, clean it up using CloseHandle() as follows:

```
CloseHandle(process);
```

You can reuse handles as much as you want, so you can leave one open until you're completely done using it or until your bot is exited.

Now that you've seen how to open a process handle in preparation for manipulating game memory, let's dig into how to actually access the memory of that process.

Accessing Memory

The Windows API exposes two functions that are crucial to memory access: ReadProcessMemory() and WriteProcessMemory(). You can use these functions to externally manipulate a game's memory.

Working with ReadProcessMemory() and WriteProcessMemory()

The prototypes for these two functions (shown in Listing 6-3) resemble each other closely, and you'll follow almost exactly the same steps to use them.

```
BOOL ReadProcessMemory(
    HANDLE Process, LPVOID Address,
    LPVOID Buffer, DWORD Size,
    DWORD *NumberOfBytesRead
);
BOOL WriteProcessMemory(
    HANDLE Process, LPVOID Address,
    LPCVOID Buffer, DWORD Size,
```

```
    DWORD *NumberOfBytesWritten
);
```

Listing 6-3: ReadProcessMemory() and WriteProcessMemory() prototypes

Both functions expect Process to be a process handle and Address to be the target memory address. When the function is reading from memory, Buffer is expected to point to an object that will hold the read data. When the function is writing to memory, Buffer is expected to point to the data to write. In both cases, Size defines the size of Buffer, in bytes. The final parameter to both functions is used to optionally return the number of bytes that were accessed; you can safely set it to NULL. Unless the function fails, the value returned in the final parameter should be equal to Size.

Accessing a Value in Memory with ReadProcessMemory() and WriteProcessMemory()

The code in Listing 6-4 shows how you might use these functions to access a value in memory.

```
DWORD val;
ReadProcessMemory(proc, adr, &val, sizeof(DWORD), 0);
printf("Current mem value is %d\n", val);

val++;

WriteProcessMemory(proc, adr, &val, sizeof(DWORD), 0);
ReadProcessMemory(proc, adr, &val, sizeof(DWORD), 0);
printf("New mem value is confirmed as %d\n", val);
```

Listing 6-4: Reading from and writing to process memory using the Windows API

Before code like this appears in a program, you need to find the PID (proc) as described in "Obtaining the Game's Process Identifier" on page 120, as well as the memory address (adr) you want to read from or write to. With those values in place, the ReadProcessMemory() function stores a fetched value from memory in val. Then, the code increments val and replaces the original value by calling WriteProcessMemory(). After the write takes place, ReadProcessMemory() is called on the same address to confirm the new memory value. Notice that val isn't actually a buffer. Passing &val as the Buffer parameter works because it can be a pointer to any static memory structure, as long as Size matches.

Writing Templated Memory Access Functions

Of course, the example in Listing 6-4 assumes you already know what type of memory you're dealing with, and it hardcodes the type as DWORD. To be a versatile game hacker, it's better to have some generic code in your toolbox to avoid duplicating code for different types. Generic memory reading and writing functions that support different types might look like Listing 6-5.

```
template<typename T>
T readMemory(HANDLE proc, LPVOID adr) {
    T val;
    ReadProcessMemory(proc, adr, &val, sizeof(T), NULL);
    return val;
}

template<typename T>
void writeMemory(HANDLE proc, LPVOID adr, T val) {
    WriteProcessMemory(proc, adr, &val, sizeof(T), NULL);
}
```

Listing 6-5: Generic memory functions

These functions use C++ templates to accept arbitrary types as arguments. They allow you to access memory with whatever types you like in a very clean way. For example, given these `readMemory()` and `writeMemory()` templates I just showed, you could make the calls in Listing 6-6.

```
DWORD value = readMemory<DWORD>(proc, adr); // read
writeMemory<DWORD>(proc, adr, value++);     // increment and write
```

Listing 6-6: Calling templated memory access functions

Compare this to the calls to `WriteProcessMemory()` and `ReadProcessMemory()` in Listing 6-4. This code still reads a value, increments it, and writes the new value to memory. But since the templated functions let you specify the type when you call them, you don't need a new `readMemory()` and `writeMemory()` function for every data type you might need to work with. That's much cleaner, since you'll often want to work with all kinds of data.

Memory Protection

When memory is allocated by a game (or any program), it is placed in a *page*. In x86 Windows, pages are chunks of 4,096 bytes that store data. Because all memory must be within a page, the minimal allocation unit is 4,096 bytes. The operating system can place memory chunks smaller than 4,096 bytes as a subset of an existing page that has enough uncommitted space, in a newly allocated page, or across two contiguous pages that have the same attributes.

Memory chunks 4,096 bytes or larger span n pages, where n is

$$\frac{\text{memory size}}{4,096}.$$

The operating system typically looks for room in existing pages when allocating memory, but it allocates new pages on demand if necessary.

NOTE   *It's also possible for large chunks to span* n *+ 1 pages, as there's no guarantee that a chunk begins at the start of a page.*

The important thing to understand about memory pages is that each page has a set of specific attributes. Most of these attributes are transparent in user mode, but there's one you should be extra conscious of when working with memory: protection.

Differentiating x86 Windows Memory Protection Attributes

The memory-reading techniques you've learned so far are very basic. They assume that the memory you're accessing is protected with the PAGE_READWRITE attribute. While this assumption is correct for variable data, other types of data exist on pages with different types of protection. Table 6-1 describes the different types of memory protection in x86 Windows.

Table 6-1: Memory Protection Types

Protection type	Value	Read permission?	Write permission?	Execute permission?	Special permissions?
PAGE_NOACCESS	0x01	No	No	No	
PAGE_READONLY	0x02	Yes	No	No	
PAGE_READWRITE	0x04	Yes	No	No	
PAGE_WRITECOPY	0x08	Yes	Yes	No	Yes, copy on write
PAGE_EXECUTE	0x10	No	No	Yes	
PAGE_EXECUTE_READ	0x20	Yes	No	Yes	
PAGE_EXECUTE_READWRITE	0x40	Yes	Yes	Yes	
PAGE_EXECUTE_WRITECOPY	0x80	Yes	Yes	Yes	Yes, copy on write
PAGE_GUARD	0x100	No	No	No	Yes, guard page

If a protection type in Table 6-1 has a *Yes* in any permission column, it means the action in question can be performed on that page of memory. For example, if a page is PAGE_READONLY, then a program can read the memory on that page, but the program cannot write to that memory.

Constant strings, for example, are usually stored with PAGE_READONLY protection. Other constant data, such as virtual function tables and a module's entire *Portable Executable (PE)* header (which contains information about a program, such as the kind of application it is, library functions it uses, its size, and so on), are also stored on read-only pages. Assembly code, on the other hand, is stored on pages protected with PAGE_EXECUTE_READ.

Most protection types involve only some combination of read, write, and execute protection. For now, you can safely ignore special protection types; I cover them in "Special Protection Types" on page 126 if you're curious, but only very advanced hacks will ever require knowledge of them. The basic protection types, though, will be prevalent in your game-hacking adventures.

SPECIAL PROTECTION TYPES

Two protection types in Table 6-1 include *copy-on-write* protection. When multiple processes have pages of memory that are identical (such as pages with mapped system DLLs), copy-on-write protection is used to conserve memory. The actual data is stored in only one physical place, and the operating system virtually maps all memory pages containing that data to the physical location. If a process sharing the memory makes a change to it, a copy of the data will be made in physical memory, the change will be applied, and the memory page(s) for that process will be remapped to the new physical memory. When a copy on write happens, the protection for all affected pages changes accordingly; PAGE_WRITECOPY will become PAGE_READWRITE, and PAGE_EXECUTE_WRITECOPY will become PAGE_EXECUTE_READWRITE. I've found no game hacking–specific uses for copy-on-write pages, but it's useful to understand them.

Pages can also be created with *guard* protection. Guarded pages must have a secondary protection, defined like PAGE_GUARD | PAGE_READONLY. When the program tries to access a guarded page, the operating system will throw a STATUS_GUARD_PAGE_VIOLATION exception. Once the exception is handled, the guard protection is removed from the page, leaving only the secondary protection. One way in which the operating system uses this type of protection is to dynamically expand the call stack by placing a guarded page at the top and allocating more memory when that guarded page is hit. Some memory analysis tools place guarded pages after heap memory to detect heap corruption bugs. In the context of game hacking, a guarded page can be used as a trip wire that tells you when a game might be attempting to detect your code within its memory.

Changing Memory Protection

When you want to hack a game, you'll sometimes need to access memory in a way that is forbidden by the memory page's protection, making it important to be able to change memory protection at will. Luckily, the Windows API provides the VirtualProtectEx() function for this purpose. This is the function's prototype:

```
BOOL VirtualProtectEx(
    HANDLE Process, LPVOID Address,
    DWORD Size, DWORD NewProtect,
    PDWORD OldProtect
);
```

The parameters Process, Address, and Size take the same input as they do in the ReadProcessMemory() and WriteProcessMemory() functions. NewProtect should specify the new protection flags for the memory, and OldProtect can optionally point to a DWORD where the old protection flags will be stored.

The most granular scale for memory protection is per page, which means VirtualProtectEx() will set the new protection to every page that is on or between Address and Address + Size - 1.

The VirtualProtectEx() function has a sister called VirtualProtect(). They work the same way, but VirtualProtect() operates only on the process calling it and, thus, does not have a process handle parameter.

When you're writing your own code to change memory protections, I suggest making it flexible by creating a template. A generic wrapped function for VirtualProtectEx() should look something like Listing 6-7.

```
template<typename T>
DWORD protectMemory(HANDLE proc, LPVOID adr, DWORD prot) {
    DWORD oldProt;
    VirtualProtectEx(proc, adr, sizeof(T), prot, &oldProt);
    return oldProt;
}
```

Listing 6-7: A generic function to change memory protection

With this template in place, if you wanted to, say, write a DWORD to a memory page without write permission, you might do something like this:

```
protectMemory<DWORD>(process, address, PAGE_READWRITE)
writeMemory<DWORD>(process, address, newValue)
```

First, this sets the protection on the memory to change to PAGE_READWRITE. With write permission granted, the door is open to call writeMemory() and change the data at address.

When you're changing memory protection, it's best practice to let the change persist only as long as needed and restore the original protection as soon as possible. This is less efficient, but it ensures that a game doesn't detect your bot (for example, by noticing that some of its assembly code pages have become writable).

A typical write operation on read-only memory should look like this:

```
DWORD oldProt =
    protectMemory<DWORD>(process, address, PAGE_READWRITE);
writeMemory<DWORD>(process, address, newValue);
protectMemory<DWORD>(process, address, oldProt);
```

This code calls the protectMemory() function from Listing 6-7 to change the protection to PAGE_READWRITE. It then writes newValue to the memory before changing the protection back to oldProt, which was set to the page's original protection by the initial call to protectMemory(). The writeMemory() function used here is the same one defined in Listing 6-5.

A final important point is that when you're manipulating a game's memory, it's entirely possible that the game will access the memory at the same time as you. If the new protection that you set is not compatible with the original protection, the game process will get an ACCESS_VIOLATION exception and crash. For instance, if you change memory protection from PAGE_EXECUTE to PAGE_READWRITE, the game might try to execute the code on the page(s) when the memory is not marked as executable. In this case, you'd want to instead set the memory protection to PAGE_EXECUTE_READWRITE to ensure that you can operate on the memory while still allowing the game to execute it.

Address Space Layout Randomization

So far, I've described memory addresses as static integers that change only as the binary changes. This model is correct on Windows XP and earlier. On later Windows systems, however, memory addresses are only static relative to the base address of the game binary, because these systems enable a feature called *address space layout randomization (ASLR)* for supported binaries. When a binary is compiled with ASLR support (enabled by default on MSVC++ 2010 and many other compilers), its base address can be different every time it is run. Conversely, non-ASLR binaries will always have a base address of 0x400000.

NOTE   *Since ASLR doesn't work on XP, I'll call 0x400000 the* XP-base.

Disabling ASLR to Simplify Bot Development

To keep development simple, you can disable ASLR and use addresses with the transparent XP-base. To do so, enter a single command in the Visual Studio Command Prompt:

```
> editbin /DYNAMICBASE:NO "C:\path\to\game.exe"
```

To re-enable it, enter:

```
> editbin /DYNAMICBASE "C:\path\to\game.exe"
```

Bypassing ASLR in Production

Disabling ASLR is suitable for bot development, but it is a no-no for production; end users cannot be expected to turn off ALSR. Instead, you can write a function to dynamically rebase addresses at runtime. If you use addresses with the XP-base, the code to do a rebase would look like this:

```
DWORD rebase(DWORD address, DWORD newBase) {
    DWORD diff = address - 0x400000;
    return diff + newBase;
}
```

When you know the base address of the game (newBase), this function allows you to essentially ignore ASLR by rebasing address.

To find newBase, however, you need to use the GetModuleHandle() function. When the parameter to GetModuleHandle() is NULL, it always returns a handle to the main binary in a process. The function's returned type is HMODULE, but the value is actually just the address where the binary is mapped. This is the base address, so you can directly cast it to a DWORD to get newBase. Since you're looking for the base address in another process, though, you need a way to execute the function in the context of that process.

To do this, call GetModuleHandle() using the CreateRemoteThread() API function, which can be used to spawn threads and execute code in a remote process. It has the prototype shown in Listing 6-8.

```
HANDLE CreateRemoteThread(
    HANDLE Process,
    LPSECURITY_ATTRIBUTES ThreadAttributes,
    DWORD StackSize,
    LPTHREAD_START_ROUTINE StartAddress,
    LPVOID Param,
    DWORD CreationFlags,
    LPDWORD ThreadId
);
```

Listing 6-8: A function that spawns a thread

The spawned thread will start execution on StartAddress, treating it as a single-parameter function with Param as input and setting the value returned as the thread exit code. This is ideal, as the thread can be started with StartAddress pointing to the address of GetModuleHandle() and Param set to NULL. You can then use the API function WaitForSingleObject() to wait until the thread is done executing and get the returned base address using the API function GetExitCodeThread().

Once all of these things are tied together, the code to get newBase from an external bot should look like Listing 6-9.

```
DWORD newBase;

// get the address of kernel32.dll
HMODULE k32 = GetModuleHandle("kernel32.dll");

// get the address of GetModuleHandle()
LPVOID funcAdr = GetProcAddress(k32, "GetModuleHandleA");
if (!funcAdr)
    funcAdr = GetProcAddress(k32, "GetModuleHandleW");

// create the thread
HANDLE thread =
    CreateRemoteThread(process, NULL, NULL,
        (LPTHREAD_START_ROUTINE)funcAdr,
        NULL, NULL, NULL);
```

```
// let the thread finish
WaitForSingleObject(thread, INFINITE);

// get the exit code
GetExitCodeThread(thread, &newBase);

// clean up the thread handle
CloseHandle(thread);
```

Listing 6-9: Finding the base address of a game with API functions

The GetModuleHandle() function is part of *kernel32.dll*, which has the same base address in every process, so first this code gets the address for *kernel32.dll*. Since the base address of *kernel32.dll* is the same in every process, the address of GetModuleHandle() will be the same in the game as it is in the external bot. Given the base address of *kernel32.dll*, this code finds the address of GetModuleHandle() easily with the API function GetProcAddress(). From there, it calls the CreateRemoteThread() function from Listing 6-8, lets the thread do its job, and fetches the exit code to obtain newBase.

Closing Thoughts

Now that you've seen how to manipulate memory from your own code, I'll show you how to apply the skills from Parts I and II to games. These skills are paramount to the concepts you'll explore in the coming chapters, so make sure you have a firm grasp on what's happening. If you're having trouble, play with the example code as you review concepts, as it provides a safe sandbox for testing and tweaking how the methods in this and earlier chapters behave.

The way Listing 6-9 tricks the game into executing GetModuleHandle() is a form of code injection. But that's just a glimpse into what injection can do. If you're excited to learn more about it, dive into Chapter 7, which explores this topic in detail.

PART 3

PROCESS PUPPETEERING

7

CODE INJECTION

Imagine being able to walk into a game company's office, sit down, and start adding code to their game client. Imagine that you can do this for any game you want, whenever you want, and for any functionality you want. Almost any gamer you talk to will have ideas on how to improve a game, but, as far as they know, it's just a pipe dream. But you know that dreams are meant to be fulfilled, and now that you've learned a bit about how memory works, you're ready to start throwing the rules out the window. Using code injection, you can, for all intents and purposes, become as powerful as any game's developers.

Code injection is a means of forcing any process to execute foreign code within its own memory space and execution context. I touched on this topic previously in "Bypassing ASLR in Production" on page 128, where I showed you how to remotely subvert ASLR using CreateRemoteThread(), but that example only scratched the surface. In the first part of this chapter, you'll learn how to create code caves, inject new threads, and hijack thread execution to force games to execute small snippets of assembly code. In the second part, you'll learn how to inject foreign binaries directly into games, forcing those games to execute entire programs that you've created.

Injecting Code Caves with Thread Injection

The first step to injecting code into another process is writing position-agnostic assembly code, known as *shellcode*, in the form of a byte array. You can write shellcode to remote processes to form *code caves*, which act as the entry point for a new thread that you want a game to execute. Once a code cave is created, you can execute it using either *thread injection* or *thread hijacking*. I'll show you an example of thread injection in this section, and I'll illustrate thread hijacking in "Hijacking a Game's Main Thread to Execute Code Caves" on page 138.

You'll find example code for this chapter in this book's resource files in the directory *GameHackingExamples/Chapter7_CodeInjection*. Open *main-codeInjection.cpp* to follow along as I explain how to build a simplified version of the function injectCodeUsingThreadInjection() from that file.

Creating an Assembly Code Cave

In "Bypassing ASLR in Production" on page 128, I used thread injection to call the function GetModuleHandle() by way of CreateRemoteThread() and obtain a process handle. In that case, GetModuleHandle() acted as the code cave; it had the proper code structure to act as the entry point for a new thread. Thread injection isn't always that easy, though.

For example, say you want your external bot to remotely call a function within a game, and the function has this prototype:

```
DWORD __cdecl someFunction(int times, const char* string);
```

A few things make remotely calling this function tricky. First, it has two parameters, meaning you need to create a code cave that will both set up the stack and properly make the call. CreateRemoteThread() allows you to pass one argument to the code cave, and you can access that argument relative to ESP, but the other one would still need to be hardcoded into the code cave. Hardcoding the first argument, times, is easiest. Additionally, you'd need to make sure that the cave properly cleans the stack.

> **NOTE** *Recall that when bypassing ASLR in Chapter 6, I used CreateRemoteThread() to start new threads by executing any arbitrary code at a given address and passing that code a single parameter. That's why these examples can pass one parameter using the stack.*

Ultimately, the code cave to inject that call to someFunction into a running game process would look something like this pseudocode:

```
PUSH DWORD PTR:[ESP+0x4] // get second arg from stack
PUSH times
CALL someFunction
ADD ESP, 0x8
RETN
```

This code cave is almost perfect, but it could be less complex. The CALL operation expects one of two operands: either a register with an absolute function address or an immediate integer that holds an offset to a function, relative to the return address. This means you'd have to do a bunch of offset calculations, which can be tedious.

To keep the cave position agnostic, modify it to use a register instead, as in Listing 7-1.

```
PUSH DWORD PTR:[ESP+0x4] // get second arg from stack
PUSH times
MOV EAX, someFunction
CALL EAX
ADD ESP, 0x8
RETN
```

Listing 7-1: A code cave to call someFunction

Since a caller knows that a function it calls will overwrite EAX with its return value, the caller should ensure that EAX doesn't hold any critical data. Knowing this, you can use EAX to hold the absolute address of someFunction.

Translating the Assembly to Shellcode

Because code caves need to be written to another process's memory, they cannot be written directly in assembly. Instead, you'll need to write them byte by byte. There's no standard way to determine which bytes represent which assembly code, but there are a few hacky approaches. My personal favorite is to compile an empty C++ application with the assembly code in a function and use OllyDbg to inspect that function. Alternatively, you could open OllyDbg on any arbitrary process and scan through the disassembly until you find the bytes for all of the operations you need. This method is actually really good, as your code caves should be written as simply as possible, meaning all of the operations should be very common. You can also find charts of assembly opcodes online, but I find that they're all pretty hard to read; the methods I just described are easier overall.

When you know what your bytes should be, you can use C++ to easily generate the proper shellcode. Listing 7-2 shows the finished shellcode skeleton for the assembly in Listing 7-1.

```
BYTE codeCave[20] = {
    0xFF, 0x74, 0x24, 0x04,        // PUSH DWORD PTR:[ESP+0x4]
    0x68, 0x00, 0x00, 0x00, 0x00,  // PUSH 0
    0xB8, 0x00, 0x00, 0x00, 0x00,  // MOV EAX, 0x0
    0xFF, 0xD0,                    // CALL EAX
    0x83, 0xC4, 0x08,              // ADD ESP, 0x08
    0xC3                           // RETN
};
```

Listing 7-2: Shellcode skeleton

This example creates a BYTE array containing the needed bytes of shell-code. But the times argument needs to be dynamic, and it's impossible to know the address of someFunction at compile time, which is why this shell-code is written as a skeleton. The two groups of four sequential 0x00 bytes are placeholders for times and the address of someFunction, and you can insert the real values into your code cave at runtime by calling memcpy(), as in the snippet in Listing 7-3.

```
memcpy(&codeCave[5], &times, 4);
memcpy(&codeCave[10], &addressOfSomeFunc, 4);
```

Listing 7-3: Inserting times and the location of someFunction into the code cave

Both times and the address of someFunction are 4 bytes each (recall that times is an int and addresses are 32-bit values), and they belong at codeCave[5-8] and codeCave[10-13], respectively. The two calls to memcpy() pass this information as parameters to fill the blanks in the codeCave array.

Writing the Code Cave to Memory

With the proper shellcode created, you can place it inside the target process using VirtualAllocEx() and WriteProcessMemory(). Listing 7-4 shows one way to do this.

```
  int stringlen = strlen(string) + 1; // +1 to include null terminator
  int cavelen = sizeof(codeCave);
❶ int fulllen = stringlen + cavelen;
  auto remoteString = // allocate the memory with EXECUTE rights
❷     VirtualAllocEx(process, 0, fulllen, MEM_COMMIT, PAGE_EXECUTE);

  auto remoteCave = // keep a note of where the code cave will go
❸     (LPVOID)((DWORD)remoteString + stringlen);

  // write the string first
❹ WriteProcessMemory(process, remoteString, string, stringlen, NULL);

  // write the code cave next
❺ WriteProcessMemory(process, remoteCave, codeCave, cavelen, NULL);
```

Listing 7-4: Writing the final shellcode to a code cave memory

First, this code determines exactly how many bytes of memory it will need to write the string argument and the code cave into the game's memory, and it stores that value in fulllen ❶. Then, it calls the API function VirtualAllocEx() to allocate fulllen bytes inside of process with PAGE_EXECUTE protection (you can always use 0 and MEM_COMMIT, respectively, for the second and fourth parameters), and it stores the address of the memory in remoteString ❷. It also increments remoteString by stringlen bytes and stores the result in remoteCave ❸, as the shellcode should be written directly to the memory following the string argument. Finally, it uses WriteProcessMemory() to fill the allocated buffer with string ❹ and the assembly bytes ❺ stored in codeCave.

Table 7-1 shows how a memory dump of the code cave might look, assuming that it is allocated at 0x030000, someFunction is at 0xDEADBEEF, times is set to 5, and string is pointing to the injected! text.

Table 7-1: Code Cave Memory Dump

Address	Code representation	Raw data	Data meaning
0x030000	remoteString[0-4]	0x69 0x6E 0x6A 0x65 0x63	injec
0x030005	remoteString[5-9]	0x74 0x65 0x64 0x0A 0x00	ted!\0
0x03000A	remoteCave[0-3]	0xFF 0x74 0x24 0x04	PUSH DWORD PTR[ESP+0x4]
0x03000E	remoteCave[4-8]	0x68 0x05 0x00 0x00 0x00	PUSH 0x05
0x030013	remoteCave[9-13]	0xB8 0xEF 0xBE 0xAD 0xDE	MOV EAX, 0xDEADBEEF
0x030018	remoteCave[14-15]	0xFF 0xD0	CALL EAX
0x03001A	remoteCave[16-18]	0x83 0xC4 0x08	ADD ESP, 0x08
0x03001D	remoteCave[19]	0xC3	RETN

The Address column shows where each piece of the cave is located in memory; the Code representation column tells you which indexes of remoteString and remoteCave correspond to the bytes in the Raw data column; and the Data meaning column shows what the bytes represent, in human-readable format. You can see the injected! string at 0x030000, the value of times at 0x03000E, and the address of someFunction at 0x030014.

Using Thread Injection to Execute the Code Cave

With a complete code cave written to memory, the only thing left to do is execute it. In this example, you could execute the cave using the following code:

```
HANDLE thread = CreateRemoteThread(process, NULL, NULL,
                (LPTHREAD_START_ROUTINE)remoteCave,
                remoteString, NULL, NULL);
```

```
WaitForSingleObject(thread, INFINITE);
CloseHandle(thread);
VirtualFreeEx(process, remoteString, fulllen, MEM_RELEASE)
```

The calls to `CreateRemoteThread()`, `WaitForSingleObject()`, and `CloseHandle()` work to inject and execute the code cave, and `VirtalFreeEx()` covers the bot's tracks by freeing the memory allocated in code like Listing 7-4. In the simplest form, that's all there is to executing a code cave injected into a game. In practice, you should also check return values after calling `VirtualAllocEx()`, `WriteProcessMemory()`, and `CreateRemoteThread()` to make sure that everything was successful.

For instance, if `VirtualAllocEx()` returns 0x00000000, it means that the memory allocation failed. If you don't handle the failure, `WriteProcessMemory()` will also fail and `CreateRemoteThread()` will begin executing with an entry point of 0x00000000, ultimately crashing the game. The same is true for the return values of `WriteProcessMemory()` and `CreateRemoteThread()`. Typically, these functions will only fail when the process handle is opened without the required access flags.

Hijacking a Game's Main Thread to Execute Code Caves

In some cases, injected code caves need to be in sync with the main thread of the game process. Solving this problem can be very tricky because it means that you must control the existing threads in an external process.

You could simply suspend the main thread until the code cave finishes executing, which might work, but that would prove very slow. The overhead required to wait for a code cave and then resume a thread is pretty heavy. A faster alternative is to force the thread to execute the code for you, a process called *thread hijacking*.

NOTE   *Open the* main-codeInjection.cpp *file in this book's source code files to follow along with building this thread-hijacking example, which is a simplified version of* injectCodeUsingThreadHijacking()*.*

Building the Assembly Code Cave

As with thread injection, the first step to thread hijacking is knowing what you want to happen in your code cave. This time, however, you don't know what the thread will be executing when you hijack it, so you'll need to make sure to save the thread's state when the code cave starts and restore the state when you're done hijacking it. This means your shellcode needs to be wrapped in some assembly, as in Listing 7-5.

```
PUSHAD // push general registers to the stack
PUSHFD // push EFLAGS to the stack
```

```
// shellcode should be here

POPFD  // pop EFLAGS from the stack
POPAD  // pop general registers to the stack

// resume the thread without using registers here
```

Listing 7-5: A framework for the thread-hijacking code cave

If you were to call the same someFunction that you did with thread injection, you could use shellcode similar to that in Listing 7-2. The only difference is that you couldn't pass the second parameter to your bot using the stack because you wouldn't be using CreateRemoteThread(). But that's no problem; you could just push it the same way you'd push the first parameter. The part of the code cave that executes the function you want to call would need to look like Listing 7-6.

```
PUSH string
PUSH times
MOV EAX, someFunction
CALL EAX
ADD ESP, 0x8
```

Listing 7-6: Assembly skeleton for calling someFunction

All that's changed here from Listing 7-1 is that this example pushes string explicitly and there's no RETN. You don't call RETN in this case because you want the game thread to go back to whatever it was doing before you hijacked it.

To resume the execution of the thread normally, the cave needs to jump back to the thread's original EIP without using registers. Fortunately, you can use the GetThreadContext() function to fetch EIP, filling the shellcode skeleton in C++. Then you can push it to the stack inside your code cave and do a return. Listing 7-7 shows how your code cave would need to end.

```
PUSH originalEIP
RETN
```

Listing 7-7: Jumping to EIP indirectly

A return jumps to the value on the top of the stack, so doing this immediately after pushing EIP will do the trick. You should use this method instead of a jump, because jumps require offset calculation and make the shellcode a bit more complex to generate. If you tie Listings 7-5 through 7-7 together, you come up with the following code cave:

```
//save state
PUSHAD       // push general registers to the stack
PUSHFD       // push EFLAGS to the stack
```

```
// do work with shellcode
PUSH string
PUSH times
MOV EAX, someFunction
CALL EAX
ADD ESP, 0x8

// restore state
POPFD              // pop EFLAGS from the stack
POPAD              // pop general registers to the stack

// un-hijack: resume the thread without using registers
PUSH originalEIP
RETN
```

Next, follow the instructions in "Translating the Assembly to Shellcode" on page 135 and plug those bytes into an array representing your code cave.

Generating Skeleton Shellcode and Allocating Memory

Using the same method shown in Listing 7-2, you could generate the shellcode for this cave, as shown in Listing 7-8.

```
BYTE codeCave[31] = {
    0x60,                              // PUSHAD
    0x9C,                              // PUSHFD
    0x68, 0x00, 0x00, 0x00, 0x00,      // PUSH 0
    0x68, 0x00, 0x00, 0x00, 0x00,      // PUSH 0
    0xB8, 0x00, 0x00, 0x00, 0x00,      // MOV EAX, 0x0
    0xFF, 0xD0,                        // CALL EAX
    0x83, 0xC4, 0x08,                  // ADD ESP, 0x08
    0x9D,                              // POPFD
    0x61,                              // POPAD
    0x68, 0x00, 0x00, 0x00, 0x00,      // PUSH 0
    0xC3                               // RETN
};

// we'll need to add some code here to place
// the thread's EIP into threadContext.Eip

memcpy(&codeCave[3], &remoteString, 4);
memcpy(&codeCave[8], &times, 4);
memcpy(&codeCave[13], &func, 4);
memcpy(&codeCave[25], &threadContext.Eip, 4);
```

Listing 7-8: Creating the thread-hijacking shellcode array

As in Listing 7-3, memcpy() is used to put the variables into the skeleton. Unlike in that listing, though, there are two variables that cannot be copied right away; times and func are known immediately, but remoteString is a result of allocation and threadContext.Eip will be known only once the thread is frozen. It also makes sense to allocate memory before freezing the thread, because you don't want the thread to be frozen any longer than it has to be. Here's how this might look:

```
int stringlen = strlen(string) + 1;
int cavelen = sizeof(codeCave);
int fulllen = stringlen + cavelen;

auto remoteString =
    VirtualAllocEx(process, 0, fulllen, MEM_COMMIT, PAGE_EXECUTE);
auto remoteCave =
    (LPVOID)((DWORD)remoteString + stringlen);
```

The allocation code is the same as it was for thread injection, so you can reuse the same snippet.

Finding and Freezing the Main Thread

The code to freeze the main thread is a bit trickier. First, you get the thread's unique identifier. This works much like getting a PID, and you can do it using CreateToolhelp32Snapshot(), Thread32First(), and Thread32Next() from *TlHelp32.h*. As discussed in "Obtaining the Game's Process Identifier" on page 120, these functions are used to essentially iterate over a list. A process can have many threads, but the following example assumes that the first thread the game process created is the one that needs to be hijacked:

```
DWORD GetProcessThreadID(HANDLE Process) {
    THREADENTRY32 entry;
    entry.dwSize = sizeof(THREADENTRY32);
    HANDLE snapshot = CreateToolhelp32Snapshot(TH32CS_SNAPTHREAD, 0);

    if (Thread32First(snapshot, &entry) == TRUE) {
        DWORD PID = GetProcessId(Process);
        while (Thread32Next(snapshot, &entry) == TRUE) {
            if (entry.th32OwnerProcessID == PID) {
                CloseHandle(snapshot);
                return entry.th32ThreadID;
            }
        }
    }
    CloseHandle(snapshot);
    return NULL;
}
```

This code simply iterates over the list of all threads on the system and finds the first one that matches the game's PID. Then it gets the thread identifier from the snapshot entry. Once you know the thread identifier, fetch the thread's current register state like this:

```
HANDLE thread = OpenThread(
    (THREAD_GET_CONTEXT | THREAD_SUSPEND_RESUME | THREAD_SET_CONTEXT),
    false, threadID);
SuspendThread(thread);
```

```
CONTEXT threadContext;
threadContext.ContextFlags = CONTEXT_CONTROL;
GetThreadContext(thread, &threadContext);
```

This code uses `OpenThread()` to get a thread handle. It then suspends the thread using `SuspendThread()` and obtains the values of its registers using `GetThreadContext()`. After this, the `memcpy()` code in Listing 7-8 should have all of the variables it needs to finish generating the shellcode.

With the shellcode generated, the code cave can be written to the allocated memory in the same fashion as in Listing 7-4:

```
WriteProcessMemory(process, remoteString, string, stringlen, NULL);
WriteProcessMemory(process, remoteCave, codeCave, cavelen, NULL);
```

Once the cave is ready and waiting in memory, all you need to do is set the thread's `EIP` to the address of the code cave and let the thread resume execution, as follows:

```
threadContext.Eip = (DWORD)remoteCave;
threadContext.ContextFlags = CONTEXT_CONTROL;
SetThreadContext(thread, &threadContext);
ResumeThread(thread);
```

This code causes the thread to resume execution at the address of the code cave. Because of the way the code cave is written, the thread has no clue that anything has changed. The cave stores the thread's original state, executes the payload, restores the thread's original state, and then returns to the original code with everything intact.

When you're using any form of code injection, it is also important to understand what data your code caves touch. For example, if you were to create a code cave that calls a game's internal functions to create and send a network packet, you'd need to make sure that any global variables that the functions touch (like a packet buffer, packet position marker, and so on) are safely restored once you're done. You never know what the game is doing when your code cave is executed—it could be calling the same function as you!

Injecting DLLs for Full Control

Code caves are very powerful (you can make a game do anything using assembly shellcode), but handcrafting shellcode isn't practical. It would be much more convenient to inject C++ code, wouldn't it? That's possible, but the process is far more complex: the code must be compiled to assembly, packaged in a position-agnostic format, made aware of any external dependencies, entirely mapped into memory, and then executed on some entry point.

Luckily, all of these things are already taken care of in Windows. By changing a C++ project to compile as a dynamic library, you can create a self-contained, position-agnostic binary called a *dynamic link library (DLL)*. Then you can use a mix of thread injection or hijacking and the LoadLibrary() API function to map your DLL file into a game's memory.

Open *main-codeInjection.cpp* in the *GameHackingExamples/Chapter7_CodeInjection* directory and *dllmain.cpp* under *GameHackingExamples/Chapter7_CodeInjection_DLL* to follow along with some example code as you read this section. In *main-codeInjection.cpp*, look at the LoadDLL() function specifically.

Tricking a Process into Loading Your DLL

Using a code cave, you can trick a remote process into invoking LoadLibrary() on a DLL, effectively loading foreign code into its memory space. Because LoadLibrary() takes only a single parameter, you could create a code cave to call it as follows:

```
// write the dll name to memory
wchar_t* dllName = "c:\\something.dll";
int namelen = wcslen(dllName) + 1;
LPVOID remoteString =
    VirtualAllocEx(process, NULL, namelen * 2, MEM_COMMIT, PAGE_EXECUTE);
WriteProcessMemory(process, remoteString, dllName, namelen * 2, NULL);

// get the address of LoadLibraryW()
HMODULE k32 = GetModuleHandleA("kernel32.dll");
LPVOID funcAdr = GetProcAddress(k32, "LoadLibraryW");

// create a thread to call LoadLibraryW(dllName)
HANDLE thread =
    CreateRemoteThread(process, NULL, NULL,
        (LPTHREAD_START_ROUTINE)funcAdr,
        remoteString, NULL, NULL);

// let the thread finish and clean up
WaitForSingleObject(thread, INFINITE);
CloseHandle(thread);
```

This code is somewhat a mix of the thread injection code from "Bypassing ASLR in Production" on page 128 and the code cave created to call someFunction in Listings 7-2 and 7-3. Like the former, this example uses the body of a single-parameter API function, namely LoadLibrary, as the body of the code cave. Like the latter, though, it has to inject a string into memory, since LoadLibrary expects a string pointer as its first argument. Once the thread is injected, it forces LoadLibrary to load the DLL whose name was injected into memory, effectively putting foreign code into a game.

Give any DLL you plan to inject a unique name, like MySuperBotV2Hook.dll. *Simpler names, such as* Hook.dll *or* Injected.dll, *are dangerously generic. If the name conflicts with a DLL that is already loaded,* LoadLibrary() *will assume that it is the same DLL and not load it!*

Once the LoadLibrary() code cave loads your DLL into a game, the DLL's entry point—known as DllMain()—will be executed with DLL_PROCESS_ATTACH as the reason. When the process is killed or FreeLibrary() is called on the DLL, its entry point will be called with the DLL_PROCESS_DETACH reason. Handling these events from the entry point might look like this:

```
BOOL APIENTRY DllMain(HMODULE hModule,
                      DWORD  ul_reason_for_call,
                      LPVOID lpReserved) {
    switch (ul_reason_for_call) {
        case DLL_PROCESS_ATTACH:
            printf("DLL attached!\n");
            break;
        case DLL_PROCESS_DETACH:
            printf("DLL detached!\n");
            break;
    }
    return TRUE;
}
```

This example function starts by checking why DllMain() was called. It then outputs text indicating whether it was called because the DLL was attached or detached, returning TRUE either way.

Keep in mind that the entry point of a DLL is executed inside a *loader lock*, which is a global synchronization lock used by all functions that read or modify the list of modules loaded in a process. This loader lock gets used by functions like GetModuleHandle(), GetModuleFileName(), Module32First(), and Module32Next(), which means that running nontrivial code from a DLL entry point can lead to deadlocks and should be avoided.

If you need to run code from a DLL entry point, do so from a new thread, as follows:

```
DWORD WINAPI runBot(LPVOID lpParam) {
    // run your bot
    return 1;
}

// do this from DllMain() for case DLL_PROCESS_ATTACH
auto thread = CreateThread(NULL, 0, &runBot, NULL, 0, NULL);
CloseHandle(thread);
```

From DllMain(), this code creates a new thread starting on the function runBot(). It then immediately closes its handle to the thread, as doing any further operations from DllMain() can lead to serious problems. From inside this runBot(), you can begin executing your bot's code. The code runs inside the game, meaning you can directly manipulate memory using the typecasting methods. You can also do a lot more, as you'll see in Chapter 8.

When injecting DLLs, make sure you have no dependency issues. If your DLL relies on some nonstandard DLLs, for example, you have to either inject those DLLs into the game first or put them in a folder that LoadLibrary() will search, such as any folder in the PATH environment variable. The former will work only if the DLLs have no dependencies of their own, whereas the latter is a bit tricky to implement and subject to name collisions. The best option is to link all external libraries statically so that they are compiled directly into your DLL.

Accessing Memory in an Injected DLL

When you're trying to access a game's memory from an injected DLL, process handles and API functions are a hindrance. Because a game shares the same memory space as all code injected into it, you can access a game's memory directly from injected code. For example, to access a DWORD value from injected code, you could write the following:

```
DWORD value = *((DWORD*)adr); // read a DWORD from adr
*((DWORD*)adr) = 1234;        // write 1234 to DWORD adr
```

This simply typecasts the memory address adr to a DWORD* and dereferences that pointer to a DWORD. Doing typecasts in place like that is fine, but your memory access code will look cleaner if the functions are abstracted and made generic, just like the Windows API wrappers.

The generic functions for accessing memory from inside injected code look something like this:

```
template<typename T>
T readMemory(LPVOID adr) {
    return *((T*)adr);
}

template<typename T>
void writeMemory(LPVOID adr, T val) {
    *((T*)adr) = val;
}
```

Using these templates is just like using the functions under "Writing Templated Memory Access Functions" on page 123. Here's an example:

```
DWORD value = readMemory<DWORD>(adr); // read
writeMemory<DWORD>(adr, value++);     // increment and write
```

These calls are nearly identical to the calls in Listing 6-6 on page 124; they just don't need to take the process handle as an argument because they're being called from inside the process itself. You can make this method even more flexible by creating a third templated function called pointMemory(), as follows:

```
template<typename T>
T* pointMemory(LPVOID adr) {
    return ((T*)adr);
}
```

This function skips the dereferencing step of a memory read and simply gives you the pointer to the data. From there, you're free to both read from and write to the memory by dereferencing that pointer yourself, like this:

```
DWORD* pValue = pointMemory<DWORD>(adr); // point
DWORD value = *pValue;                   // 'read'
(*pValue)++;                             // increment and 'write'
```

With a function like pointMemory() in place, you could eliminate the calls to readMemory() and writeMemory(). You'd still need to find adr ahead of time, but from there, the code to read a value, change it, and write it back would be much simpler to follow.

Bypassing ASLR in an Injected DLL

Similarly, since the code is injected, there's no need to inject a thread into the game to get the base address. Instead, you can just call GetModuleHandle() directly, like so:

```
DWORD newBase = (DWORD)GetModuleHandle(NULL);
```

A faster way to get the base address is to utilize the game's FS memory segment, which is another superpower you get from injected code. This memory segment points to a structure called the *thread environment block (TEB)*, and 0x30 bytes into the TEB is a pointer to the *process environment block (PEB)* structure. These structures are used by the operating system and contain a ton of data about the current thread and the current process, but we're interested only in the base address of the main module, which is stored 0x8 bytes into the PEB. Using inline assembly, you can traverse these structures to get newBase, like this:

```
DWORD newBase;
__asm {
    MOV EAX, DWORD PTR FS:[0x30]
    MOV EAX, DWORD PTR DS:[EAX+0x8]
    MOV newBase, EAX
}
```

The first command stores the PEB address in EAX, and the second command reads the main module's base address and stores it in EAX. The final command then copies EAX to newBase.

Closing Thoughts

In Chapter 6, I showed you how to read from memory remotely and how an injected DLL can directly access a game's memory using pointers. This chapter demonstrated how to inject all types of code, from pure assembly byte code to entire C++ binaries. In the next chapter, you'll learn just how much power being in a game's memory space actually gives you. If you thought assembly code injection was cool, you'll love what you can do when you mix injected C++ with control flow manipulation.

The example code for this chapter contains proofs of concept for everything we've discussed. If you're still unclear about any of the topics, you can poke at the code to learn exactly what's going on and see all of the tricks in action.

8

MANIPULATING CONTROL FLOW IN A GAME

Forcing a game to execute foreign code is definitely powerful, but what if you could alter the way a game executes its own code? What if you could force the game to bypass the code that draws the fog of war, trick it into making enemies visible through walls, or manipulate the arguments it passes to functions? *Control flow manipulation* lets you do exactly that, allowing you to change what a process does by intercepting code execution and monitoring, modifying, or preventing it.

There are many ways to manipulate the control flow of a process, but almost all require you to modify the process's assembly code. Depending on your goals, you'll need to either completely remove code from the process (called *NOPing*) or force the process to redirect execution to injected functions (called *hooking*). In the beginning of this chapter, you'll learn about

NOPing, several types of hooking, and other control flow manipulation techniques. Once I've explained the basics, I'll show you how I've applied these principles to common game libraries like Adobe AIR and Direct3D.

Open the directory *GameHackingExamples/Chapter8_ControlFlow* in this book's resource files to see the complete sample code for the next section and "Hooking to Redirect Game Execution" on page 153.

NOPing to Remove Unwanted Code

Chapter 7 described how to inject new code into a game, but the opposite—removing code from a game—can also be useful. Some hacks require you to stop some of a game's original code from being executed, and to do that, you'll have to get rid of it. One way to eliminate code from a game process is NOPing, which involves overwriting the original x86 assembly code with NOP instructions.

When to NOP

Consider a game that won't show the health bars of cloaked enemies. It's pretty hard to see cloaked enemies coming, and you'd have a huge advantage in combat if you could at least see their health bars. The code to draw health bars often looks like Listing 8-1.

```
for (int i = 0; i < creatures.size(); i++) {
    auto c = creatures[i];
    if (c.isEnemy && c.isCloaked) continue;
    drawHealthBar(c.healthBar);
}
```

Listing 8-1: The loop from the `drawCreatureHealthBarExample()` function

When drawing health bars, a game with cloaked creatures might use a for loop to check whether the creatures within the screen's bounds are cloaked. If an enemy isn't cloaked, the loop calls some function (drawHealthBar() in this example) to display the enemy's health bar.

Given the source code, you could force the game to draw even cloaked enemies' health bars by simply removing if (c.isEnemy && c.isCloaked) continue; from the code. But as a game hacker, you have only the assembly code, not the source code. When simplified, the assembly that Listing 8-1 translates into looks something like this pseudocode:

```
startOfLoop:                        ; for
    MOV i, 0                        ; int i = 0
    JMP condition                   ; first loop, skip increment
increment:
    ADD i, 1                        ; i++
condition:
    CMP i, creatures.Size()         ; i < creatures.size()
    JNB endOfLoop                   ; exit loop if i >= creatures.size()
```

```
body:
    MOV c, creatures[i]              ; auto c = creatures[i]
    TEST c.isEnemy, c.isEnemy        ; if c.isEnemy
    JZ drawHealthBar                 ; draw bar if c.isEnemy == false
    TEST c.isCloaked, c.isCloaked    ; && c.isCloaked
    JZ drawHealthBar                 ; draw bar if c.isCloaked == false
❶  JMP increment                    ; continue
drawHealthBar:
    CALL drawHealthBar(c.healthBar)  ; drawHealthBar(c.healthBar)
    JMP increment                    ; continue
endOfLoop:
```

To trick the game into drawing all enemy health bars, regardless of cloaking, you'd need to remove the JMP increment command ❶ that executes when c.isEnemy && c.isCloaked evaluates to true. In assembly, though, replacing unwanted code with instructions that do nothing is easier than deleting code. That's where the NOP command comes in. Since NOP is a single byte (0x90), you can overwrite the 2-byte JMP increment command with two NOP commands. When the processor reaches those NOP commands, it rolls over them and falls into drawHealthBar() even when c.isEnemy && c.isCloaked evaluates to true.

How to NOP

The first step to NOPing a chunk of assembly code is making the memory chunk where the code lives writable. It's possible for the code on the same memory page to be executed while you're writing the NOP commands, though, so you also want to make sure the memory is still executable. You can accomplish both of these tasks by setting the memory's protection to PAGE_EXECUTE_READWRITE. Once the memory is properly protected, you can write the NOP commands and be done. It technically doesn't hurt to leave the memory writable, but it's good practice to also restore the original protection when you're finished.

Provided you have facilities in place for writing and protecting memory (as described in Chapter 6), you can write a function like the one shown in Listing 8-2 to write NOP commands to game memory. (Follow along by opening the project's *NOPExample.cpp* file.)

```cpp
template<int SIZE>
void writeNop(DWORD address)
{
    auto oldProtection =
        protectMemory<BYTE[SIZE]>(address, PAGE_EXECUTE_READWRITE);

    for (int i = 0; i < SIZE; i++)
        writeMemory<BYTE>(address + i, 0x90);

    protectMemory<BYTE[SIZE]>(address, oldProtection);
}
```

Listing 8-2: Proper NOPing, complete with memory protection

In this example, the writeNop() function sets the appropriate memory protection, writes a number of NOP commands equal to SIZE, and reapplies the original memory protection level.

The writeNop() function takes the number of NOP instructions to place as a template parameter, since the memory functions require a correctly sized type at compile time. Passing an integer SIZE tells the memory functions to operate on a type of BYTE[SIZE] at compile time. To specify a dynamic size at runtime, simply drop the loop and instead call protectMemory<BYTE> and pass address and address + SIZE as arguments. As long as the size isn't larger than a page (and really, you shouldn't be NOPing a full page), this will ensure that the memory gets properly protected even if it's on a page boundary.

Call this function with the address where you want to place your NOPs and the number of NOP commands to place:

```
writeNop<2>(0xDEADBEEF);
```

Keep in mind that the number of NOP commands should match the size in bytes of the command being removed. This call to writeNop() writes two NOP commands to the address 0xDEADBEEF.

PRACTICE NOPING

If you haven't already, open *NOPExample.cpp* in this chapter's example code now and play around with it for a bit. You'll find a working implementation of the writeNop() function and an interesting function called getAddressforNOP() that scans the example program's memory to find where the NOP command should be placed.

To see the NOP command in action, run the compiled NOPapplication in Visual Studio's debugger with breakpoints at the start and end of the writeNop() function. When the first breakpoint is hit, press ALT-8 to open the disassembly window, enter **address** in the input box, and press ENTER. This brings you to the NOP's target address, where you'll see the assembly code fully intact. Press F5 to continue execution, which triggers the second breakpoint after allowing the application to place the NOPs. Finally, jump back to address in the disassembly tab to see that the code was replaced by NOPs.

You can rework this code to do other cool stuff. For example, you might try placing NOPs on the comparisons instead of the jump or even modifying the jump's type or destination.

These and other alternative approaches may work, but note that they introduce more room for error than overwriting the single JMP with NOP commands. When modifying foreign code, make as few changes as possible to minimize the potential for errors.

Hooking to Redirect Game Execution

So far, I've shown you how to manipulate games by adding code to them, hijacking their threads, creating new threads, and even removing existing code from their execution flow. These methods are very powerful on their own, but when combined, they form an even more potent method of manipulation called *hooking*. Hooking allows you to intercept precise branches of execution and redirect them to injected code that you've written to dictate what the game should do next, and it comes in a variety of flavors. In this section, I'll teach you about four of the most powerful hooking methods for game hacking: call hooking, virtual function table hooking, import address table hooking, and jump hooking.

Call Hooking

A *call hook* directly modifies the target of a CALL operation to point to a new piece of code. There are a few variations of the CALL operation in x86 assembly, but call hooks are generally used on only one: the *near call*, which takes an immediate address as an operand.

Working with Near Calls in Memory

In an assembly program, a near call looks like this:

```
CALL 0x0BADF00D
```

This near call is represented by the byte 0xE8, so you might assume it is stored in memory like this:

```
0xE8 0x0BADF00D
```

Or, when split into single bytes and swapped for endianness, like this:

```
0xE8 0x0D 0xF0 0xAD 0x0B
```

But the anatomy of a near call in memory is not that simple. Instead of storing the callee's absolute address, a near call stores an offset to the callee relative to the address immediately after the call. Since a near call is 5 bytes, the address immediately after the call is 5 bytes later in memory. Given that, the address stored can be computed as follows:

```
calleeAddress - (callAddress + 5)
```

If CALL 0x0BADF00D lives at 0xDEADBEEF in memory, then the value after 0xE8 is this:

```
0x0BADF00D - (0xDEADBEEF + 5) = 0x2D003119
```

In memory, then, that CALL instruction looks like this:

```
0xE8 0x19 0x31 0x00 0x2D
```

To hook a near call, you first need to change the offset following 0xE8 (that is, the little-endian 0x19 0x31 0x00 0x2D) to point to your new callee.

Hooking a Near Call

Following the same memory protection rules shown in Listing 8-2, you hook a near call like so (follow along by opening *CallHookExample.cpp*):

```
DWORD callHook(DWORD hookAt, DWORD newFunc)
{
    DWORD newOffset = newFunc - hookAt - 5;

    auto oldProtection =
        protectMemory<DWORD>(hookAt + 1, PAGE_EXECUTE_READWRITE);

    DWORD originalOffset = readMemory<DWORD>(❶hookAt + 1);
    writeMemory<DWORD>(hookAt + 1, newOffset);
    protectMemory<DWORD>(hookAt + 1, oldProtection);

❷   return originalOffset + hookAt + 5;
}
```

This function takes as arguments the address of the CALL to hook (hookAt) and the address to redirect execution to (newFunc), and it uses them to calculate the offset required to call the code at the address newFunc contains. After you apply the correct memory protections, the callHook() function writes the new offset to the memory at hookAt + 1 ❶, applies the old memory protections, calculates the address of the original call ❷, and returns that value to the caller.

Here's how you might actually use a function like this in a game hack:

```
DWORD origFunc = callHook(0xDEADBEEF, (DWORD)&someNewFunction);
```

This hooks the near call to 0x0BADF00D at 0xDEADBEEF and redirects it to the address of someNewFunction, which is the code your hack will execute. After this is called, the origFunc value will hold 0x0BADF00D.

Cleaning Up the Stack

The new callee must also properly handle the stack, preserve registers, and pass proper return values. At the least, this means your replacement function must match the game's original function in both calling convention and argument count.

Let's say this is the original full function call, in assembly:

```
PUSH 1
PUSH 456
```

```
PUSH 321
CALL 0x0BADF00D
ADD ESP, 0x0C
```

You can tell the function has the C++ __cdecl convention because the stack is being reset by the caller. Additionally, the 0x0C bytes being cleaned from the stack show that there are three arguments, which you can calculate as follows:

$$\frac{0x0C}{\text{sizeof(DWORD)}} = 3$$

Of course, you can also obtain the number of arguments by checking how many things are pushed to the stack: there are three PUSH commands, one for each argument.

Writing a Call Hook

In any case, the new callee, someNewFunction, must follow the __cdecl convention and have three arguments. Here's an example skeleton for the new callee:

```
DWORD __cdecl someNewFunction(DWORD arg1, DWORD arg2, DWORD arg3)
{

}
```

In Visual Studio, C++ programs use the __cdecl convention by default, so technically you could omit it from your function definition; however, I've found it's better to be verbose so you get into the habit of being specific. Also keep in mind that if the caller expects a value to be returned, the return type of your function should match as well. This example assumes the return type is always a DWORD or smaller. Since return types in this size range will all be passed back on EAX, further examples will also use a return type of DWORD.

In most cases, a hook finishes by calling the original function and passing its return value back to the caller. Here's how all of that might fit together:

```
typedef DWORD (__cdecl _origFunc)(DWORD arg1, DWORD arg2, DWORD arg3);

_origFunc* originalFunction =
    (_origFunc*)hookCall(0xDEADBEEF, (DWORD)&someNewFunction);

DWORD __cdecl someNewFunction(DWORD arg1, DWORD arg2, DWORD arg3)
{
    return originalFunction(arg1, arg2, arg3);
}
```

This example uses typedef to declare a type representing the original function's prototype and creates a pointer with this type to the original function. Then `someNewFunction()` uses this pointer to call the original function with the original arguments and pass the returned value back to the caller.

Right now, all `someNewFunction()` does is return to the original function. But you can do whatever you want from inside the `someNewFunction()` call from here. You can modify the parameters being passed to the original function or intercept and store interesting parameters for later use. If you know the caller isn't expecting a return value (or if you know how to spoof the return value), you can even forget about the original function and completely replace, replicate, or improve its functionality inside the new callee. Once you've perfected this skill, you can add your own native C or C++ code to any part of a game that you wish.

VF Table Hooking

Unlike call hooks, *virtual function (VF) table hooks* don't modify assembly code. Instead, they modify the function addresses stored in the VF tables of classes. (If you need a refresher on VF tables, see "A Class with Virtual Functions" on page 75.) All instances of the same class type share a static VF table, so VF table hooks will intercept all calls made to a member function, regardless of which class instance the game is calling the function from. This can be both powerful and tricky.

THE TRUTH ABOUT VF TABLES

To simplify the explanation, I lied a little when I said that VF table hooks could intercept all calls made to a function. In reality, the VF table is traversed only when a virtual function is called in a way that leaves the compiler with some plausible type ambiguity. For example, a VF table will be traversed when a function is called through the `inst->function()` call format. A VF table won't be traversed when a virtual function is invoked in such a way that the compiler is sure about the type, as in `inst.function()` or similar calls, since the compiler will know the function's address. Conversely, calling `inst.function()` from a scope where inst is passed in as a reference would trigger a VF table traversal. Before you try to deploy VF table hooking, make sure the function calls you want to hook have type ambiguity.

Writing a VF Table Hook

Before we go any deeper into how to place a VF table hook, we need to talk about those pesky calling conventions again. VF tables are used by class instances to call virtual member functions, and all member functions will have the __thiscall convention. The name __thiscall is derived from the this pointer that member functions use to reference the active class instance. Thus, member functions are given this as a pseudoparameter on ECX.

It's possible to match the prototype of a __thiscall by declaring a class that acts as a container for all __thiscall hook callbacks, but I don't prefer this method. Instead, I find it easier to control the data using inline assembly. Let's explore how you control the data when placing a VF hook on a class that looks like this:

```
class someBaseClass {
    public:
        virtual DWORD someFunction(DWORD arg1) {}
};
class someClass : public someBaseClass {
    public:
        virtual DWORD someFunction(DWORD arg1) {}
};
```

The someBaseClass class just has one member (a public virtual function), and the someClass class inherits from someBaseClass and overrides the someBaseClass::someFunction member. To hook someClass::someFunction, you replicate the prototype in your VF table hook, as shown in Listing 8-3 (follow along in the *VFHookExample.cpp* file of the project).

```
DWORD __stdcall someNewVFFunction(DWORD arg1)
{
❶   static DWORD _this;
    __asm MOV _this, ECX
}
```

Listing 8-3: The start of a VF table hook

This function works as a hook because __thiscall only differs from __stdcall in that the former is given this on ECX. To reconcile this small difference, the callback function uses inline assembly (denoted by __asm) to copy this from ECX to a static variable ❶. Since the static variable is actually initialized as a global, the only code that executes before MOV _this, ECX is the code that sets up the stack frame—and that code never touches ECX. That ensures that the proper value is in ECX when the assembly is executed.

NOTE *If multiple threads start calling the same VF function, the someNewVFFunction() hook will break because _this might be modified by one call while still being used by another call. I've never personally run into this problem, as games don't typically throw around multiple instances of critical classes between threads, but an efficient remedy would be to store _this in thread local storage, ensuring each thread would have its own copy.*

Before returning, a VF table callback must also restore ECX, to keep with the __thiscall convention. Here's how that process looks:

```
DWORD __stdcall someNewVFFunction(DWORD arg1)
{
    static DWORD _this;
    __asm MOV _this, ECX

    // do game modifying stuff here

    __asm ❶MOV ECX, _this
}
```

After executing some game-hacking code, this version of the function someNewVFFunction() restores ECX ❶ with a reversed version of the first MOV instruction from Listing 8-3.

Unlike with __cdecl functions, however, you shouldn't call functions that use the __thiscall convention from pure C++ using only a function pointer and typedef (as you would for a call hook). When calling the original function from a VF table hook, you must use inline assembly—that's the only way to be sure you're passing data (specifically _this) around properly. For example, this is how you continue to build the someNewVFFunction() hook:

```
DWORD __stdcall someNewVFFunction(DWORD arg1)
{
    static DWORD _this, _ret;
    __asm MOV _this, ECX

    // do pre-call stuff here

    __asm {
        PUSH arg1
        MOV ECX, _this
❶      CALL [originalVFFunction]
❷      MOV _ret, EAX
    }

    // do post-call stuff here

❸  __asm MOV ECX, _this
    return _ret;
}
```

Now, someNewVFFunction() stores this in the _this variable, allows some code to execute, calls the original game function ❶ that's being hooked, stores that function's return value in _ret ❷, allows some more code to execute, restores this to ECX ❸, and returns the value stored in _ret. The callee cleans the stack for __thiscall calls, so unlike a call hook, the pushed argument doesn't need to be removed.

If you want to remove a single pushed argument at any point, use the assembly instruction ADD ESP, 0x4 *because a single argument is 4 bytes.*

Using a VF Table Hook

With the calling convention established and a skeleton callback in place, it's time to move on to the fun part: actually using a VF table hook. A pointer to a class's VF table is the first member of every class instance, so placing a VF table hook requires only a class instance address and the index of the function to be hooked. Using these two pieces of information, you need only a modest amount of code to place a hook. Here's an example:

```
DWORD hookVF(DWORD classInst, DWORD funcIndex, DWORD newFunc)
{
    DWORD VFTable = ❶readMemory<DWORD>(classInst);
    DWORD hookAt = VFTable + funcIndex * sizeof(DWORD);

    auto oldProtection =
        protectMemory<DWORD>(hookAt, PAGE_READWRITE);
    DWORD originalFunc = readMemory<DWORD>(hookAt);
    writeMemory<DWORD>(hookAt, newFunc);
    protectMemory<DWORD>(hookAt, oldProtection);

    return originalFunc;
}
```

The hookVF() function finds the VF table by reading the first member of the class instance ❶ and storing it in VFTable. Since the VF table is just an array of DWORD-sized addresses, this code finds the function address by multiplying the function's index in the VF table (funcIndex in this example) by the size of a DWORD, which is 4, and adding the result to the VF table's address. From there, hookVF() acts similar to a call hook: it makes sure the memory is properly accessible by setting appropriate protections, stores the original function address for later, writes the new function address, and finally, restores the original memory protection.

You'll typically hook the VF table of a class instantiated by the game, and calling a function like hookVF() for a VF table hook looks like this:

```
DWORD origVFFunction =
    hookVF(classInstAddr, 0, (DWORD)&someNewVFFunction);
```

As usual, you need to find classInstAddr and the funcIndex argument ahead of time.

There are some very niche cases in which VF table hooks are useful, and it can be really hard to find the right class pointers and functions. Given that, instead of showing contrived use cases, I'll come back to VF table hooks in "Applying Jump Hooks and VF Hooks to Direct3D" on page 175, once I've discussed other types of hooking.

If you want to play with VF hooks before reading more, add new virtual functions to the example classes in this book's resource files and practice hooking them. You might even create a second class that derives from someBaseClass and place a hook on its virtual table to demonstrate how you can have two completely separate VF hooks on two classes that inherit the same base class.

IAT Hooking

IAT hooks actually replace function addresses in a specific type of VF table, called the *import address table (IAT)*. Each loaded module in a process contains an IAT in its PE header. A module's IAT holds a list of all the other modules on which the module depends, as well as a list of functions that the module uses from each dependency. Think of an IAT as a lookup table for APIs to call one another.

When a module is loaded, its dependencies are also loaded. Dependency loading is a recursive process that continues until all dependencies for all modules are loaded. As each dependency is loaded, the operating system finds all functions used by the dependent module and fills any blank spaces in its IAT with the function addresses. Then, when a module calls a function from a dependency, it makes that call by resolving the function's address from the IAT.

Paying for Portability

Function addresses are always resolved from the IAT in real time, so hooking the IAT is similar to hooking VF tables. Since function pointers are stored in the IAT beside their actual names, there's no need to do any reverse engineering or memory scanning; as long as you know the name of the API you want to hook, you can hook it! Moreover, IAT hooking lets you easily hook Windows API calls on a module-specific basis, allowing your hooks to intercept only API calls from a game's main module.

This portability has a cost, though; the code to place an IAT hook is much more complex than what you've seen so far. First, you need to locate the PE header of the game's main module. Since the PE header is the first structure in any binary, you can find it at the base address of each module, as shown in Listing 8-4 (follow along in the *IATHookExample.cpp* file of the project).

```
DWORD baseAddr = (DWORD)GetModuleHandle(NULL);
```

Listing 8-4: Fetching the module's base address

Once you've found the base address, you must verify that the PE header is valid. This validation can be very important, as some games try to prevent these types of hooks by scrambling nonessential parts of their PE header after they load. A valid PE header is prefixed by a DOS header, which indicates the file is a DOS MZ executable; the DOS header is identified by the magic value 0x5A4D. A member of the DOS header called e_lfanew then points to the optional header, which contains values like the size of the code, a version number, and so on and is identified by the magic value 0x10B.

The Windows API has PE structures called IMAGE_DOS_HEADER and IMAGE_OPTIONAL_HEADER that correspond to the DOS header and optional header, respectively. You can use them to validate the PE header with code like Listing 8-5.

```
auto dosHeader = pointMemory<IMAGE_DOS_HEADER>(baseAddr);
if (dosHeader->e_magic != 0x5A4D)
    return 0;

auto optHeader =
    pointMemory<IMAGE_OPTIONAL_HEADER>(baseAddr + dosHeader->e_lfanew + 24);
if (optHeader->Magic != 0x10B)
    return 0;
```

Listing 8-5: Confirming the DOS and optional headers are valid

The calls to pointMemory() create pointers to the two headers that need to be checked. If either if() statement returns 0, then the corresponding header has the wrong magic number, meaning the PE header isn't valid.

References to the IAT from assembly are hardcoded, meaning assembly references don't traverse the PE header to locate the IAT. Instead, each function call has a static location indicating where to find the function address. That means overwriting the PE header to say that there are no imports is a viable way to protect against IAT hooks, and some games have this protection.

To account for that, you also need to make sure the game's IAT still exists. Listing 8-6 shows how to add such a check to the code in Listing 8-5.

```
auto IAT = optHeader->DataDirectory[IMAGE_DIRECTORY_ENTRY_IMPORT];
if (IAT.Size == 0 || IAT.VirtualAddress == 0)
    return 0;
```

Listing 8-6: Checking that the IAT actually exists

The PE header contains many sections that store information about the application's code, embedded resources, relocations, and so on. The piece of code in Listing 8-6 is particularly interested in the data section, which—as you might guess—stores many different types of data. Each type of data is stored in its own directory, and the DataDirectory member of IMAGE_OPTIONAL_HEADER is an array of directory headers that describes the size and virtual address of each directory in the data section. The Windows API defines a constant called IMAGE_DIRECTORY_ENTRY_IMPORT, which happens to be the index of the IAT header within the DataDirectory array.

Thus, this code uses optHeader->DataDirectory[IMAGE_DIRECTORY_ENTRY_IMPORT] to resolve the header of the IAT and check that the header's Size and VirtualAddress are nonzero, essentially confirming its existence.

Traversing the IAT

Once you know the IAT is still intact, you can start traversing it, and this is where IAT hooking starts to get ugly. The IAT is an array of structures called *import descriptors*. There is one import descriptor for each dependency, each import descriptor points to an array of structures called *thunks*, and each thunk represents a function imported from the dependency.

Luckily, the Windows API exposes both the import descriptors and thunks through the IMAGE_IMPORT_DESCRIPTOR and IMAGE_THUNK_DATA structures, respectively. Having the structures predefined saves you from creating your own, but it doesn't make the code to traverse the IAT any prettier. To see what I mean, look at Listing 8-7, which builds on Listings 8-4 through 8-6.

```
auto impDesc =
    pointMemory<IMAGE_IMPORT_DESCRIPTOR>(❶baseAddr + IAT.VirtualAddress);

❷ while (impDesc->FirstThunk) {
❸     auto thunkData =
           pointMemory<IMAGE_THUNK_DATA>(baseAddr + impDesc->OriginalFirstThunk);
       int n = 0;
❹     while (thunkData->u1.Function) {
           // the hook happens in here
           n++;
           thunkData++;
       }
       impDesc++;
}
```

Listing 8-7: Iterating over the IAT to find a function

Keeping in mind that the import descriptors are stored relative to the start of the PE header, this code adds the module's base address to the virtual address found in the IAT's directory header ❶, creating a pointer, impDesc, that points to the module's first import descriptor.

Import descriptors are stored in a sequential array, and a descriptor with a FirstThunk member set to NULL signifies the end of the array. Knowing this, the code uses a while loop ❷ that continues until impDesc->FirstThunk is NULL, incrementing the descriptor by executing impDesc++ each iteration.

For each import descriptor, the code creates a pointer called thunkData ❸ that points to the first thunk inside the descriptor. Using a familiar loop, the code iterates over thunks ❹ until one is found with a Function member set to NULL. The loop also uses an integer, n, to keep track of the current thunk index, as the index is important when placing the hook.

Placing the IAT Hook

From here, placing the hook is just a matter of finding the proper function name and replacing the function address. You can find the name inside the nested while loop, as shown in Listing 8-8.

```
char* importFunctionName =
    pointMemory<char>(baseAddr + (DWORD)thunkData->u1.AddressOfData + 2);
```

Listing 8-8: Finding the function name

The function name for each thunk is stored at `thunkData->u1.AddressOfData + 2` bytes into the module, so you can add that value to the module's base address to locate the function name in memory.

After obtaining a pointer to the function name, use `strcmp()` to check whether it's the target function, like so:

```
if (strcmp(importFuncName, funcName) == 0) {
    // the final step happens in here
}
```

Once you've located the target function using its name, you simply need to overwrite the function address with the address of your own function. Unlike function names, function addresses are stored in an array at the start of each import descriptor. Using n from the thunk loop, you can finally set the hook, as shown in Listing 8-9.

```
auto vfTable = pointMemory<DWORD> (baseAddr + impDesc->FirstThunk);
DWORD original = vfTable[n];

❶ auto oldProtection = protectMemory<DWORD>((DWORD)&vfTable[n], PAGE_READWRITE);
❷ vfTable[n] = newFunc;
  protectMemory<DWORD>((DWORD)&vfTable[n], oldProtection);
```

Listing 8-9: Finding the function address

This code locates the VF table for the current descriptor by adding the address of the first thunk to the module base address. The VF table is an array of function addresses, so the code uses the n variable as an index to locate the target function address.

Once the address is found, the code in Listing 8-9 works just like a typical VF hook: it stores the original function address, sets the protection of index n in the VF table to `PAGE_READWRITE` ❶, inserts the new function address into the VF table ❷, and finally restores the old protection.

If you stitch together the code from Listings 8-4 through 8-9, the final IAT hooking function looks like Listing 8-10.

```
DWORD hookIAT(const char* funcName, DWORD newFunc)
                {
   DWORD baseAddr = (DWORD)GetModuleHandle(NULL);
```

```
auto dosHeader = pointMemory<IMAGE_DOS_HEADER>(baseAddr);
if (dosHeader->e_magic != 0x5A4D)
    return 0;

auto optHeader =
    pointMemory<IMAGE_OPTIONAL_HEADER>(baseAddr + dosHeader->e_lfanew + 24);
if (optHeader->Magic != 0x10B)
    return 0;

auto IAT =
    optHeader->DataDirectory[IMAGE_DIRECTORY_ENTRY_IMPORT];
if (IAT.Size == 0 || IAT.VirtualAddress == 0)
    return 0;

auto impDesc =
    pointMemory<IMAGE_IMPORT_DESCRIPTOR>(baseAddr + IAT.VirtualAddress);

while (impDesc->FirstThunk) {
    auto thunkData =
        pointMemory<IMAGE_THUNK_DATA>(baseAddr + impDesc->OriginalFirstThunk);
    int n = 0;
    while (thunkData->u1.Function) {
        char* importFuncName = pointMemory<char>
            (baseAddr + (DWORD)thunkData->u1.AddressOfData + 2);
        if (strcmp(importFuncName, funcName) == 0) {
            auto vfTable = pointMemory<DWORD>(baseAddr + impDesc->FirstThunk);
            DWORD original = vfTable[n];
            auto oldProtection =
                protectMemory<DWORD>((DWORD)&vfTable[n], PAGE_READWRITE);
            vfTable[n] = newFunc;
            protectMemory<DWORD>((DWORD)&vfTable[n], oldProtection);
            return original;
        }
        n++;
        thunkData++;
    }
    impDesc++;
}
}
```

Listing 8-10: The complete IAT hooking function

This is the most complex code that we've put together so far, and it's pretty hard to read when squished to fit on a page. If you haven't yet wrapped your head around what it's doing, you might want to study the example code from this book's resource files before continuing.

Using an IAT Hook to Sync with a Game Thread

With the code in Listing 8-10, hooking any Windows API function is as simple as knowing the function name and the proper prototype. The Sleep() API is a common API to hook when game hacking, as bots can use a Sleep() hook to thread-sync with a game's main loop.

Here's one way to use hookIAT() to hook the Sleep() API:

```
VOID WINAPI newSleepFunction(DWORD ms)
{
    // do thread-sensitive things
    originalSleep(ms);
}

typedef VOID (WINAPI _origSleep)(DWORD ms);
_origSleep* originalSleep =
    (_origSleep*)hookIAT("Sleep", (DWORD)&newSleepFunction);
```

Here's why this works. At the end of a game's main loop, it might call Sleep() to rest until it's ready to draw the next frame. Since it's sleeping, it's safe for you to do anything you want without worrying about synchronization issues. Some games might not do this, or they might call Sleep() from multiple threads, and those games will require a different method.

A more portable alternative is to hook the PeekMessageA() API function, because games often call that function from the main loop while waiting for input. Then, your bot can do thread-sensitive operations from within the PeekMessageA() hook, ensuring that they're done from the game's main thread. You may also want your bot to use this method to hook the send() and recv() API functions, as intercepting these allows you to create a packet sniffer relatively simply.

Jump Hooking

Jump hooking allows you to hook code in places where there is no branching code to manipulate. A jump hook replaces the code being hooked with an unconditional jump to a *trampoline function*. When the jump is hit, the trampoline function stores all current register and flag values, calls a callback function of your choice, restores the registers, restores the flags, executes the code that was replaced by the hook, and finally jumps back to the code just below the hook. This process is shown in Figure 8-1.

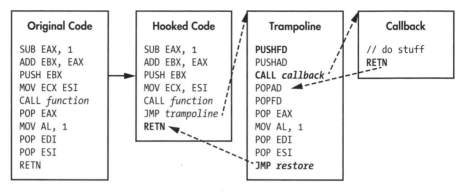

Figure 8-1: A jump hook

The original code shows an example of some unmodified assembly you might find in a game, and the hooked code shows how that assembly might look after being hooked by a jump hook. The trampoline box shows an example trampoline function, in assembly, and the callback represents the code you're trying to execute through hooking. In the original code, the assembly executes from top to bottom. In the hooked code, to get from the SUB EAX,1 instruction to the RETN instruction, execution must follow the path shown by the dashed arrows.

NOTE *If your callback code is simple, it can be integrated into the trampoline instead. It's also not always necessary to store and restore the registers and flags, but doing so is good practice.*

Placing a Jump

The byte code of an unconditional jump resembles that of a near call, but the first byte is 0xE9 instead of 0xE8. (See "Working with Near Calls in Memory" on page 153 for a refresher.) In Figure 8-1, the unconditional jump JMP trampoline replaces the following four operations:

```
POP EAX
MOV AL, 1
POP EDI
POP ESI
```

In this case, you need to replace multiple sequential operations to accommodate the 5-byte size of the unconditional jump. You may come across cases where the size of the operation (or operations) being replaced is larger than 5 bytes. When this happens, replace the remaining bytes with NOP instructions.

Now, let's look at how to replace those operations. Listing 8-11 shows the code to place a jump hook.

```
DWORD hookWithJump(DWORD hookAt, DWORD newFunc, int size)
{
    if (size > 12) // shouldn't ever have to replace 12+ bytes
        return 0;
❶  DWORD newOffset = newFunc - hookAt - 5;

    auto oldProtection =
        protectMemory<DWORD[3]>(hookAt + 1,PAGE_EXECUTE_READWRITE);
❷  writeMemory<BYTE>(hookAt, 0xE9);
❸  writeMemory<DWORD>(hookAt + 1, newOffset);
    for (unsigned int i = 5; i < size; i++)
        writeMemory<BYTE>(hookAt + i, 0x90);
    protectMemory<DWORD[3]>(hookAt + 1, oldProtection);

    return hookAt + 5;
}
```

Listing 8-11: How to place a jump hook

This function takes the address to hook at, the address of the callback function, and the size of the memory to overwrite (in bytes) as arguments. First, it calculates the offset between the hook site and the trampoline and stores the result in newOffset ❶. Next, PAGE_EXECUTE_READWRITE permissions are applied to the memory to be changed. The unconditional jump (0xE9) ❷ and the address of the callback function ❸ are then written to memory, and a for loop writes NOP instructions (0x90) to any abandoned bytes. After the old protections are reapplied, hookWithJump() returns to the original address.

Notice that the hookWithJump() function ensures that size is not above 12 before placing the jump. This check is important because a jump takes up 5 bytes, meaning it can replace up to five commands if the first four are each a single byte. If the first four commands are each a single byte, the fifth command would need to be more than 8 bytes to trigger the if (size > 12) clause. Because 9-byte operations are very, very rare, 12 is a safe but flexible limit. Having this limit can stop all sorts of bugs from happening, especially if your bot is dynamically detecting the size parameter. If the bot messes up and passes a size of 500,000,000, for instance, the check will stop you from NOPing the whole universe.

Writing the Trampoline Function

Using the function in Listing 8-11, you can replicate the hook shown in Figure 8-1, but first you'll have to create the trampoline function as follows:

```
DWORD restoreJumpHook = 0;
void __declspec(naked) myTrampoline()
{
```

```
       __asm {
❶          PUSHFD
❷          PUSHAD
❸          CALL jumpHookCallback
❹          POPAD
❺          POPFD
❻          POP EAX
           MOV AL, 1
           POP EDI
❼          POP ESI
❽          JMP [restoreJumpHook]
       }
}
```

Just like the trampoline described alongside Figure 8-1, this trampoline
stores all current flag ❶ and register values ❷, calls a callback function ❸,
restores the registers ❹, restores the flags ❺, executes the code that was
replaced by the hook at ❻ and ❼, and finally jumps back to the original
code just below the jump and NOPs ❽.

NOTE *To ensure that the compiler doesn't autogenerate any extra code within the trampoline,
always declare the trampoline using the __declspec(naked) convention.*

Finishing the Jump Hook

Once you create the trampoline, define the callback and set the hook
like so:

```
void jumpHookCallback() {
    // do stuff
}
restoreJumpHook = hookWithJump(0xDEADBEEF, &myTrampoline, 5);
```

Finally, inside the jumpHookCallback() function, execute the code that
relies on the hook. If your code needs to read or write the values of the
registers as they were when the hook executed, you're in luck. The PUSHAD
command pushes them to the stack in the order EAX, ECX, EDX, EBX,
original ESP, EBP, ESI, and EDI. The trampoline calls PUSHAD directly before
the jumpHookCallback() call, so you can reference the register values as arguments, like this:

```
void jumpHookCallback(DWORD EDI, DWORD ESI, DWORD EBP, DWORD ESP,
                      DWORD EBX, DWORD EDX, DWORD ECX, DWORD EAX) {
    // do stuff
}
restoreJumpHook = hookWithJump(0xDEADBEEF, &myTrampoline, 5);
```

Since the trampoline uses POPAD to directly restore the registers from
these values on the stack, any modifications you make to the parameters
will be applied to the actual registers when they are restored from the
stack.

Like VF table hooks, jump hooks are rarely needed, and they can be tricky to simulate with a simple example. To help you wrap your head around them, I'll explore a real-world, practical use case in "Applying Jump Hooks and VF Hooks to Direct3D" on page 175.

PROFESSIONAL API HOOKING LIBRARIES

There are prewritten hooking libraries, like Microsoft's Detours and MadCHook, that use only jump hooks. These libraries can automatically detect and follow other hooks, they know how many instructions to replace, and they generate trampoline functions for you. The libraries are able to do this because they understand how to disassemble and walk through assembly instructions to determine lengths, jump destinations, and so on. If you need to use hooks with that much power, it is arguably better to use one of those libraries than to create your own.

Applying Call Hooks to Adobe AIR

Adobe AIR is a development framework that can be used to make cross-platform games in an environment similar to Abode Flash. AIR is a common framework for online games, as it allows developers to write cross-platform code in a versatile, high-level language called ActionScript. ActionScript is an interpreted language, and AIR runs the code inside a virtual machine, which makes it infeasible to hook game-specific code with AIR. Instead, it is easier to hook AIR itself.

The example code for this section can be found in *GameHackingExamples/ Chapter8_AdobeAirHook* in this book's source files. The code comes from an old project of mine, and it works on any game running *Adobe AIR.dll* version 3.7.0.1530. I've gotten it working on other versions as well, but I can't guarantee it will work with much newer or much older versions, so treat this as a case study.

Accessing the RTMP Goldmine

The *Real Time Messaging Protocol (RTMP)* is a text-based network protocol that ActionScript uses to serialize and send entire objects over the network. RTMP sits on top of the *HyperText Transfer Protocol (HTTP)*, and a secure version, RTMPS, sits on top of *HTTP Secure (HTTPS)*. RTMPS allows game developers to easily send and receive entire object instances over a secure connection with little complication, making it the network protocol of choice for any games running on AIR.

NOTE   *Data sent over RTMP/RTMPS is serialized through* Action Message Format (AMF), *and parsing AMF packets is beyond the scope of this book. Search online for "AMF3 Parser," and you'll find a lot of code that does it.*

Data sent over RTMP and RTMPS is very rich. The packets contain information about object types, names, and values. This is a gold mine. If you can intercept this data in real time, you can instantaneously respond to changes in game state, see a wealth of critical information without ever reading it from memory, and find useful pieces of data that you might not even know exist.

A while back, I was working on a tool that required a ton of insight into the state of a game. Obtaining such a large amount of data directly from memory would have been extremely hard, if not impossible. After some research, I realized that the game was using RTMPS to communicate with the server, and that prompted me to start digging into this gold mine.

Since RTMPS is encrypted, I knew I had to somehow hook the cryptographic functions used by AIR before I could get any usable data. After searching online, I found source code for a small tool called airlog, created by another game hacker who, like me, was trying to log packets sent over RTMPS. Although the tool hooked the exact functions I needed, the code was outdated, messy, and, worst of all, didn't work on the version of AIR I was trying to hook.

But that didn't mean it was useless. Not only did airlog hook the two functions I needed, but it also located them by scanning for certain byte patterns within the Adobe AIR library. These byte patterns were three years old, though, so they weren't working anymore. The newer versions of Adobe AIR had changed enough that the assembly bytes were no longer the same. The difference in bytes was a problem for the code in airlog, but not for me.

Inside an inline assembly block, you can specify raw bytes with the following function call:

```
_emit BYTE
```

If you replace *BYTE* with, say, 0x03, the code will be compiled in a way that treats 0x03 as a byte in the assembly code, regardless of whether that makes sense. Using this trick, I compiled the byte arrays back to assembly code. The code didn't do anything, and it wasn't meant to; using this trick simply allowed me to attach to my dummy application with OllyDBG and inspect bytes, which were conveniently presented as a clean disassembly.

Since these bytes represented the code surrounding the functions I needed, so, too, did their disassembly. The code was pretty standard and didn't seem likely to change, so I turned my attention to the constants. The code had a few immediate values passed as offsets in commands. Knowing how commonly these can change, I rewired airlog's pattern-matching algorithm to support wildcards, updated the patterns to treat any constants as wildcards, and then ran the match. After some tweaks to the patterns and a bit of digging through duplicate search results, I tracked down the functions I wanted to hook. I appropriately named them encode() and decode() and began working on a tool similar to airlog—but better.

Hooking the RTMPS encode() Function

I discovered that the encode() function, which is used to encrypt the data for outgoing packets, is a nonvirtual __thiscall, meaning it's called by a near call. Moreover, the call happens inside a loop. The entire loop looks like Listing 8-12, taken directly from the OllyDBG disassembly pane.

```
loop:
        MOV EAX, [ESI+3C58]
        SUB EAX,EDI
        PUSH EAX
❶      LEA EAX, [ESI+EDI+1C58]
        PUSH EAX
        MOV ECX,ESI
❷      CALL encode
        CMP EAX,-1
❸      JE SHORT endLoop
        ADD EDI,EAX
❹      CMP EDI, [ESI+3C58]
        JL loop
endLoop:
```

Listing 8-12: The encode() loop

With a bit of analysis and some guidance from airlog, I determined that the encode() function called at ❶ takes a byte array and buffer length (let's call them buffer and size, respectively) as parameters. The function returns -1 when it fails and returns size otherwise. The function operates on chunks of 4,096 bytes, which is why this happens in a loop.

Turned into more readable pseudocode, the loop calling encode() looks like this (the numbers refer to the relevant assembly instructions in Listing 8-12):

```
for (EDI = 0; EDI < ❹[ESI+3C58]; ) {
    EAX = ❷encode(❶&[ESI+EDI+1C58], [ESI+3C58] - EDI);
    if (EAX == -1) ❸break;
    EDI += EAX;
}
```

I wasn't interested in what encode() did, but I needed the entire buffer it was looping over, and hooking encode() was my means of getting that buffer. Looking at the real loop in Listing 8-12, I knew that the calling object instance's full buffer was stored at ESI+0x1C58, that the full size was stored at ESI+0x3C58, and that EDI contained the loop counter. I devised the hook with these things in mind, ultimately creating a two-part hook.

The first part of my hook was a reportEncode() function that logs the entire buffer on the first loop iteration. Here's the reportEncode() function in full:

```
DWORD __stdcall reportEncode(
    const unsigned char* buffer,
    unsigned int size,
```

```
    unsigned int loopCounter)
{
    if (loopCounter == 0)
        printBuffer(buffer, size);
    return origEncodeFunc;
}
```

This function takes buffer, size, and loopCounter as parameters and returns the address of the function I dubbed encode(). Before fetching that address, however, the second part of my hook, a myEncode() function, does all of the dirty work to obtain buffer, size, and loopCounter, as follows:

```
void __declspec(naked) myEncode()
{
    __asm {
        MOV EAX, DWORD PTR SS:[ESP + 0x4]      // get buffer
        MOV EDX, DWORD PTR DS:[ESI + 0x3C58]  // get full size
        PUSH ECX               // store ecx
        PUSH EDI               // push current pos (loop counter)
        PUSH EDX               // push size
        PUSH EAX               // push buffer
        CALL reportEncode  // report the encode call
        POP ECX            // restore ecx
        JMP EAX            // jump to encode
    }
}
```

The myEncode() function is a pure assembly function that replaces the original encode() function call using a near call hook. After storing ECX on the stack, myEncode() obtains buffer, size, and loopCounter and passes them to the reportEncode() function. After calling the reportEncode() function, the myEncode() function restores ECX and jumps directly into encode(), causing the original function to execute and return gracefully to the loop.

Since myEncode() cleans everything it uses from the stack, the stack still contains the original parameters and return address in the correct spot after myEncode() runs. That's why myEncode() jumps directly into encode() instead of using a function call: that stack is already set up with the proper return address and parameters, so the encode() function will think everything happened as normal.

Hooking the RTMPS decode() Function

The function I named decode(), which is used to decrypt incoming data, was also a __thiscall that was called in a loop. It worked on chunks of 4,096 bytes and took a buffer and size as parameters. The loop was quite a bit more complex, containing multiple function calls, nested loops, and loop escapes, but hooking worked much the same as hooking the so-called encode() function. The reason for the added complexity is not relevant to hooking the function, but it makes the code difficult to summarize, so I won't show the original function here. The bottom line is this: once all the complexity was rubbed away, the decode() loop was the encode() loop in reverse.

Once again, I devised a two-part near call hook. The first part, reportDecode(), is shown here:

```
void __stdcall reportDecode(const unsigned char* buffer, unsigned int size)
{
    printBuffer(buffer, size);
}
```

The function logs each packet that comes through. I didn't have a loop index at the time, so I decided that it was okay to log every single partial packet.

The second part of the hook, the myDecode() function, acts as the new callee and does all of the dirty work, as follows:

```
void __declspec(naked) myDecode()
{
    __asm {
        MOV EAX, DWORD PTR SS:[ESP + 0x4]  // get buffer
        MOV EDX, DWORD PTR SS:[ESP + 0x8]  // get size
        PUSH EDX                           // push size
        PUSH EAX                           // push buffer
❶      CALL [origDecodeFunc]

        MOV EDX, DWORD PTR SS:[ESP + 0x4]  // get the buffer

        PUSH EAX                           // store eax (return value)
        PUSH ECX                           // store ecx
        PUSH EAX                           // push size
        PUSH EDX                           // push buffer
        CALL reportDecode                  // report the results now
        POP ECX                            // restore ecx
❷      POP EAX                            // restore eax (return value)
❸      RETN 8                            // return and clean stack
    }
}
```

I knew the buffer was decrypted in place, meaning the encrypted chunk would be overwritten with the decrypted one once the call to decode() was complete. This meant that myDecode() had to call the original decode() function ❶ before calling the reportDecode() function, which would give the results of the decoding. Ultimately, myDecode() also needed to return with the same value that the original decode() function would and clean up the stack, and the final POP ❷ and RETN ❸ instructions took care of that.

Placing the Hooks

The next problem I ran into was that the hooks were for code inside the module *Adobe AIR.dll*, which was not the main module of the game. Because of the code's location, I needed to find the base addresses for the hooks a bit differently. Additionally, since I needed these hooks to work across a few different versions of Adobe AIR, I also had to find the right addresses for each version. Instead of trying to get my hands on all of the different versions of Adobe AIR, I took another page out of airlog's playbook and decided to programmatically locate the addresses by writing a small memory scanner. Before I could write the memory scanner, I needed both the base address and size of *Adobe AIR.dll* so I could limit my memory search to only that area.

I found these values using `Module32First()` and `Module32Next()` as follows:

```
MODULEENTRY32 entry;
entry.dwSize = sizeof(MODULEENTRY32);
HANDLE snapshot = CreateToolhelp32Snapshot(TH32CS_SNAPMODULE, NULL);

DWORD base, size;
if (Module32First(snapshot, &entry) == TRUE) {
❶   while (Module32Next(snapshot, &entry) == TRUE) {
        std::wstring binaryPath = entry.szModule;
❷       if (binaryPath.find("Adobe AIR.dll") != std::wstring::npos) {
            size = (DWORD)entry.modBaseSize;
            base = (DWORD)entry.modBaseAddr;
            break;
        }
    }
}

CloseHandle(snapshot);
```

This code loops through all modules in the process until it finds *Adobe AIR.dll* ❶. When it finds the correct module entry ❷, it fetches the `modBaseSize` and `modBaseAddr` properties from it and breaks out immediately.

The next step was finding a sequence of bytes I could use to identify the functions. I decided to use the byte code surrounding each call. I also had to make sure that each sequence was unique while avoiding the use of any constants in the patterns to ensure the code's portability. Listing 8-13 shows the byte sequences I ended up with.

```
const char encodeSeq[16] = {
    0x8B, 0xCE,                   // MOV ECX, ESI
    0xE8, 0xA6, 0xFF, 0xFF, 0xFF, // CALL encode
    0x83, 0xF8, 0xFF,             // CMP EAX, -1
    0x74, 0x16,                   // JE SHORT endLoop
    0x03, 0xF8,                   // ADD EDI, EAX
    0x3B, 0xBE};                  // part of CMP EDI, [ESI+0x3C58]
const char decodeSeq[12] = {
    0x8B, 0xCE,                   // MOV ECX, ESI
    0xE8, 0x7F, 0xF7, 0xFF, 0xFF, // CALL decode
    0x83, 0xF8,  0xFF,            // CMP EAX, -1
    0x89, 0x86};                  // part of MOV [ESI+0x1C54], EAX
```

Listing 8-13: The encode() and decode() byte sequences

Notice the CALL instruction in each pattern; these are the calls to the Adobe AIR functions I named encode() and decode(). I scanned for these sequences with the following function:

```
DWORD findSequence(
    DWORD base, DWORD size,
    const char* sequence,
    unsigned int seqLen){
    for (DWORD adr = base; adr <= base + size - seqLen; adr++) {
        if (memcmp((LPVOID)sequence, (LPVOID)adr, seqLen) == 0)
            return adr;
    }
    return 0;
}
```

Treating the memory of *Adobe AIR.dll* as a byte array, the findSequence() function looks for a sequence of bytes as a subset of that byte array and returns the address of the first match it finds. With the findSequence() function written, finding the addresses I needed to hook encode() and decode() was simple. Here's how those calls looked:

```
DWORD encodeHookAt =
    findSequence(base, size, encodeSeq, 16) + 2;
DWORD decodeHookAt =
    findSequence(base, size, decodeSeq, 12) + 2;
```

Since each target call was 2 bytes into its receptive search sequence, all I had to do was locate each sequence and add 2. After that, the final step was to place the hooks using the method described in "Call Hooking" on page 153.

With my hook finished, I could see every single piece of data that went between the game's client and server. Moreover, since the RTMPS protocol sends serialized ActionScript objects, the data was basically self-documenting. Every single piece of information was accompanied by a variable name. Every variable existed as a member of a well-described object. Every object had a consistent name. Like I said—it was a gold mine.

Applying Jump Hooks and VF Hooks to Direct3D

Unlike the Adobe AIR hook I just described, hooks for Direct3D (the 3D graphics component of Microsoft's DirectX API) are very common and highly documented. Direct3D is ubiquitous in the world of gaming: a majority of PC games use the library, which means that hooking it gives you a very powerful method for intercepting data and manipulating the graphics layers of many different games. You can use a Direct3D hook for a number of tasks, such as detecting locations of hidden enemy players, increasing the lighting of dark in-game environments, and seamlessly displaying additional graphical information. Making effective use of a Direct3D hook requires you to learn about the API, but there's more than enough information in this book to get you started.

In this section, I'll give you a high-level introduction to a game loop that uses Direct3D before diving right into the implementation of a Direct3D hook. Rather than detailing the internals and giving you the analytical backstory as I did with the Adobe AIR hook, I'll go over the most popular Direct3D hook method, as it is well documented and used by the majority of game hackers.

The online resources for this book include two pieces of example code for this section; find those files now if you want to follow along. The first part, an example Direct3D 9 application for you to hack on, can be found under *GameHackingExamples/Chapter8_Direct3DApplication*. The second part, the actual hook, is under *Chapter8_Direct3DHook*.

There are multiple versions of Direct3D in use at any given time, and there are ways to hook each one. For this book, I'll focus on hooking Direct3D 9, because it is the only commonly used version that is supported by Windows XP.

NOTE *Even though XP has reached end of life, many people in less developed countries still use it as a primary gaming system. Direct3D 9 works on all versions of Windows and is nearly as powerful as its successors, so many game companies still prefer to use it over newer versions that don't have as much backward compatibility.*

The Drawing Loop

Let's jump right in with a crash course on how Direct3D works. Inside a Direct3D game's source code, you'll find an infinite loop that processes input and renders graphics. Each iteration in this drawing loop is called a *frame*. If we cut out all the extraneous code and focus simply on a bare skeleton, we can visualize a game's main loop with the following code:

```
int WINAPI WinMain(args)
{
    /* Some code here would be called
       to set up Direct3D and initialize
       the game. Leaving it out for brevity. */
    MSG msg;
    while(TRUE) {
        /* Some code would be here to handle incoming
           mouse and keyboard messages. */
        drawFrame(); // this is the function we care about
    }
    /* Some code here would be called to
       clean up everything before exiting. */
}
```

This function is the entry point of the game. Simply put, it initializes the game and then enters the game's main loop. Inside the main loop, it executes code responsible for processing user input before calling drawFrame() to redraw the screen using Direct3D. (Check out the code in *GameHackingExamples/Chapter8_Direct3DApplication* to see a fully functional game loop.)

Each time it is called, the drawFrame() function redraws the entire screen. The code looks something like this:

```
void drawFrame()
{
❶    device->Clear(0, NULL, D3DCLEAR_TARGET, D3DCOLOR_XRGB(0, 0, 0), 1.0f, 0);
    device->BeginScene();
    // drawing will happen here
    device->EndScene();
    device->Present(NULL, NULL, NULL, NULL);
}
```

After clearing the screen with device->Clear ❶, the drawFrame() function calls device->BeginScene() to unlock the scene for drawing. It then executes some drawing code (what that drawing code actually does isn't important right now) and locks the scene with a device->EndScene() call. To finish up, it renders the scene to the screen by calling the device->Present() function.

Notice that all of these functions are called as members of some instance called device. This is simply an object instance representing the Direct3D device, which is used to invoke all sorts of drawing calls. Also, notice that this function is devoid of any actual drawing code, but that's okay. It's really only important for you to understand the high-level concepts of drawing loops, frames, and the Direct3D device. To recap, games have a main loop with two responsibilities:

- Handling incoming messages
- Drawing the game to the screen

Each iteration in this loop is called a frame, and each frame is drawn by a device. Taking control of the device gives you access to the most sensitive and descriptive details of the game's state; that is, you'll be able to peek into the game's state after the data has been parsed, processed, and rendered to the screen. Moreover, you'll be able to modify the output of this state. These two superpowers enable you to pull off all kinds of awesome hacks.

Finding the Direct3D Device

To take control of a Direct3D device, you hook the member functions in the device's VF table. Unfortunately, however, using the Direct3D API to instantiate your own instance of the same device class from injected code doesn't mean you'll share a VF table with the game's instance. Direct3D devices use a customized runtime implementation of VF tables, and each device gets its own unique VF table. Additionally, devices sometimes rewrite their own VF tables, removing any hooks and restoring the original function addresses.

Both of these Direct3D quirks leave you with one inevitable option: you must find the address of the game's device and modify its VF table directly. Here's how:

1. Create a Direct3D device and traverse its VF table to locate the true address of EndScene().

2. Place a temporary jump hook on EndScene().

3. When the jump hook callback is executed, store the address of the device that was used to call the function, remove the hook, and restore execution normally.

4. From there, use VF hooks to hook any member function of the Direct3D device.

Jump Hooking EndScene()

Since every device will call EndScene() at the end of each frame, you can hook EndScene() using a jump hook and intercept the game's device from your hook callback. Unique devices may have their own unique VF tables, but the different tables still point to the same functions, so you can find the address of EndScene() in the VF table of any arbitrary device. Using standard Direct3D API calls, you can create your own device like this:

```
LPDIRECT3D9 pD3D = Direct3DCreate9(D3D_SDK_VERSION);
if (!pD3D) return 0;

D3DPRESENT_PARAMETERS d3dpp;
ZeroMemory( &d3dpp, sizeof(d3dpp) );
d3dpp.Windowed = TRUE;
d3dpp.SwapEffect = D3DSWAPEFFECT_DISCARD;
d3dpp.hDeviceWindow = hWnd;

LPDIRECT3DDEVICE9 device;
HRESULT res = pD3D->CreateDevice(
    D3DADAPTER_DEFAULT,
    D3DDEVTYPE_HAL,
    hWnd,
    D3DCREATE_SOFTWARE_VERTEXPROCESSING,
    &d3dpp, &device);
if (FAILED(res)) return 0;
```

Explaining how everything in Direct3D works is outside the scope of this book, so just know that you can copy this code to create a Direct3D device that contains the EndScene() function as a member. The EndScene() address is at index 42 in the VF table of device (see "The Meaning of Device,

Direct3D, and VF Hooks" box to learn how to find that index), and you can read it using a subset of the VF table hooking code from "Using a VF Table Hook" on page 159, as follows:

```
DWORD getVF(DWORD classInst, DWORD funcIndex)
{
    DWORD VFTable = readMemory<DWORD>(classInst);
    DWORD hookAddress = VFTable + funcIndex * sizeof(DWORD);
    return readMemory<DWORD>(hookAddress);
}
DWORD EndSceneAddress = getVF((DWORD)device, 42);
```

Once you've obtained the address, your discovery device has served its purpose, and it can be destroyed with a call to the Release() function:

```
pD3D->Release();
device->Release();
```

With the address of EndScene() in hand, you'd be ready to start thinking about how to place your hook in memory. But since you just have a function address, your only option is to place a jump hook at the top of the function.

THE MEANING OF DEVICE, DIRECT3D, AND VF HOOKS

If you're wondering how I know that the index of the EndScene() function is 42, you've come to the right box. Since Direct3D 9 is a freely available library, you can actually see quite a bit of what goes on under the hood. The main header file for the library is *d3d9.h*. If you open this file in your editor and search for "EndScene," you'll end up in the middle of a large class definition that specifies several functions using C macros. This is the base class for all Direct3D 9 device implementations, and it defines the virtual functions used by the class.

The VF table is constructed in the same order as the functions are defined in code, so you can determine the index of any member function by simply counting the lines. You can scroll to the top of the class definition (at line 426 in my version of the library, and probably yours too), note the line where the first function is declared (line 429), and then scroll to the EndScene() definition and note that line (line 473). Finally, count the number of blank or commented lines (two for me) and do some math: $473 - 429 - 2 = 42$.

Presto! The EndScene() function is the 43rd function declared, so it sits at the 42nd spot in the VF table. Another advantage to having this header is that you can see the name, argument types, argument names, and return type of every single function in the device class. So when you're writing your own hooks in the future, you'll know exactly where to look.

Placing and Removing the Jump Hook

Since you're just using the hook to find the device, you need to call it only once. After obtaining the device, you'll remove the jump hook and restore execution back to the start of EndScene() so that the drawing loop can carry on its work. Believe it or not, this makes your life much easier. Since the code will be restored immediately, there's no need for your trampoline to execute the commands that are replaced by the jump, and there's no need to pad the jump with NOPs. All you need to do is store the original bytes and place the hook. To do so, you use a slightly tweaked version of the jump-hooking code from Listing 8-11:

```
unsigned char* hookWithJump(DWORD hookAt, DWORD newFunc)
{
    DWORD newOffset = newFunc - hookAt - 5;
❶    auto oldProtection = protectMemory<BYTE[5]>(hookAt, PAGE_EXECUTE_READWRITE);
    unsigned char* originals = new unsigned char[5];
    for (int i = 0; i < 5; i++)
❷        originals[i] = readMemory<unsigned char>(hookAt + i);
❸    writeMemory<BYTE>(hookAt, 0xE9);
    writeMemory<DWORD>(hookAt + 1, newOffset);
    protectMemory<BYTE[5]>(hookAt, oldProtection);
    return originals;
}
```

Like the function in Listing 8-11, this function makes the memory writable ❶, places the hook ❸, and restores the memory protection. Before placing the hook, it allocates a 5-byte buffer called originals ❷ and fills it with the original bytes. After the hook is placed, it returns originals to the calling function.

When it's time to remove the hook, pass originals to the following function:

```
void unhookWithJump(DWORD hookAt, unsigned char* originals)
{
    auto oldProtection = protectMemory<BYTE[5]>(hookAt, PAGE_EXECUTE_READWRITE);
    for (int i = 0; i < 5; i++)
        writeMemory<BYTE>(hookAt + i, originals[i]);
    protectMemory<BYTE[5]>(hookAt, oldProtection);
    delete [] originals;
}
```

This code simply iterates over originals and quietly places those 5 bytes back where they were found so that everything is as expected when execution returns to the EndScene() function. When the time comes, you can place and remove your actual hook using two lines of code, like this:

```
auto originals = hookWithJump(EndSceneAddress, (DWORD)&endSceneTrampoline);
unhookWithJump(EndSceneAddress, originals);
```

Once you have the `hookWithJump()` and `unhookWithJump()` functions, it's time to prepare the callback and find the device.

Writing the Callback and Trampoline

Even though you can obtain the `EndScene()` address from a VF table, the `EndScene()` function doesn't actually follow the __thiscall convention. Direct3D classes are simple wrappers around a C API, and all of the member function calls are forwarded to __stdcall functions that take a class instance as a first parameter. This means that your trampoline only needs to grab the device from the stack, pass it to the callback, and then jump back to `EndScene()`. The callback only has to remove the jump hook before returning to the trampoline.

The final code for the callback and trampoline to this jump hook looks something like this:

```
LPDIRECT3DDEVICE9 discoveredDevice;
DWORD __stdcall reportInitEndScene(LPDIRECT3DDEVICE9 device)
{
    discoveredDevice = device;
    unhookWithJump(EndSceneAddress, originals);
    return EndSceneAddress;
}
__declspec(naked) void endSceneTrampoline()
{
    __asm {
        MOV EAX, DWORD PTR SS:[ESP + 0x4]
        PUSH EAX  // give the device to the callback
❶       CALL reportInitEndScene
        JMP EAX   // jump to the start of EndScene
    }
}
```

Using the `hookWithJump()` function, you can place a jump hook on `EndScene()` that calls the `endSceneTrampoline()` function. When the game's device calls the `EndScene()` function, the trampoline function calls the `reportInitEndScene()` function ❶. The `reportInitEndScene()` function stores the captured device pointer to a global variable called `discoveredDevice`, removes the hook by calling `unhookWithJump()`, and returns the address of `EndScene()` to the trampoline. To finish up, the trampoline jumps directly to EAX, which will be holding the address that was returned from the reporting function.

NOTE *You can use jump hooks to completely skip the VF table hooking that I'll show you, but it's very unreliable to use "dumb" jump hooks on commonly hooked API functions. Consistently obtaining good results with only jump hooks requires professional hooking libraries, and I'd rather teach you how to do it completely on your own.*

At this point, all that's left to do is hook the VF table of `discoveredDevice` to hack the game. The next two sections will walk you through hooks on the `EndScene()` and `Reset()` functions, which are required if you want a stable hook.

Writing a Hook for EndScene()

A hook on EndScene() is useful because it allows you to intercept a completed frame just before it is rendered; you can effectively execute your own rendering code inside the game loop. As you saw when locating this function's address in "Jump Hooking EndScene()" on page 178, this function is at index 42 in the VF table. You can hook EndScene() using a VF hook as follows:

```
typedef HRESULT (WINAPI* _endScene)(LPDIRECT3DDEVICE9 pDevice);
_endScene origEndScene =
    (_endScene)hookVF((DWORD)discoveredDevice, 42,(DWORD)&myEndScene);
HRESULT WINAPI myEndScene(LPDIRECT3DDEVICE9 pDevice)
{
    // draw your own stuff here
    return origEndScene(pDevice);
}
```

This code uses the hookVF() function from "Using a VF Table Hook" on page 159 to hook EndScene() at index 42 of discoveredDevice, using myEndScene() as the callback function. A direct Direct3D device will occasionally repatch its own VF table and restore the original function addresses. This typically happens from within the EndScene() function, meaning you also have to repatch the VF table after calling the original EndScene() function. There are a few changes you can make to this hook to handle that, as shown in Listing 8-14.

```
_endScene origEndScene = NULL;
void placeHooks()
{
    auto ret = hookVF((DWORD)discoveredDevice, 42, (DWORD)&myEndScene);
    if (ret != (DWORD)&myEndScene) // don't point to your hook
        origEndScene = (_endScene)ret;
}
placeHooks();

HRESULT WINAPI myEndScene(LPDIRECT3DDEVICE9 pDevice)
{
    // draw your own stuff here
    auto ret = origEndScene(pDevice);
    placeHooks(); // update hooks
    return ret;
}
```

Listing 8-14: Final code to hook EndScene()

The code to place the hook has been moved into a function called placeHooks() so it can be called multiple times with ease. The callback function still forwards the call to the original function, but it makes sure to call placeHooks() before returning. This ensures that the hook is always active, even if the original EndScene() function removes it.

Another point to notice is that placeHooks() updates the address of origEndScene() every time the hook is replaced, as long as the address returned from hookVF() isn't the address of the myEndScene() function. This does two distinct things. First, it allows other applications to hook EndScene() without stepping on their toes, since it will update origEndScene() to whatever is seen in the VF table. Second, it makes sure that the value of origEndScene() can never be the address of our callback, preventing a potential infinite loop. An infinite loop is possible otherwise, because origEndScene() doesn't always fix the device's VF table, meaning placeHooks() can be called when the VF table still contains the myEndScene() function.

Writing a Hook for Reset()

When you're using a Direct3D hook in production, you'll be doing all kinds of tasks like drawing custom text, displaying images related to your bot, and interacting with function calls from the game. These tasks will require you to create your own Direct3D objects that are tied to the game's device, and that can be a problem. From time to time, the game may completely reset its device through a Reset() function. When a device is reset, you'll need to update any objects (most commonly fonts and sprites) that you've created for the device, using their OnLostDevice() member functions.

Since Reset() is called from the VF table of the device, you can use a hook on it to tell you when the device has been reset. Reset() takes two parameters and is at index 16 in the VF table. You can add this code to placeHooks() in Listing 8-14 to hook the Reset() function:

```
auto ret = hookVF((DWORD)discoveredDevice, 16, (DWORD)&myReset);
if (ret != (DWORD)&myReset)
    origReset = (_reset)ret;
```

And this is the declaration to use for origReset:

```
typedef HRESULT (WINAPI* _reset)(
    LPDIRECT3DDEVICE9 pDevice,
    D3DPRESENT_PARAMETERS* pPresentationParameters);
_reset origReset = NULL;
```

When a reset is successful, the original function returns D3D_OK. Your hook function recognizes this and calls OnLostDevice() accordingly:

```
HRESULT WINAPI myReset(
    LPDIRECT3DDEVICE9 pDevice,
    D3DPRESENT_PARAMETERS* pPresentationParameters)
{
    auto result = origReset(pDevice, pPresentationParameters);
    if (result == D3D_OK) {
        // call onLostDevice() for all of your objects
    }
    return result;
}
```

Once you fill in the contents of the if() statement, all of your objects are ready to use again.

What's Next?

Now that I've shown you how to take control of a game's Direct3D device, you're probably wondering what you can do with it. Unlike the other examples in the book, the code in this section and the example code don't have a one-to-one correlation, but the functionality is still the same. Here's a high-level view of the correlation between this chapter and the code in the *Chapter8_Direct3DHook* example project.

The file *DirectXHookCallbacks.h* contains the callbacks for the EndScene() and Reset() functions, two callbacks for other common functions, and the trampoline and reporter functions for the temporary jump hook. These functions are all pretty much as described in this chapter, except they call into a singleton class defined in *DirectXHook.h* and *DirectXHook.cpp*. This singleton class is responsible for forwarding the calls to the original functions.

The class is also responsible for all of the heavy lifting, and it contains the code to create the discovery device, place the hooks, draw text, handle device resets, and display images. Furthermore, it allows external code to add custom callbacks for each hook, as you can see in *main.cpp*. Here, you'll see a number of different callbacks that are drawing custom text, adding new images to the screen, and changing the textures of models that are drawn by the game. I recommend poking around in the code to get a better understanding of what's going on, but don't get too carried away. We'll dive into this code in Chapter 9 to talk about all the cool hacks it can do.

OPTIONAL FIXES FOR STABILITY

The Reset() and EndScene() hooks described in this chapter should work well for any game running Direct3D 9, but it is slightly unstable. If the game tries to execute EndScene() when the jump hook is placed, it will crash because the bytes are being modified. There are two ways to fix this. First, you can place the jump hook from within an IAT hook on PeekMessage(). This will work because placing an IAT hook is a thread-safe operation, but it assumes that PeekMessage() is called only from the same thread that does the Direct3D drawing.

A safer, but more complex, alternative is to iterate over every thread in the game (similar to how it worked for thread hijacking) and use SuspendThread() to pause all threads in the game (except for the one placing the hook, of course). Before pausing a thread, you must make sure its EIP is not executing the first 5 bytes of EndScene(). After the hook is placed, you must use ResumeThread() to restore execution with your hook in place.

Closing Thoughts

Control flow manipulation is a very important skill in game hacking, and a lot of the hacks in this book rely on it. Throughout the next two chapters you'll learn how to create common hacks using the Direct3D hook, and you'll get a better idea of the general use cases of hooking. Even if you feel a little shaky, continue to Chapter 9. The code examples there center on the Direct3D hook and will get you even more familiar with hooking techniques.

PART 4

CREATING BOTS

9

USING EXTRASENSORY PERCEPTION TO WARD OFF FOG OF WAR

Fog of war (often shortened to just *fog*) is a mechanism that game developers commonly use to limit a player's situational awareness and hide information about the game environment. Fog is often a literal lack of sight in massive online battle arena (MOBA) games, but the concept also includes any lack or obscurity of pertinent gameplay information. Cloaked figures, dark rooms, and enemies hiding behind walls are all forms of fog.

Game hackers can reduce or even completely remove fog using an *extrasensory perception (ESP)* hack. An ESP hack uses hooking, memory manipulation, or both to force a game to display hidden information. These hacks take advantage of the fact that some types of fog are often implemented on the client side, as opposed to the server side, meaning that the game clients still contain information (partial or complete) about what is being hidden.

In this chapter, you will learn how to implement different types of ESP hacks. First, you'll learn to light up dark environments. Next, you'll use x-ray vision to see through walls. Finally, you'll learn about zoom hacking, tweaking heads-up displays, and other simple ESP hacks that can reveal all sorts of useful (but otherwise hidden) information about the game you're playing.

Background Knowledge

This chapter starts the transition from hacking, puppeteering, and reverse engineering to coding. From here on out, you'll be learning how to actually code your own hacks. To keep on topic, everything I've talked about thus far will be treated as background knowledge. If you see a technique used that you don't quite remember, such as memory scanning, setting memory breakpoints, hooking, or writing memory, flip back to the relevant chapters and study them a bit more before continuing. Throughout the text, you'll find notes to remind you where you can brush up on certain topics.

Specifically, this chapter will talk a lot about Direct3D. In "Applying Jump Hooks and VF Hooks to Direct3D" on page 175, I explained how to hook into a game's Direct3D drawing loop. The example code for that chapter includes a fully featured Direct3D hooking engine in *GameHackingExamples/Chapter8_Direct3DHook*. A lot of the hacks in this chapter build on that hook, and their example code can be found in the *main.cpp* file of the Direct3D hook code. You can run the compiled application from *GameHackingExamples/Chapter8_Direct3DApplication* to see the hacks in action on a test application.

Revealing Hidden Details with Lighthacks

Lighthacks increase lighting in dark environments, allowing you to clearly see enemies, treasure chests, pathways, and anything else that is normally obscured by darkness. Lighting is often a cosmetic change that's added at a game's graphical layer, and it can usually be directly modified with a hook on the graphics layer.

Optimal lighting depends on camera orientation, environment layout, and even specific traits of a game's engine, and you can manipulate any of these factors to create lighthacks. But the easiest way is simply to add more light to a room.

Adding a Central Ambient Light Source

The online resources for this book include two small lighthack examples. The first is the enableLightHackDirectional() function in *main.cpp*, which is shown in Listing 9-1.

```
void enableLightHackDirectional(LPDIRECT3DDEVICE9 pDevice)
{
    D3DLIGHT9 light;
```

```
    ZeroMemory(&light, sizeof(light));
    light.Type = D3DLIGHT_DIRECTIONAL;
    light.Diffuse = D3DXCOLOR(0.5f, 0.5f, 0.5f, 1.0f);
    light.Direction = D3DXVECTOR3(-1.0f, -0.5f, -1.0f);

    pDevice->SetLight(0, &light);
    pDevice->LightEnable(0, TRUE);
}
```

Listing 9-1: A directional lighthack

This code is called from the EndScene() hook, and it adds light to the scene by creating a light source called light. The code sets light.Type to directional, which means the light source will act like a spotlight and project light in a specific direction. The code then sets the red, green, and blue values of light.Diffuse to 0.5, 0.5, and 0.5, giving the light an off-white shine when reflected from a surface. Next, it sets light.Direction to an arbitrary point in the three-dimensional space. Finally, the code uses the game's Direct3D device to set up the light at index 0 and enable lighting effects.

NOTE *In the example application, the light shines up and to the right from the bottom left of the scene. You may need to change this location depending on how your target game is rendered.*

Note that inserting the light at index 0 works for this proof of concept, but it won't always work. Games typically have multiple light sources defined, and setting your light at an index the game uses might override critical lighting effects. In practice, you might try setting the index to an arbitrarily high number. There's an issue with this type of lighthack, though: directional lights will be blocked by objects such as walls, creatures, and terrain, meaning shadows can still be cast. Directional lights work great for wide-open spaces, but not so well for tightly wound corridors or underground caves.

Increasing the Absolute Ambient Light

The other lighthack method, seen in the enableLightHackAmbient() function, is far more aggressive than the one in Listing 9-1. It affects the light level globally, rather than adding an extra light source. Here's what the code looks like:

```
void enableLightHackAmbient(LPDIRECT3DDEVICE9 pDevice)
{
    pDevice->SetRenderState(D3DRS_AMBIENT, D3DCOLOR_XRGB(100, 100, 100));
}
```

This lighthack sets the absolute ambient light (which you indicate by passing D3DRS_AMBIENT to the SetRenderState() function) to a medium-strength white. The D3DCOLOR_XRGB macro sets that strength, taking 100 as its parameters for the red, green, and blue levels. This lights up objects using an omnidirectional white light, effectively revealing everything at the cost of shadows and other lighting-based details.

Creating Other Types of Lighthacks

There are many other ways to create lighthacks, but they differ from game to game. One creative way to affect the light in a game is to NOP the code that the game uses to call the `device->SetRenderState()` function. Since this function is used to set up the global ambient light strength, disabling calls to it leaves Direct3D at the default light settings and makes everything visible. This is perhaps the most powerful type of lighthack, but it requires your bot to know the address of the lighting code to NOP.

There are also memory-based lighthacks. In some games, players and creatures emit light of different colors and strengths, often depending on attributes like their equipment, mount, or active spells. If you understand the structure of the game's creature list, you can directly modify the values that determine a creature's light level.

For instance, imagine a game in which characters emit a bluish ball of light when under a healing or strengthening spell. Somewhere in the game's memory are values associated with each creature that tell the game the color and intensity of light the creature should emit. If you can locate these values in memory, you can change them so that the creatures effectively emit orbs of light. This type of lighthack is commonly used in games with a 2D top-down style, since the orbs around individual creatures produce a cool artistic effect while shedding light on important parts of the screen. In 3D games, however, this sort of hack just turns creatures into blobs of light that run around.

You can also hook the `SetLight()` member function at index 51 in the VF table of the game's Direct3D device. Then, whenever your hook callback is invoked, you can modify the properties of the intercepted `D3DLIGHT9` light structure before passing it to the original function. You might, for instance, change all lights to the `D3DLIGHT_POINT` type, causing any existing light sources in the game to radiate light in every direction like a light bulb. This type of lighthack is very powerful and accurate, but it can produce some disturbing visuals. It also tends to break in any environment that has no lighting, and opaque obstacles still block point light sources.

Lighthacks are very powerful, but they don't reveal anything. If information is hidden behind an obstacle, rather than by darkness, you'll need a wallhack to reveal it.

Revealing Sneaky Enemies with Wallhacks

You can use *wallhacks* to show enemies that are hidden by walls, floors, and other obstacles. There are a few ways to create these hacks, but the most common method takes advantage of a type of rendering known as *z-buffering*.

Rendering with Z-Buffering

Most graphics engines, including Direct3D, support z-buffering, which is a way to make sure that when there are overlapping objects in a scene, only the top object is drawn. Z-buffering works by "drawing" the scene to a two-dimensional array that describes how close the object at each pixel on the screen is to the viewer. Think of the array's indices as axes: they correspond to the x-axis (right and left) and y-axis (up and down) for each pixel on the screen. Each value stored in the array is the z-axis value for a pixel.

When a new object appears, whether it is actually drawn on the screen is decided by the z-buffer array. If the spot at the object's x- and y-position is already filled in the array, that means there's another object at that pixel on the screen. The new object will appear only if it has a lower z-axis value (that is, if it's closer to the viewer) than the pixel already there. When the scene is finished being drawn to the array, it is flushed to the screen.

To illustrate this, imagine a three-dimensional space that needs to be drawn to a two-dimensional canvas by some game with 4×4-pixel viewport. The z-buffer for this scenario would look like Figure 9-1.

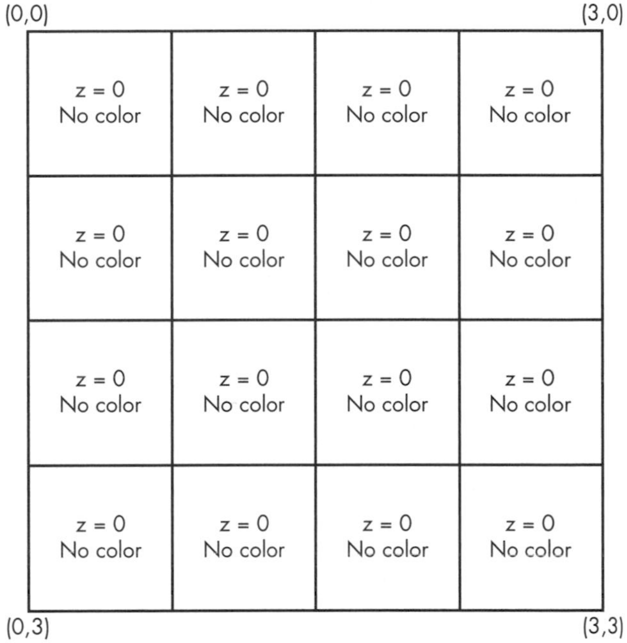

(0,0)   (3,0)

$z = 0$ No color	$z = 0$ No color	$z = 0$ No color	$z = 0$ No color
$z = 0$ No color	$z = 0$ No color	$z = 0$ No color	$z = 0$ No color
$z = 0$ No color	$z = 0$ No color	$z = 0$ No color	$z = 0$ No color
$z = 0$ No color	$z = 0$ No color	$z = 0$ No color	$z = 0$ No color

(0,3)   (3,3)

Figure 9-1: An empty z-buffer

To start, the game draws a blue background that completely fills the viewport and is located as far away on the z-axis as possible; let's say the highest z-value is 100. Next, the game draws a 2×2-pixel red rectangle at position (0,0) with a z-position of 5. Finally, the game draws a 2×2-pixel green rectangle at position (1,1) with a z-position of 3. The z-buffer would now look like Figure 9-2.

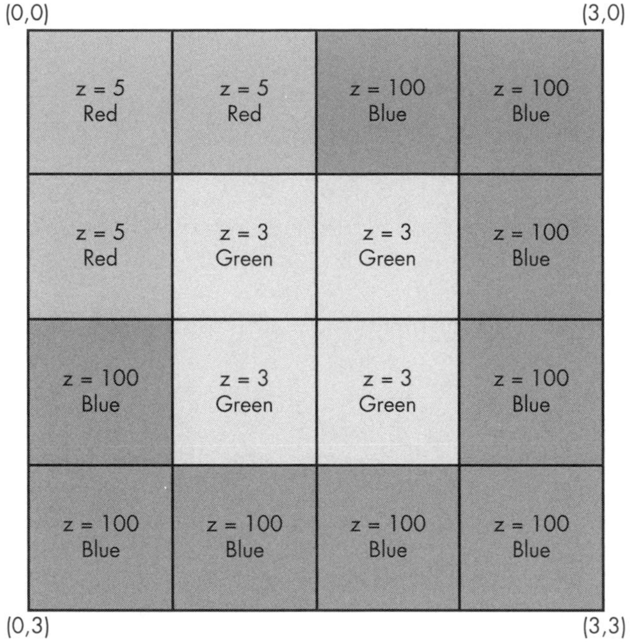

(0,0)   (3,0)

z = 5 Red	z = 5 Red	z = 100 Blue	z = 100 Blue
z = 5 Red	z = 3 Green	z = 3 Green	z = 100 Blue
z = 100 Blue	z = 3 Green	z = 3 Green	z = 100 Blue
z = 100 Blue	z = 100 Blue	z = 100 Blue	z = 100 Blue

(0,3)   (3,3)

Figure 9-2: A filled z-buffer

The z-buffer neatly handled overlapping objects based on their z-positions. The green square that's closest on the z-axis overlaps the red square that's a bit farther away, and both squares overlap the blue background, which is very far away.

This behavior allows a game to draw its map, players, creatures, details, and particles without worrying about what is actually visible to the player. This is a huge optimization for game developers, but it exposes a large area of attack. Since all game models are *always* given to the graphics engine, you can use hooks to detect objects that the player can't actually see.

Creating a Direct3D Wallhack

You can create wallhacks that manipulate z-buffering in Direct3D using a hook on the `DrawIndexedPrimitive()` function, which is called when a game draws a 3D model to the screen. When an enemy player model is drawn, a wallhack of this type disables z-buffering, calls the original function to draw the model, and then reenables z-buffering. This causes the enemy model to be drawn on top of everything else in the scene, regardless of what's in front of it. Some wallhacks can also render specific models in a solid color, such as red for enemies and green for allies.

Toggling Z-Buffering

The Direct3D hook in *main.cpp* from *GameHackingExamples/Chapter8_ Direct3DHook* has this example wallhack in the onDrawIndexedPrimitive() function:

```
void onDrawIndexedPrimitive(
    DirectXHook* hook,
    LPDIRECT3DDEVICE9 device,
    D3DPRIMITIVETYPE primType,
    INT baseVertexIndex, UINT minVertexIndex,
    UINT numVertices, UINT startIndex, UINT primCount)
{
    if (numVertices == 24 && primCount == 12) {
        // it's an enemy, do the wallhack
    }
}
```

This function is used as a callback for a hook on DrawIndexedPrimitive() at VF index 82 of the game's Direct3D device. Every model the game draws passes through this function, accompanied by some model-specific properties. By inspecting a subset of the properties, namely the numVertices and primCount values, the hook detects when an enemy model is drawn and commences the wallhack. In this example, the values representing an enemy model are 24 and 12.

The magic happens inside the if() statement. Using just a few lines of code, the wallhack draws the model in a way that ignores z-buffering, like so:

```
device->SetRenderState(D3DRS_ZENABLE, false); // disable z-buffering
DirectXHook::origDrawIndexedPrimitive(         // draw model
    device, primType, baseVertexIndex,
    minVertexIndex, numVertices, startIndex, primCount);
device->SetRenderState(D3DRS_ZENABLE, true);  // enable z-buffering
```

Simply put, this code disables z-buffering when drawing the enemy model and reenables it afterward. With z-buffering off, the enemy is drawn in front of everything.

Changing an Enemy Texture

When a model is rendered onscreen, a *texture* is used to skin the model. Textures are 2D images that are stretched around 3D models to apply the colors and patterns that make up the model's 3D artwork. To change the way an enemy looks when it's drawn in your wallhack, you can set it to be drawn with a different texture, as in this example:

```
// when hook initializes
LPDIRECT3DTEXTURE9 red;
D3DXCreateTextureFromFile(device, "red.png", &red);
```

```
// just before drawing the primitive
device->SetTexture(0, red);
```

The first block of this code loads the texture from a file and is executed only once—when the hook is initialized. The full example code does this in an initialize() function, which gets called the first time the EndScene() hook callback is invoked. The second block of this code happens right before the call to the original DrawIndexedPrimitive() function in the wallhack, and it causes the model to be drawn with the custom texture.

Fingerprinting the Model You Want to Reveal

The trickiest part to creating a good wallhack is finding the right values for numVertices and primCount. To do this, you can create a tool that logs every unique combination of the two variables and allows you to iterate over the list using your keyboard. Working example code for this tool won't be useful in the example application provided with this chapter, but I'll give you some high-level implementation details.

First, in the global scope, you'd declare a structure that has members to store the following:

- numVertices and primCount
- A std::set of this structure (let's call it seenParams)
- An instance of that structure (let's call it currentParams)

The std::set requires a comparator for this structure, so you'd also declare a comparison functor that calls memcmp() to compare two of the structures using memcmp(). Each time the DrawIndexedPrimitive() callback is invoked, your hack could create a structure instance with the intercepted values and pass it to a seenParams.insert() function, which should insert the parameter pair into the list only if the pair isn't already there.

Using the GetAsyncKeyState() Windows API function, you could then detect when the spacebar is pressed and execute something similar to this pseudocode:

```
auto current = seenParams.find(currentParam);
if (current == seenParams.end())
    current = seenParams.begin();
else
    current++;
currentParams = *current;
```

This would set currentParams to the next pair in seenParams when the spacebar is pressed. With this code in place, you could use code similar to a wallhack to change the texture of models matching currentParams.numVertices and currentParams.primCount. The tool could also draw those values on the screen so you could see them and write them down.

With a tool like this, finding the proper models is as easy as starting up a game in a mode where your character won't die (against a friend, in a customization mode, and so on), running the bot, and pressing the space-bar until each model you need is highlighted. Once you have the values for your target models, you'll modify the numVertices and primCount check in your wallhack so it knows which models to highlight.

NOTE *Character models are commonly made up of smaller models for individual body segments, and games often show different models of a character at different distances. That means a game may have 20 or more models for one type of character. Even in that case, selecting only one model (say, the enemy's torso) to show in your wallhack may be enough.*

Getting a Wider Field of Vision with Zoomhacks

Many games in the MOBA and real-time strategy (RTS) genres use a 3D top-down style that makes them immune to wallhacks. They also use dark-ness on the map as a type of fog, but showing the dark areas using a light-hack doesn't give any extra information; models hidden inside the fog are known only to the game server, not to the client.

This style makes most types of ESP hacks useless: there's little unknown information to reveal, so these hacks only augment your view of the information you can already see. One type of ESP hack, however, can still be helpful. *Zoomhacks* let you zoom out much farther than a game normally allows, effectively revealing large portions of the map that you couldn't see otherwise—and thus getting around the game's wallhack and lighthack immunity.

Using NOPing Zoomhacks

MOBA and RTS games typically allow players a variable but limited amount of zoom. The simplest type of zoomhack finds the value of the *zoom factor* (a multiplier that changes as the zoom level changes, typically a float or double) and overwrites it with a larger value.

To find the zoom factor, fire up Cheat Engine and search for a float with an unknown initial value. (To brush up on Cheat Engine, head over to "Cheat Engine's Memory Scanner" on page 5.) For rescans, repeat the following process until there are only a few values left to find the zoom factor:

1. Go to the game window and zoom in.
2. Search for an increased value in Cheat Engine.
3. Go to the game window and zoom out.
4. Search for a decreased value in Cheat Engine.

Try to get the value list down to one option. To confirm that the remaining value is the zoom factor, freeze it in Cheat Engine and see how zoom behaves in-game; freezing the proper value will disable zooming. If you fail to find the zoom factor using a float search, retry the search using a `double`. If both searches fail, try them again but correspond zooming in with decreased values and zooming out with increased values instead. Once you've found the zoom factor in memory, you can write a small bot to overwrite it to the zoom factor that best suits you.

More advanced zoomhacks NOP the game code responsible for making sure the zoom factor is within a set range. You should be able to find this code with OllyDbg. Set a memory on-write breakpoint on the zoom factor, zoom in-game to trigger the breakpoint, and inspect the code at the breakpoint. (To hone your OllyDbg memory breakpoint skills, flip to "Controlling OllyDbg Through the Command Line" on page 43.) You should see the code that modified the zoom factor. Zoom limitation code is typically easy to spot: constants that match the minimum and maximum zoom values are a dead giveaway.

If you can't find the limitation code using this method, then the limitation may be applied when the graphics are redrawn at a new zoom level, rather than when the zoom factor changes. In this case, switch your breakpoint to memory on-read and look for the same clues.

Scratching the Surface of Hooking Zoomhacks

You can also create zoomhacks by using a Direct3D hook on the function `device->SetTransform(type, matrix)`, but this requires a deep understanding of how a game sets up the player's perspective. There are a few different ways to manage perspective, but you control zoom level using either *view* (transform type `D3DTS_VIEW`) or *projection* (transform type `D3DTS_PROJECTION`).

Properly manipulating transform matrices that control view and projection requires some pretty extensive knowledge of the mathematics behind 3D graphics, though, so I stay away from this method at all costs—and I've never had trouble simply manipulating the zoom factor. If you're interested in this kind of hack, though, I recommend reading a 3D game programming book to learn more about 3D mathematics first.

But sometimes, even a zoomhack isn't enough. Some useful information may remain hidden as a part of a game's internal state or may simply be hard for a player to determine at a moment's glance. For these situations, a heads-up display is the tool for the job.

Displaying Hidden Data with HUDs

A *heads-up display (HUD)* is a type of ESP hack that displays critical game information in an overlay. HUDs often resemble a game's existing interface for displaying information like your remaining ammunition, a mini-map, your current health level, any active ability cooldowns, and so on. HUDs typically display either historical or aggregated information, and they're mostly used on MMORPGs. They are often text based, but some also contain sprites, shapes, and other small visual effects.

The HUDs you can create depend on what data is available in the game. Common data points are these:

- Experience gain per hour (exp/h)
- Creature kills per hour (KPH)
- Damage per second (DPS)
- Gold looted per hour (GPH)
- Healing per minute
- Estimated time until next level
- Amount of gold spent on supplies
- Overall gold value of items looted

More advanced custom HUDs may display large tables containing items looted, supplies used, the number of kills for each type of creature, and the names of players that have recently been seen.

Beyond what you've already learned about reading memory, hooking graphics engines, and displaying customized data, there's not much else I can teach you about how to create a HUD. Most games have a simple enough architecture that you can easily obtain most of the information you need from memory. Then, you can run some basic hourly, percentage, or summation calculations to get the data into a usable format.

Creating an Experience HUD

Imagine you want a HUD that displays your current level, hourly experience, and how long you'll have to play before your character levels up. First, you could use Cheat Engine to find the variables that contain your level and experience. When you know those values, you can use either a game-specific algorithm or a hardcoded experience table to calculate the experience required to reach the next level.

When you know how much experience you need to level up, you can calculate your hourly experience. Put into pseudocode, that process might look like this:

```
// this example assumes the time is stored in milliseconds
// for seconds, remove the "1000 * "
timeUnitsPerHour = 1000 * 60 * 60
timePassed = (currentTime - startTime)
❶ timePassedToHourRatio = timeUnitsPerHour / timePassed
❷ expGained = (currentExp - startExp)
hourlyExp = expGained * timePassedToHourRatio

❸ remainingExp = nextExp - currentExp
❹ hoursToGo = remainingExp / hourlyExp
```

To find your hourly experience, hourlyExp, you'd store your experience and the time when your HUD first starts; these are startExp and startTime, respectively. This example also assumes currentLevel and currentExp are previously defined, where currentLevel is the character's level and currentExp is the current amount of experience.

With these values, hourlyExp can be calculated by multiplying a ratio ❶ of the time units in an hour to the time that has passed by the experience gained since startTime ❷. In this case, the time unit is a millisecond, so the time units get multiplied by 1,000.

Next, currentExp is subtracted from nextExp to determine the remaining experience ❸ to level up. To calculate how many hours are left to level up, your remaining experience is divided by your hourly experience ❹.

When you have all this information, you can finally display it onscreen. Using the Direct3D hooking engine provided in this book's example code, you'd draw the text using this call inside the EndScene() hook callback:

```
hook->drawText(
    10, 10,
    D3DCOLOR_ARGB(255, 255, 0, 0),
    "Will reach level %d in %0.20f hours (%d exp per hour)",
    currentLevel, hoursToGo, hourlyExp);
```

That's all you need for a working, experience-tracking HUD. Variations of these same equations can be used to calculate KPH, DPS, GPH, and other useful time-based measures. Furthermore, you can use the drawText() function of the Direct3D hook to display any information you can locate and normalize. The hook also contains addSpriteImage() and drawSpriteImage() functions that you can use to draw your own custom images, allowing you to make your HUDs as fancy as you want.

Using Hooks to Locate Data

Memory reading isn't the only way to get data for a custom HUD. You can also gather information by counting the number of times a specific model is drawn by the DrawIndexedPrimitive() function, hooking the game's internal functions responsible for drawing certain types of text, or even intercepting function calls responsible for processing data packets from the game server. The methods you use to do this will be drastically different for every game, and finding those methods will require you to pair everything you've learned from this book with your own ingenuity and programming instincts.

For instance, to create a HUD that displays how many enemies are on the map, you could use the model-fingerprinting methods used by wallhacks to count the number of enemies and output that number to the screen. This method is better than creating a way to read the list of enemies from memory, since it doesn't require new memory addresses every time the game patches.

Another example is displaying a list of enemy cooldowns, which would require you to intercept incoming packets that tell the client which spell effects to display. You could then correlate certain spells with certain enemies based on spell and enemy location, spell type, and so on, and use that information to track spells each enemy has used. If you correlate the data with a database of cooldown times, you can display exactly when each enemy spell can be used again. This is especially powerful because most games don't store enemy cooldowns in memory.

An Overview of Other ESP Hacks

In addition to the hacks discussed in this chapter, there are a number of ESP hacks that don't have common names and are specific to certain genres or even certain games. I'll quickly take you through the theory, background, and architecture of some of these hacks.

Range Hacks

Range hacks use a method similar to wallhacks to detect when the models for different types of champions or heroes are drawn. Then they draw circles on the ground around each hero model. The radius of each circle corresponds to the maximum attack range of the champion or hero it surrounds, effectively showing you areas where you can be damaged by each enemy.

Loading-Screen HUDs

Loading-screen HUDs are common in MOBA and RTS games that require all players to sit through a loading screen while everyone's game is starting up. These hacks take advantage of the fact that such games often have websites where historical player statistics can be queried. You can write a bot that automatically queries the statistics of each player in the game and seamlessly displays the information as an overlay on your loading screen, allowing you to study your enemies before launching into battle.

Pick-Phase HUDs

Pick-phase HUDs are similar to their loading-screen cousins, but they are displayed during the pregame phase when each player is picking a champion or hero to play. Instead of showing enemy statistics, pick-phase HUDs show statistics about allies. This allows you to quickly assess the strengths and weaknesses of your allies so you can make better decisions about which character to play.

Floor Spy Hacks

Floor spy hacks are common in older 2D top-down games that have different distinct floors or platforms. If you're on the top floor, you might want to know what's going on downstairs before you go charging in. You can write floor spy hacks that modify the current floor value (typically an unsigned int) to a different floor above or below you, allowing you to spy on other floors.

Games often recalculate the current floor value every frame based on player position, so NOPs are sometimes required to keep the value from being reset every time a frame is redrawn. Finding the current floor value and the code to NOP would be similar to finding the zoom factor, as discussed in "Using NOPing Zoomhacks" on page 197.

Closing Thoughts

ESP hacks are powerful ways to obtain extra information about a game. Some of them can be done pretty easily through Direct3D hooks or simple memory editing. Others require you to learn about a game's internal data structures and hook proprietary functions, giving you a reason to employ your reverse engineering skills.

If you want to experiment with ESP hacks, study and tweak the example code for this chapter. For practice with more specific ESP hacks, I encourage you to go out and find some games to play around with.

10

RESPONSIVE HACKS

The average gamer has a reaction time of 250 milliseconds, or a quarter of a second. Professional gamers average a fifth of a second, but some can react in a sixth of a second. These figures are based on online tests that measure players' reaction times to singular, predictable events. In actual games, though, players must react to dozens of different events, like health loss, incoming skill shots, abilities coming off of cooldown, enemy attacks, and many others. Only very skilled gamers can maintain a fourth- or fifth-of-a-second reaction time in such dynamic environments; the only way to be faster is to be a computer.

In this chapter, you'll learn how to make bots that react faster than any player. First, I'll show you some code patterns you can incorporate into a bot to detect when certain events happen within a game. Next, you'll learn how to make a bot that moves your character, heals, or casts spells all on its own. Once you've explored those fundamental techniques, I'll help you tie them together to implement some of the most common, and most powerful, responsive hacks.

Observing Game Events

Within just a few seconds of playing a game, most people can make essential observations about the game environment. You can clearly see when missiles are flying toward your character, when your health is too low, and when abilities come off of cooldown. For a bot, though, these seemingly intuitive observations are not as easy to make. The bot must detect each event by looking for changes in memory, detecting visual cues, or intercepting network traffic.

Monitoring Memory

To detect simple events, such as your health bar dropping low, you can program a bot to periodically read your health from memory and compare it to some minimum acceptable value, as in Listing 10-1.

```
// do this every 10 milliseconds (100 times a second)
auto health = readMemory<int>(HEALTH_ADDRESS);
if (health <= 500) {
    // some code to tell the bot how to react
}
```

Listing 10-1: An if statement that checks health

Given the address of your character's health, you can check the value there as often as you need; every 10 milliseconds is typically a good rate. (Flip back to Chapter 1 if you need a refresher on locating values in memory.) Once health drops below a certain value, you'll want to run some reaction code to cast a healing spell or drink a potion. I'll talk about how you can do this later in the chapter.

If you want your bot to have more granular information and the chance for a greater variety of responses, you can program it to react to *any* change in health, instead of only after a set threshold. To do so, change the code in Listing 10-1 to compare your current health to the amount you had during the previous execution, as follows:

```
// still do this every 10 milliseconds
static int previousHealth = 0;
auto health = readMemory<int>(HEALTH_ADDRESS);
if (health != previousHealth) {
    if (health > previousHealth) {
        // react to increase
    } else {
        // react to decrease
    }
    previousHealth = health;
}
```

Now, this code uses a static variable called previousHealth to track the value of health on the previous iteration. If previousHealth and health differ, the bot not only reacts to the change in health but also reacts differently to health increases and decreases. This technique is the simplest, and most common, way to react to changes in a game state. With the proper memory addresses, you can use this code pattern to observe changes in health, mana, ability cooldowns, and other critical information.

Detecting Visual Cues

Health is relatively simple for a bot to check because it's just a number, but some game elements have to be relayed to the bot differently. For example, when status ailments or buffs are affecting a character, the easiest way for you to tell is to simply look for an onscreen status indicator, and the same is true for bots.

When reading memory isn't enough, you can detect certain events by hooking a game's graphics engine and waiting for the game to render a specific model. (Refer back to "Applying Jump Hooks and VF Hooks to Direct3D" on page 175 and "Creating a Direct3D Wallhack" on page 194 to get refreshed on Direct3D hooks.) When the model is drawn, you can queue up a reaction to be executed after the frame is drawn, like this:

```
// below is the drawIndexedPrimitive hook
void onDrawIndexedPrimitive(...) {
    if (numVertices == EVENT_VERT && primCount == EVENT_PRIM) {
        // react, preferably after drawing is done
    }
}
```

Using the same model-fingerprinting trick as the wallhack code in Chapter 9, this code detects when a specific model is drawn to the screen and reacts accordingly. This code reacts to the event every single frame, though, and that can make your game unplayable. You'll probably want some internal cooldown to avoid spamming a reaction. In cases where the indicator model is persistently drawn (that is, not blinking), you can actually track it across frames to determine when it appears and disappears.

Here's a code snippet that also handles tracking:

```
bool eventActive = false;
bool eventActiveLastFrame = false;
// below is the drawIndexedPrimitive hook
void onDrawIndexedPrimitive(...) {
    if (numVertices == EVENT_VERT && primCount == EVENT_PRIM)
        eventActive = true;
}

// below is the endScene hook
void onDrawFrame(...) {
    if (eventActive) {
        if (!eventActiveLastFrame) {
            // react to event model appear
        }
        eventActiveLastFrame = true;
```

```
    } else {
        if (eventActiveLastFrame) {
            // react to event model disappear
        }
        eventActiveLastFrame = false;
    }
    eventActive = false;
}
```

The onDrawIndexedPrimitive() function still checks whether a certain model was drawn, but now, two Booleans track whether the model was drawn this frame or the previous frame. Then, when the frame is completely drawn, the bot can check these variables and react to the model either appearing or disappearing.

This method works great for detecting visual status indicators that appear only when your character is affected by stuns, movement slows, snares, poisons, and so on. You can also use it to detect when enemies appear and disappear in MOBA and RTS games, as these games draw only enemies that are explicitly in the sight range of an allied unit or player.

Intercepting Network Traffic

One of the most reliable ways to observe events is the same way the game client does: by waiting for the game server to tell you that they occurred. In this type of communication, the game server sends byte arrays called *packets* over the network to the client, using sockets. The packets are typically encrypted and contain blobs of data serialized through a proprietary format.

A Typical Packet-Parsing Function

To receive and process packets, a game client does something like Listing 10-2 before it draws a frame.

```
void parseNextPacket() {
    if (!network->packetReady()) return;

    auto packet = network->getPacket();
    auto data = packet->decrypt();
    switch (data->getType()) {
        case PACKET_HEALTH_CHANGE:
            onHealthChange(data->getMessage());
            break;
        case PACKET_MANA_CHANGE:
            onManaChange(data->getMessage());
            break;
        // more cases for more packet types
    }
}
```

Listing 10-2: A simplified look at how a game parses packets

The exact code for any particular game might look different, but the control flow is always the same: receive a packet, decrypt it, decide what kind of message it contains, and call a function that knows what to do with it. Some game hackers intercept raw network packets and replicate this functionality in their bots. This technique works, but it requires extensive knowledge of encryption, a complete understanding of how the game stores data inside a packet, the ability to man-in-the-middle the network connection, and a way to locate the decryption keys being used by the game client.

Hooking the functions responsible for handling the packets after they are decrypted and parsed is a much better approach; in Listing 10-2, those functions are the onHealthChange() and onManaChange() functions. This method leverages the game's inherent ability to process packets, allowing a bot to remain ignorant of the various network facilities the game uses. It also gives you discretion over which network data you intercept, as you need to hook only the handlers that meet your needs.

NOTE   *Intercepting entire packets can sometimes be advantageous—for example, in any game that uses Adobe AIR and communicates using RTMPS. Since RTMPS is so heavily documented, there's no need to reverse engineer the format or encryption. Chapter 8 explains how to hook RTMPS in detail.*

There are a few tricks you can use to easily find the parser function and, ultimately, the switch() statement that dispatches packets to their handlers. The most useful method I've found is to place a breakpoint on the function the game uses to receive data from the network, and then analyze the flow of the application when the breakpoint is hit.

Let's walk through how you might do this with OllyDbg attached to your target game. In Windows, recv() is the API function to receive data from a socket. From the OllyDbg command line, you can set a breakpoint on recv() by entering the bp recv command. When the breakpoint is hit, you can climb the call stack using CTRL-F9, the shortcut for execute until return, and F8, the shortcut for step over. This combination essentially lets the program execute until the callee has returned to the caller, allowing you to climb the call stack in tandem with the game. At each stack level, you can inspect the code of each caller until you find one that has a big switch() statement; this should be the packet parser.

A Trickier Parser

Depending on the game's architecture, though, finding the parser function may not be that simple. Consider a game with a parser function that looks like this:

```
packetHandlers[PACKET_HEALTH_CHANGE] = onHealthChange;
packetHandlers[PACKET_MANA_CHANGE] = onManaChange;

void parseNextPacket()
{
    if (!network->packetReady()) return;
```

```
    auto packet = network->getPacket();
    auto data = packet->decrypt();
    auto handler = packetHandlers[data->getType()];
    handler->invoke(data->getMessage());
}
```

Since the parseNextPacket() function doesn't have a switch() statement, there's no obvious way to identify it in memory. Unless you pay very close attention, you'll likely climb right past it on the call stack. When a game has a parser function like this, trying to figure out what the parser function looks like might be pointless. If you don't see a switch() statement when climbing the recv() call stack, you'll have to note every callee on the call stack instead.

Instead of climbing up the call stack from the breakpoint, you'd go to every address marked as a RETURN below ESP in the OllyDbg stack pane. These are the return addresses into each caller for each callee. At each return address, you'd need to find the top of the caller in OllyDbg's disassembly pane and note the address. As a result, you'd have a list of every function call leading up to the recv() call.

Next, you'd repeat the same list-making process from breakpoints placed on a few of the game's handler functions. You can find a handler function by monitoring memory that it will inevitably use. The handler for a health change packet, for instance, will update your health in memory. Using OllyDbg, you can set a *memory on write* breakpoint to the health address. When the breakpoint gets triggered, it means the game updated the health value from a handler function. This should work the same way for most values that are controlled by the server. The server will control any game-critical values, such as health, mana, level, items, and so on.

Once you've recorded the call stack from recv() and a few handler functions, you can correlate them to locate the parser function. For example, consider the three pseudo–call stacks in Table 10-1.

Table 10-1: Pseudo–Call Stacks for Three Packet-Related Functions

recv() stack	onHealthChange() stack	onManaChange() stack
0x0BADF00D	0x101E1337	0x14141414
0x40404040	0x50505050	0x60606060
0xDEADBEEF	0xDEADBEEF	0xDEADBEEF
0x30303030	0x30303030	0x30303030
0x20202020	0x20202020	0x20202020
0x10101010	0x10101010	0x10101010

These stacks show what memory might look like during a call to recv() and to a game's hypothetical onHealthChange() and onManaChange() functions. Notice that each function originates from a chain of four common function calls (shown in boldface). The deepest common address, 0xDEADBEEF, is the address of the parser. For a better understanding of this structure, look at the call stacks laid out in a tree view, as in Figure 10-1.

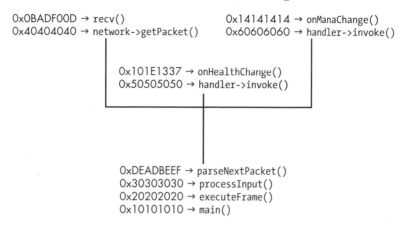

```
0x0BADF00D → recv()              0x14141414 → onManaChange()
0x40404040 → network->getPacket()  0x60606060 → handler->invoke()


          0x101E1337 → onHealthChange()
          0x50505050 → handler->invoke()




          0xDEADBEEF → parseNextPacket()
          0x30303030 → processInput()
          0x20202020 → executeFrame()
          0x10101010 → main()
```

Figure 10-1: Tree view of our three call stacks

Each function's call stack branches out from the function at 0xDEADBEEF, meaning that function is a common point of origin for all three calls. The example parseNextPacket() function is responsible for calling these functions, so it must be the most recent common ancestor at 0xDEADBEEF.

NOTE *These call stacks are hypothetical, and they're simplified beyond what you'll typically encounter. Real call stacks will probably have quite a few more function calls, and comparing them won't be as easy.*

A Hybrid Parsing System

A third variation of the parsing loop might be a hybrid of the previous two that uses a switch() statement after a function call. Here's another hypothetical function:

```
void processNextPacket()
{
    if (!network->packetReady()) return;
    auto packet = network->getPacket();
    auto data = packet->decrypt();
    dispatchPacket(data);
}

void dispatchPacket(data)
{
    switch (data->getType()) {
    case PACKET_HEALTH_CHANGE:
        processHealthChangePacket(data->getMessage());
        break;
```

```
    case PACKET_MANA_CHANGE:
        processManaChangePacket(data->getMessage());
        break;
        // more cases for more data types
    }
}
```

The processNextPacket() function fetches a new packet and calls dispatchPacket() to handle the data. In this case, the dispatchPacket() function exists in the call stack of each handler, but not in the one for the recv() function. Look at the hypothetical stacks in Table 10-2, for example.

Table 10-2: Pseudo–Call Stacks for Three Packet-Related Functions

recv() stack	onHealthChange() stack	onManaChange() stack
0x0BADF00D	0x101E1337	0x14141414
0x40404040	0x00ABCDEF	0x00ABCDEF
0xDEADBEEF	0xDEADBEEF	0xDEADBEEF
0x30303030	0x30303030	0x30303030
0x20202020	0x20202020	0x20202020
0x10101010	0x10101010	0x10101010

Although these three functions have the same first four addresses in their call stacks, only the two handlers have one more address in common (again shown in boldface). That's 0x00ABCDEF, and it's the address of the dispatchPacket() function. Once again, you can imagine these laid out in a tree view, as in Figure 10-2.

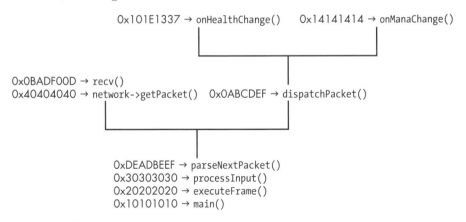

Figure 10-2: Tree view of our three call stacks

A Parser Hack

Once you've located the function responsible for dispatching packets to their handlers, you'll be able to spot every handler that can be called. You can deduce a handler's purpose by placing a breakpoint on it and watching what values change in memory when it executes. Then, you can hook any handlers that your bot needs to react to. (Flip back to Chapter 8 if you need a refresher on how you might hook these functions.)

Of course, there are endless ways to implement network behavior. I can't cover them all, but seeing these three common techniques should help you understand the methodology. No matter what game you're dealing with, a breakpoint on recv() should be a step in the right direction.

Performing In-Game Actions

Before a bot can react to events, you have to teach it to play the game. It needs to be able to cast spells, move around, and activate items. On this front, bots aren't much different from people: they can just be told which buttons to press. Pressing buttons is simple and suffices in many cases, but in more intricate situations, a bot may have to communicate on the network and tell the server what it's trying to do.

To follow along with the examples in this section and explore on your own afterward, open the files in the *GameHackingExamples/Chapter10_ResponsiveHacks/* folder in this book's resource files.

Emulating the Keyboard

The most common buttons you'll press in a game are keyboard keys, and there are a couple of ways you can teach your bot to type.

The SendInput() Function

One common way to emulate the keyboard is with the SendInput() Windows API function. This function, which sends keyboard and mouse input to the topmost window, has the following prototype:

```
UINT SendInput(UINT inputCount, LPINPUT inputs, int size);
```

The first parameter, inputCount, is the number of inputs being sent. For the examples in this book, I'll always use a value of 1. The second parameter, inputs, is a pointer to a structure (or an array of structures whose length matches the inputCount value) with the predefined type INPUT. The final parameter is the size of inputs in memory, as calculated with the formula size = inputCount × sizeof(INPUT).

The INPUT structure tells the SendInput() function what type of input to send, and the following code shows how you might initialize an instance of INPUT to press the F1 key:

```
INPUT input = {0};
input.type = INPUT_KEYBOARD;
input.ki.wVk = VK_F1;
```

To have your bot actually press F1, you'd need to send this input twice, like so:

```
SendInput(1, &input, sizeof(input));
// change input to key up
input.ki.dwFlags |= KEYEVENTF_KEYUP;
SendInput(1, &input, sizeof(input));
```

The first call to SendInput() presses F1, and the second releases it. The release happens not because the input was sent twice, but because the second call was made with the KEYEVENTF_KEYUP flag enabled in the input parameter's keyboard flags field. Since setting up input for even a single key is a bit messy, it's best to wrap everything inside a function. The result looks something like Listing 10-3.

```
void sendKeyWithSendInput(WORD key, bool up)
{
    INPUT input = {0};
    input.type = INPUT_KEYBOARD;
    input.ki.wVk = key;
    input.ki.dwFlags = 0;

    if (up)
        input.ki.dwFlags |= KEYEVENTF_KEYUP;
    SendInput(1, &input, sizeof(input));
}
sendKeyWithSendInput(VK_F1, false); // press
sendKeyWithSendInput(VK_F1, true);  // release
```

Listing 10-3: A wrapper for emulating keystrokes with SendInput()

This function initializes input with the given key, enables the flag KEYEVENTF_KEYUP if up is set, and calls the SendInput() function. This means sendKeyWithSendInput() must be called a second time to send the key release, even though the release is always required. The function is written this way because key combinations that involve modifiers like SHIFT, ALT, or CTRL must be sent a bit differently; the modifier's press must come before the key's press, but its release must come after the key's release.

The following code shows how you'd use the sendKeyWithSendInput() function to tell a bot to press SHIFT-F1:

```
sendKeyWithSendInput(VK_LSHIFT, false); // press shift
sendKeyWithSendInput(VK_F1, false);     // press F1
sendKeyWithSendInput(VK_F1, true);      // release F1
sendKeyWithSendInput(VK_LSHIFT, true);  // release shift
```

You'd have to call sendKeyWithSendInput() four times, but that's still easier than using the code without a wrapper function.

The SendMessage() Function

An alternative method for sending keystrokes relies on the `SendMessage()` Windows API function. This function allows you to send input to any window, even if it's minimized or hidden, by posting data directly to the target window's message queue. This advantage makes it the method of choice for game hackers, because it enables users to do other things while their bot plays the game in the background. `SendMessage()` has the following prototype:

```
LRESULT SendMessage(
    HWND window,
    UINT message,
    WPARAM wparam,
    LPARAM lparam);
```

The first parameter, `window`, is a handle to the window that the input is being sent to. The second parameter, `message`, is the type of input being sent; for keyboard input, this parameter is `WM_KEYUP`, `WM_KEYDOWN`, or `WM_CHAR`. The third parameter, `wparam`, should be the key code. The final parameter, `lparam`, should be 0 when the message is `WM_KEYDOWN` and 1 otherwise.

Before you can use the `SendMessage()` function, you must obtain a handle to the target process's main window. Given the title of the window, you can obtain a handle using the `FindWindow()` Windows API function, as follows:

```
auto window = FindWindowA(NULL, "Title Of Game Window");
```

With a valid window handle, making a call to `SendMessage()` looks something like this:

```
SendMessageA(window, WM_KEYDOWN, VK_F1, 0);
SendMessageA(window, WM_KEYUP, VK_F1, 0);
```

The first call presses the F1 key, and the second call releases it. Keep in mind, however, that this series of calls works only for keys that don't input text, like F1, INSERT, or TAB. To have your bot press keys that input text, you must also send a `WM_CHAR` message between the down and up messages. To type W, for instance, you'd do something like this:

```
DWORD key = (DWORD)'W';
SendMessageA(window, WM_KEYDOWN, key, 0);
SendMessageA(window, WM_CHAR, key, 1);
SendMessageA(window, WM_KEYUP, key, 1);
```

This creates a key variable so the letter key to press can be changed easily. Then it follows the same steps the F1 example used, just with a `WM_CHAR` message in between.

You can actually send nothing but the WM_CHAR *message and get the same result, but it's best practice to send all three messages. Game developers can easily shut down bots by patching the game to ignore* WM_CHAR *messages that don't follow* WM_KEYDOWN, *and they can even use it as a way to detect your bot and ban you.*

As I showed with the SendInput() technique, you can create a wrapper around this functionality to make your bot code easier to work with. The wrapper looks something like this:

```
void sendKeyWithSendMessage(HWND window, WORD key, char letter)
{
    SendMessageA(window, WM_KEYDOWN, key, 0);
    if (letter != 0)
        SendMessageA(window, WM_CHAR, letter, 1);
    SendMessageA(window, WM_KEYUP, key, 1);
}
```

Unlike Listing 10-3, this wrapper actually sends both the press and release. This is because SendMessage() can't be used to send keystrokes with modifiers, so there's never any need to insert code between the two calls.

There are multiple ways a game might check whether a modifier key is pressed, though. You might be able to send modifier keys to certain games by calling the SendMessage() *function, but it depends on how those games detect modifiers.*

You can use this wrapper in a similar way as the one in Listing 10-3. For example, this code sends F1 followed by W:

```
sendKeyWithSendMessage(window, VK_F1, 0);
sendKeyWithSendMessage(window, 'W', 'W');
```

This example, like all of the SendMessage() code I've shown so far, simply gets the job done. It can input text, but it doesn't exactly send proper messages.

There are a lot of small details you have to get right if you want to send 100 percent valid messages with the SendMessage() function. For instance, the first 16 bits of lparam should store the number of times the key has been automatically repeated as a result of being held down. The next 8 bits should store the *scan code*, a key identifier that is specific to each keyboard manufacturer. The next bit, number 24, should be set only if the button is on an extended part of the keyboard, such as the number pad. The following 4 bits are undocumented, and the next bit should be set only if the ALT key was down when the message originated. The last 2 bits are the previous state flag and the transition state flag. The previous state flag is set only if the key was previously down, and the transition state is set only if the key was previously in the state opposite its current position (that is, if the key is now up and was previously down, or vice versa).

Thankfully, the average game doesn't consider most of these values. For that matter, the average piece of software doesn't care about them either. If you have to fill all of these values with proper data to make your bot work, you're moving in the wrong direction. There are many other ways to perform actions, the majority of which are simpler than trying to emulate the exact behavior of the operating system's kernel-level keyboard input handler/dispatcher. In fact, there's already a function that does that, and I've already talked about it: the SendInput() function.

You can also control the mouse with the SendInput() and SendMessage() functions, but I highly recommend avoiding it. Any mouse commands you send will affect, and be affected by, any legitimate mouse movements, mouse clicks, or keystrokes sent by the player. The same is true for keyboard input, but the complications are much rarer.

Sending Packets

Before a game draws a frame, it checks for keyboard and mouse input. When it receives input that results in an action, such as moving around or casting a spell, it checks to make sure the action is possible and, if so, tells the game server that the action has been performed. The game code to check for events and alert the server often looks something like this:

```
void processInput() {
    do {
        auto input = getNextInput();
        if (input.isKeyboard())
            processKeyboardInput(input);
        // handle other input types (e.g., mouse)
    } while (!input.isEmpty());
}
void processKeyboardInput(input) {
    if (input.isKeyPress()) {
        if (input.getKey() == 'W')
            step(FORWARD);
        else if (input.getKey() == 'A')
            step(BACKWARD);
        // handle other keystrokes (e.g., 'S' and 'D')
    }
}
void step(int direction) {
    if (!map->canWalkOn(player->position))
        return;
    playerMovePacket packet(direction);
    network->send(packet);
}
```

The processInput() function is called every frame. The function iterates over all pending inputs and dispatches different types of inputs to their relevant handlers. In this case, when keyboard input is received, it's dispatched to the `processKeyboardInput()` function. This handler then checks whether the key is either W or S, and, if so, calls `step()` to move the player in the corresponding direction.

Since `step()` is used to perform an action, it is called an *actor* function. The invocation of an actor function is called *actuation*. You can directly call a game's actor functions from your bot to perform an action while completely bypassing the input layer.

Before you can call an actor, though, you must find its address. To do this, you can attach OllyDbg to the game, open the command line, and enter `bp send`. This will place a breakpoint on the `send()` function, which is used to send data over the network. When you play the game, every time you take a step, cast a spell, pick up loot, or do anything else, your breakpoint should trigger, and you can note each function in the call stack.

The game should call `send()` every time you do anything while playing. Pay attention to what you did before each `send()` breakpoint is hit, as that will give you a rough idea of what action each call is communicating to the server, and, ultimately, what the actor you find is responsible for.

Once you have a few different call stacks, you can compare them to locate the actor functions. To see how to spot the actor functions, let's compare the two annotated call stacks in Figure 10-3.

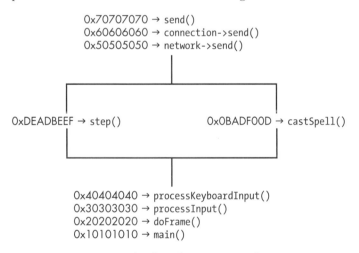

Figure 10-3: Tree view of call stacks to two actor functions

Like these two stacks, the call stacks you find should be identical at the top, sharing a couple of common functions responsible for generic network transmission. They should also be identical on the bottom, since each call to `send()` should have originated from the `processInput()` function. Each stack should have some unique functions between these identical regions, though, and those are the actor functions you're looking for. Typically, the function of interest is immediately beneath the common network calls. In this case, the two actors are the step() and castSpell() functions.

After hacking the same game for a while, you'll learn how far up the stack the actor functions are from the send() call. In Figure 10-3, for example, the actors happen three calls before the send() call. Knowing this, you could just climb the stack in OllyDbg (CTRL-F9 followed by F8) three times when your send() breakpoint is hit and be inside the actor function that sent the data.

Once you've found an actor function, you can call it from an injected DLL. Here's how you might call step() if you found it at 0xDEADBEEF:

```
typedef void _step(int direction);
auto stepActor = (_step*)0xDEADBEEF;

stepActor(FORWARD);
```

Since the bot won't know the actual name for this game function, the code assigns the contents of memory at 0xDEADBEEF to a conveniently named variable: stepActor. Then, the code just calls stepActor() like any other function.

If you've got the right address, function prototype, and parameters, this should work beautifully; you'll be able to automate actions as if you have access to the game's source code. Just make sure to call the actor functions from inside the same thread as the game, or you can run into threading issues. The best way to do this is to call the actors from a hook on a major function like Direct3D's EndScene() or the Windows API's PeekMessage() function, as these functions will usually be called only from the game's main thread.

USING THIS TO CALL __THISCALL

If you try to call an actor function that's a nonstatic member of a class, the function will have a _thiscall calling convention, which means you'll need to pass the instance of the class on the ECX register. (You can brush up on calling conventions in "Function Calls" on page 94.) Passing the instance is straightforward, but you'll have to locate a pointer chain to the class instance first.

To find the pointer chain, you can drop a breakpoint on the actor function, grab the class instance value from ECX when the breakpoint kicks, and throw that value into a Cheat Engine pointer scan. Then, to call the function, you'd walk the pointer chain, obtain the current instance address, and use inline assembly to set up ECX and make the actual function call. This process works similarly to the way VF hook callbacks call their original counterparts, as shown in "Writing a VF Table Hook" on page 156.

Tying the Pieces Together

After you've created frameworks for observing events and performing actions, you can tie them together to create responsive hacks. Responsive hacks come in many flavors, but there are a few common ones.

Making the Perfect Healer

A favorite bot among gamers is *autohealing*, a hack that automatically uses a healing spell when the player's health decreases drastically or drops below a certain threshold. Given a way to detect changes in health and an actor function to cast spells, an autohealer might look something like this:

```
void onHealthDecrease(int health, int delta) {
    if (health <= 500)      // health below 500
        castHealing();
    else if (delta >= 400) // large drop in health
        castHealing();
}
```

This autohealing function is pretty simple, but it works well. More advanced autohealers might have many more levels of healing and be able to learn as they go. You'll get working example code and an in-depth explanation of advanced autohealers in "Control Theory and Game Hacking" on page 222.

Resisting Enemy Crowd-Control Attacks

Anti-crowd-control hacks detect incoming *crowd-control attacks* and automatically cast spells that reduce their effects or completely negate them. Crowd-control attacks disable players in some way, so having enemies cast them on you can be a pain.

Given a way to detect incoming or active crowd-control effects, such as by detecting a Direct3D model or by intercepting an incoming packet, and an actor function to cast spells, you could have a bot react instantly to such attacks like so:

```
void onIncomingCrowdControl() {
    // cast a shield to block the crowd control
    castSpellShield();
}
void onReceiveCrowdControl() {
    // cleanse crowd control that has already taken effect
    castCleanse();
}
```

An onIncomingCrowdControl() function might try to stop the crowd-control spell from ever hitting you. Failing that, the bot could call an onReceiveCrowdControl() spell to remove the effects.

Avoiding Wasted Mana

Spell trainers are also quite common among botters. Spell trainers wait until the player has full mana and then cast spells to increase the player's magic level or stats. This allows players to quickly increase their magic skills, as they will never waste mana regeneration just because they have full mana.

Given a way to detect changes in mana and an actor function to cast spells, a bot might include the following pseudocode for a spell trainer:

```
void onManaIncrease(int mana, int delta) {
    if (delta >= 100) // player is using mana potions,
        return;       // they must need the mana, abort
    if (mana >= MAX_MANA - 10) // mana is nearly full, waste some
        castManaWasteSpell();
}
```

This function takes the player's mana and the increase in that player's mana (delta) as parameters. If the increase in mana is above a certain amount, it assumes the player is using potions or other items to replenish mana, and it won't cast any extra spells. Otherwise, if the player has plenty of mana, the function fires off any old spell to get the player some experience points.

Other common responsive hacks are *autoreload* to instantly reload ammo, *autododge* to evade incoming projectiles, and *autocombo* to instantly attack the same target as a nearby ally. Really, the only limit to the number of responsive hacks you can add to a bot is the number of events your bot can observe in the game, multiplied by the number of valid and helpful responses it can send for each event.

Closing Thoughts

Using hooks, memory manipulation, and keyboard simulation, you can begin creating your first responsive hacks. These hacks are your entry point into gaming autonomy, but they're only a glimpse of what's possible. Chapter 11 will be the pinnacle of your game-hacking adventure. Using everything you've learned so far, and building on the principles of responsive hacks, you'll learn how to automate advanced actions and create a truly autonomous bot.

If you're not feeling quite ready to go deeper, I strongly recommend reviewing the earlier material and then getting some practice in an isolated environment on your own machine. Implementing bots like this is a lot easier than you might think, and it's an amazingly satisfying experience. Once you're comfortable making autohealers and other basic responsive hacks, you'll be ready to start completely automating gameplay.

11

PUTTING IT ALL TOGETHER: WRITING AUTONOMOUS BOTS

The end goal of game hacking is to make a full-fledged automated bot capable of playing a game for hours on end. Such bots can heal, drink potions, farm monsters, loot corpses, walk around, sell loot, buy supplies, and more. Making bots this powerful requires you to combine your hooks and memory reads with concepts like control theory, state machines, and search algorithms, which are all covered in this chapter.

Throughout the lessons here, you'll also learn about common automated hacks and how they should behave at a high level. After covering the theory and code behind automated hacks, I'll give you a high-level look at two types of bots that rely on such code: *cavebots*, which can explore caves and bring home the loot, and *warbots*, which can fight enemies for you. By the end of the chapter, you should be ready to bust out your tools, fire up your development environment, and start making some really awesome bots.

Control Theory and Game Hacking

Control theory is a branch of engineering that provides a way to control the behavior of dynamic systems. Control theory determines the state of a *system* using *sensors*, after which a *controller* determines the set of actions needed to bring the system's current state to some other desired state. After the controller executes the first action in the set, the entire process—known as a *feedback loop*—repeats (see Figure 11-1).

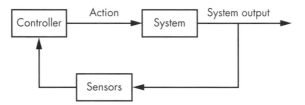

Figure 11-1: A control theory feedback loop

Let's apply this feedback loop to game hacking. To automate play within a game (the system), a bot implements some algorithms (the controller) that understand how to play the game in any state observed by the memory reads, network hooks, and so on (the sensors). The controller typically has some human inputs, like the path to walk, creatures to attack, and loot to pick up. Thus, to reach the desired state, the controller must perform some subset of these inputs that are possible given the current state.

For instance, if there are no creatures onscreen and no corpses to loot, the desired state may be for the player to reach the next location (called a *waypoint*) in the predefined path. In this case, the controller moves the player one step closer to the waypoint on each iteration. If the player encounters a creature, the controller might decide to attack the creature in the first frame and, in the following frames, switch between running from the creature (known as *kiting*) and shooting spells at it. Once the creature dies, the controller executes a set of actions to loot the body and continue to the next waypoint.

Given this example of how a feedback loop might operate, it might seem overwhelming to code such a system. Luckily, there are a few design patterns that make the task much easier than it sounds.

State Machines

State machines are mathematical models of computation that describe how a system behaves based on input. Figure 11-2 shows a simple state machine that reads a list of binary digits. The machine starts with an initial state of S_1. As it iterates over the digits in the input, it changes its state accordingly. In this case, states S_1 and S_2 repeat themselves when the machine encounters a 1 and activate one another when it encounters a 0. For example, for the binary digits 11000111, the state transitions would be S_1, S_1, S_2, S_1, S_2, S_2, S_2, and finally S_2.

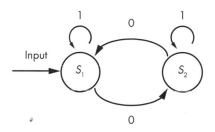

Figure 11-2: A simple state machine

With a small spin on the classical state machine theory, a state machine can be the controller in a control theory feedback loop. This tweaked version of a state machine comprises a list of states, the conditions signifying each state, and the actions that must happen to reach each state.

STATE MACHINES AND GAME HACKING

A game-hacking state machine not only must keep an internal state but also must respond to (or *actuate*) the game environment based on that state. The overall game state can change based on your bot's actuation, the behavior of other players, and other unpredictable occurrences in the game environment. For this reason, trying to persistently walk a state machine based on the observed game environment is futile; it's nearly impossible to create a set of transitions for each state to account for every possible observation that can be made between iterations. It makes more sense for the state machine to reevaluate the game environment as a fresh slate each time it considers the input. To do this, the state machine must use the game environment itself as the mechanism for transitioning between states—that is, the machine's actuation on the environment should have enough of an effect on the next iterations that it activates a new state. Classical state machines can be devised that are capable of working like this, but we're going to flatten them out and use them in a much simpler, yet still very powerful, way.

If you're familiar with classical state machines, this may not seem intuitive, but in the coming sections you'll see how state machines can be mutated and paired with control theory to achieve what we want.

The major difference is that instead of one state merely activating another, for each state in a game automation state machine, a bot will perform in-game actions that change the overall state of the game and, thus, the state that is detected on the next iteration of the feedback loop. In code, an object to represent a state in this machine might look like this:

```
class StateDefinition {
public:
    StateDefinition(){}
    ~StateDefinition(){}
    bool condition();
    void reach();
};
```

You can assemble `StateDefinition` objects into a state machine with a simple `std::vector` definition, like this:

```
std::vector<StateDefinition> stateMachine;
```

And presto, you have the skeleton of a state machine, ready to receive any `StateDefinition` objects you create. In conjunction with a feedback loop, this state machine can be used to define the flow of automation.

First, you can create a list of definitions that model your bot's desired behavior, ordered in the vector by importance. Each `StateDefinition` object can use information from your sensors as input, passing that data to the `condition()` function to determine whether or not the state should be activated. Then, you can create a controller that loops over the list of states, calling the `reach()` function of the first state whose `condition()` function returns `false`. Finally, you can wrap the controller in a feedback loop. If you don't see how this feedback loop would work yet, don't worry; I'll show you how to code it now.

NOTE *You can think of the statement in your `condition()` function as a requirement for the machine to transition to the next state. If the statement is true, it means no actuation must happen before the next state in the list can be evaluated and the loop can continue iterating. If the statement is false, it means some actuator must occur before the transition can happen.*

You'll find all of the example code for the following section and "Error Correction" on page 230 in the *GameHackingExamples/Chapter11_StateMachines* directory of this book's source files. The included projects can be compiled with Visual Studio 2010, but they should also work with any other C++ compiler. Download them at *https://www.nostarch.com/gamehacking/* and compile them if you want to follow along.

Combining Control Theory and State Machines

To tie states together with a feedback loop, first you have to provide each StateDefinition object with a generic way to access the sensors and actuators that you've implemented. The StateDefinition class then becomes the following:

```
class StateDefinition {
public:
    StateDefinition(){}
    ~StateDefinition(){}
    bool condition(GameSensors* sensors);
    void reach(GameSensors* sensors, GameActuators* actuators);
};
```

This change simply modifies the condition() and reach() functions to accept instances of the classes GameSensors and GameActuators as arguments. GameSensors and GameActuators are classes you need to define; GameSensors will contain the results of memory reads, network hooks, and other data sources your bot intercepts from the game, while GameActuators will be a collection of actor functions capable of performing actions inside the game.

Next, you need a generic way to define each individual state. You could abstract the definition of each state to its own class that inherits StateDefinition and implements condition() and reach() as virtual functions. Alternatively, if the source code needs to fit in a small space (like a book, *wink wink*), you could keep a single class to represent each definition and use std::function to implement the condition() and reach() functions outside the class definition.

Following that alternative method, the final version of StateDefinition would look like this:

```
class StateDefinition {
public:
    StateDefinition(){}
    ~StateDefinition(){}
    std::function<bool(GameSensors*)> condition;
    std::function<void(GameSensors*, GameActuators*)> reach;
};
```

With this version of the StateDefinition class, you could define a new state by creating an instance of the class and assigning condition() and reach() to functions that correspond with the intended behavior.

A Basic Healer State Machine

The next step is defining the bot's actual behavior. To keep the example code simple, let's say you're implementing an automatic healer. This healer has two healing methods: it uses strong healing if the player is at or below 50 percent health and weak healing if the player is between 51 and 70 percent health.

A state machine representing this behavior needs two states, one for strong healing and one for weak healing. To start, you need to define the state machine as a vector with two StateDefinition objects:

```
std::vector<StateDefinition> stateMachine(2);
```

This code creates a state machine called stateMachine and initializes it with two empty StateDefinition objects. Next, you define the condition() and reach() functions for these state definitions. The strong healing state is the most important because it keeps the character from dying, so it should come first in the vector, as shown in Listing 11-1.

```
   auto curDef = stateMachine.begin();
   curDef->condition = [](GameSensors* sensors) {
❶     return sensors->getHealthPercent() > 50;
   };
   curDef->reach = [](GameSensors* sensors, GameActuators* actuators) {
❷     actuators->strongHeal();
   };
```

Listing 11-1: Code for a strong healing state

This code first creates an iterator called curDef that points to the first StateDefinition object in the stateMachine vector. The object's condition() function is then defined ❶; in English, this definition says, "The state is met if the player's health percent is greater than 50." If the state isn't met, then the object's reach() function calls the strongHeal() actor function ❷ so that strong healing can be performed.

With the strong healing state defined, next you define the weak healing state, as shown in Listing 11-2.

```
   curDef++;
   curDef->condition = [](GameSensors* sensors) {
❶     return sensors->getHealthPercent() > 70;
   };
   curDef->reach = [](GameSensors* sensors, GameActuators* actuators) {
❷     actuators->weakHeal();
   };
```

Listing 11-2: Code for weak healing

After incrementing curDef so it points to the second StateDefinition object in the stateMachine vector, this code defines the object's condition()

function ❶ as, "The state is met if the player's health percent is greater than 70." It also defines the object's reach() function as an actuators->weakHeal() call ❷.

Once you've finished defining the state machine, you must implement the controller. Since the actual behavior of the controller is contained in the state machine, you only need to add a simple loop to complete it:

```
for (auto state = stateMachine.begin(); state != stateMachine.end(); state++) {
    if (❶!state->condition(&sensors)) {
        state->reach(&sensors, &actuators);
        break;
    }
}
```

This controller loop iterates over the state machine, executes the reach() function of the first state whose condition() function returns false ❶, and breaks out if any reach() function is called. The final step is to implement the feedback loop and plop the controller loop inside it, as shown in Listing 11-3.

```
while (true) {
    for (auto state = stateMachine.begin();
        state != stateMachine.end();
        state++) {
        if (!state->condition(&sensors)) {
            state->reach(&sensors, &actuators);
            break;
        }
    }
    Sleep(FEEDBACK_LOOP_TIMEOUT);
}
```

Listing 11-3: Final healing state machine and feedback loop

This loop continuously executes the controller loop and sleeps for FEEDBACK_LOOP_TIMEOUT milliseconds between each execution. The Sleep() call allows the game server to receive and process any actuation from the previous iteration and allows the game client to receive any results of the actuation from the server before executing the next controller loop.

If you're still a bit confused about what I just showed you, check out Figure 11-3, which shows how the infinitely looping code in Listing 11-3 works. First, it checks whether the strong healing condition is true, and if it is, the weak healing condition is checked. If the strong healing condition is false, then the player's health must be at or below 50 percent, so a strong healing method gets called. If the weak healing condition check is false, then the player's health must be between 51 and 70 percent, so the weak healing method is executed.

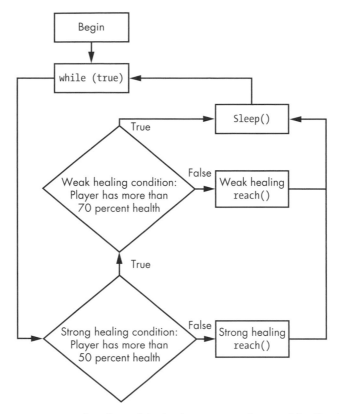

Figure 11-3: Flowchart of the healing state machine and feedback loop

After either method, the machine sleeps. If both condition checks are true, then the player needs no healing. The machine does nothing to change the state and sleeps before starting again at the top of the while loop.

A Complex Hypothetical State Machine

The behavior implemented in the healing state machine is simple, so rolling it into this kind of control structure may seem like overkill, but it's useful if you want to expand the controller. If, for example, you wanted to combine the healing state machine with the "walk, attack, loot" behavior that I discussed in "Control Theory and Game Hacking" on page 222, the control structure would be much more complex. Let's take a high-level look at the states you'd need:

Strong healing Condition met if health is over 50 percent. Reach by casting strong healing spell.

Weak healing Condition met if health is over 70 percent. Reach by casting weak healing spell.

Attack spell Condition met if no target is available or if attack spell is on cooldown. Reach by casting attack spell on target.

Kite monster   Condition met if no target is available or if distance from target is adequate. (The definition of "adequate" depends on how far away you want to be from enemies when kiting.) Reach by taking a step away from target.

Target monster   Condition met if there's no creature to attack. Reach by attacking a creature.

Loot item   Condition met if there's no corpse open or if open corpse has nothing to loot. Reach by taking an item from open corpse.

Approach corpse   Condition met if there are no corpses to open or if adjacent to a corpse. Reach by taking a step toward a corpse that will be opened.

Open corpse   Condition met if the character is not adjacent to a corpse that can be opened. Reach by opening adjacent corpse.

Follow path   Condition met if the character is unable to move to current waypoint or if standing on current waypoint. Reach by taking a step toward current waypoint.

Advance waypoint   Condition met if there are no waypoints left to follow. Reach by updating the current waypoint to the next waypoint in the list. If the character can't reach the current waypoint for some reason (say, if the character is stuck), then the Advance Waypoint state keeps it from being stuck. If the character has reached the current waypoint, Advance Waypoint selects the next waypoint to keep things moving along.

This state machine is quite a bit more complex than the healing-only state machine. If I diagrammed this state machine, there would be 23 objects in the diagram, with arrows going over 33 control paths. Compare that to Figure 11-3, which has only 7 objects and 9 control paths.

You could code the healer behavior without using a state machine or feedback loop, but I can't imagine how to easily do the same for this full-fledged bot. Each of these 10 states relies on not only its own condition but also the condition of every state preceding it. Moreover, hardcoding the logic would either require a ton of nested if() statements or a bunch of stacked if()/return() statements—and, either way, it would just behave exactly like the state machine but with no runtime flexibility.

Runtime flexibility refers to a state machine's ability to mutate. Unlike hardcoded condition checks, state definitions in a state machine can be moved, removed, and added dynamically. The state machine method allows you to plug and play different behaviors and features depending on user input.

To take this concept a step further, you could expose your sensors and actuators to a Lua environment, create Lua functions capable of adding and removing states from the state machine, and modify the StateDefinition so that its condition() and reach() functions can call Lua functions exposed by the Lua environment. Writing a control system this way would allow you to code the core of your bot (hooks, memory reading, actuation) in C++ while making Lua (a high-level, dynamic language) available to you for automation.

NOTE *You can embed Lua in your own programs by including a few headers and linking against the Lua library. This process is not difficult, but it's outside the scope of this book, so I encourage you to check out Chapter 24 of* Programming in Lua *by Roberto Ierusalimschy* (http://www.lua.org/pil/24.html) *for more information.*

Error Correction

Another piece of control theory that's useful for game hacking is *error correction*. An error correction mechanism in a controller observes the outcome of actuation, compares the outcome to an expected result, and adjusts future calculations to bring later outcomes closer to the expected one. Error correction can come in handy when you're working with *stochastic systems*, where the output generated from a given input is not fully predictable.

Games as a whole are stochastic, but, luckily for game hackers, the results of actions are mostly deterministic. Take the healing controller, for example. In most games, you can calculate exactly how much health you can heal with a given spell, and, thus, you know exactly when to heal. But imagine you're writing a healer for the small spectrum of situations where your healing is impossible to calculate; for instance, maybe the bot is supposed to work on a variety of characters spanning many levels without user input.

Error correction could enable your bot to learn how to best heal the players. In this scenario, there are two ways you can implement error correction, each of which depends on how the healing system works.

Adjusting for a Constant Ratio

If you heal for a constant ratio of health, you'll only need to adjust your controller after the first heal. Assuming that your sensors can detect how much you've healed, this adds only a few lines of code. You could easily modify the weak healing state in Listing 11-2 to something like this:

```
curDef->condition = [](GameSensors* sensors) -> bool {
    static float healAt = 70;
    static bool hasLearned = false;
    if (!hasLearned && sensors->detectedWeakHeal()) {
        hasLearned = true;
        healAt = 100 - sensors->getWeakHealIncrease();
    }
    return sensors->getHealthPercent() > healAt;
};
```

Instead of hardcoding 70 as the threshold for weak healing, this code moves the threshold to a static variable called healAt. It also adds another static variable called hasLearned so that the code knows when learning is complete.

On each invocation of this condition() function, the code checks two conditions: whether hasLearned is false and whether the sensors detected a weak healing event. When this check passes, the code sets hasLearned to true and updates healAt to heal at or below the perfect percentage; that is, if your weak healing mustered up a 20 percent increase in health, healAt would be set to 80 percent health instead of 70 percent, so each heal would bring the player back up to 100 percent health.

Implementing Adaptable Error Correction

But what if your healing power increases? If a character can gain levels, apply skill points, or increase maximum health, the amount of health it can heal may change accordingly. For example, if you start a bot on a level-10 character and let it run until the character is level 40, your healing code will need to adapt. A level-40 character healing like it did at level 10 would either immensely overheal or die quickly against on-level game enemies.

To handle this scenario, a bot needs to constantly update its healing threshold to reflect the observed healing amount. Listing 11-4 shows how you can modify the strong healing condition function in Listing 11-1 to do this.

```
curDef->condition = [](GameSensors* sensors) -> bool {
    static float healAt = 50;
❶   if (sensors->detectedStrongHeal()) {
        auto newHealAt = 100 - sensors->getStrongHealIncrease();
❷       healAt = (healAt + newHealAt) / 2.00f;
❸       sensors->clearStrongHealInfo();
    }
    return sensors->getHealthPercent() > healAt;
};
```

Listing 11-4: Tweaking the strong healing condition code

As in the modified weak healing function, the healing threshold has been moved to a static variable called healAt, but this time, the logic is a bit different. Since learning must happen continually, there's no variable to track whether the bot has already learned its true healing capacity. Instead, the code just checks whether the sensors have seen a strong healing event since its last invocation ❶. If so, the code replaces healAt with the average of healAt and newHealAt and calls a function to clear the sensors of information related to strong healing ❸.

Clearing the sensors is actually very important, because it keeps the code from constantly updating healAt against feedback from the same strong healing cast. Notice, too, that this function doesn't update healAt to a perfect value but instead slides it toward the observed optimal value. This behavior makes the new function ideal for situations where there is some amount of randomness in how much you can actually heal. If your bot needs to slide toward the new value faster, you might change the line at ❷ to something like this:

```
healAt = (healAt + newHealAt * 2) / 3.00f;
```

This code to update `healAt` uses an average weighted toward the `newHealAt` value. There are a few points to consider when using this approach, however. First, what happens when you overheal? In some games, when you heal to full health, your sensors might be able to detect only how much you actually healed. In other games, your sensors may be able to detect the actual amount healed. Put another way, if you cast a 30 percent strong heal from 85 percent health, do your sensors see a heal of 30 percent or 15 percent? If the answer is 30 percent, you're set. If the answer is 15 percent, your code needs a way to adjust downward.

One way to adjust accordingly is to decrement `healAt` when your sensors see a heal that brings you to full health, like this:

```
curDef->condition = [](GameSensors* sensors) -> bool {
    static float healAt = 50;
    if (sensors->detectedStrongHeal()) {
❶       if (sensors->getStrongHealMaxed()) {
            healAt--;
        } else {
            auto newHealAt = 100 - sensors->getStrongHealIncrease();
            healAt = (healAt + newHealAt) / 2.00f;
        }
        sensors->clearStrongHealInfo();
    }
    return sensors->getHealthPercent() > healAt;
};
```

This code is almost the same as Listing 11-4, but it adds an `if()` clause to decrement `healAt` if a max heal is detected ❶. Otherwise, the function should behave like Listing 11-4.

Healing is a simple case, but this code shows a great example of how you can use error correction to dynamically improve your bots' behavior. One more advanced use case is adjusting skillshots to account for enemy movement patterns. Every player has patterns in how they avoid skillshots, so if your sensors are able to measure the direction and distance an enemy moves when dodging a skillshot, your controller code can adjust the location where the bot initially shoots the skillshot. In this same scenario, learning would also help the bot account for differences in game server latency, character movement speed, and so on.

When using error correction, note that your code will be cleaner and more portable if your state definitions have some form of internal bookkeeping other than static variables. Moreover, to avoid cluttering your state definitions, I suggest encapsulating the error correction logic in some external modules that are easily invoked when needed.

Pathfinding with Search Algorithms

One common challenge you'll face when writing an autonomous bot is calculating a path for a character to follow from one location to another. Aside from the sheer reverse engineering challenge of creating sensors to read which coordinates on the game map are blocking forward movement or not, there's also the algorithmic challenge of calculating a path within that map. Calculating a path is called *pathfinding*, and game hackers often use a *search algorithm* to tackle it.

Two Common Search Techniques

Given a grid of tiles, a starting location *a*, and an ending location *b*, a search algorithm calculates a path from *a* to *b*. The algorithm does this by creating a *node* at *a*, adding nodes adjacent to *a* to a list of tiles to be explored (called the *frontier*), updating the node to the best tile in the frontier, and repeating the process until the node reaches *b*. Different search algorithms select the best node differently, using either a *cost*, a *heuristic*, or both.

Dijkstra's algorithm, for example, calculates the cost of a tile based on its distance from the *a* node and selects the tile with the lowest cost. Imagine an empty two-dimensional grid with *a* in the middle. In a search following Dijkstra's algorithm, the frontier will expand in a circular pattern around *a* until *b* lies on the edge of the circle, as seen in Figure 11-4.

The *greedy best-first search* algorithm, instead of prioritizing nodes by their distance from the starting point, uses a heuristic to estimate the distance from a node in the frontier to *b*. The algorithm then selects the node with the shortest estimated distance. Imagine this algorithm in the same grid as before; the frontier would be a line going almost directly from *a* to *b*, as seen in Figure 11-5.

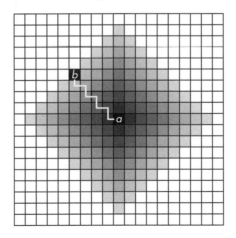

Figure 11-4: The frontier of Dijkstra's algorithm. Lighter tiles are higher cost.

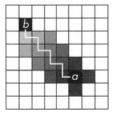

Figure 11-5: The frontier of the greedy best-first search algorithm. Lighter tiles are higher cost.

How Obstacles Disrupt Searches

The difference in how these algorithms behave becomes clearer once obstacles are added to the grid. If, for instance, a wall separates *a* and *b*, Dijkstra's algorithm will always find the quickest path, but with a huge consequence. The radius of the circular frontier around *a* will be equal to the length of the final path; let's call that radius *r*. If no grid boundaries clip the frontier, you can roughly calculate the number of nodes opened by taking the area of a circle with radius *r*. If the path around the wall is 50 tiles, the algorithm will open roughly 7,854 tiles, as shown in this equation:

$$\pi \times 50^2 = 7,854$$

In the same scenario, greedy best-first search will calculate a less-than-optimal path but open substantially fewer tiles. It's not as easy to visualize how the frontier will expand, and it's not important right now, so I won't go into it here. At the end of the day, neither of these algorithms really fits the pathfinding problem well. The optimal path is slow, and the fast path isn't optimal.

To quickly calculate an optimal path, you need to fuse Dijkstra's algorithm with greedy best-first search. Luckily, someone has already done this, and the resulting algorithm is a monster known as *A-star search* (often just called *A**).

A* uses the sum of a cost, called *g*, and a heuristic, called *h*, to select nodes. These resulting sum is called the *score*. Put simply, score = *g* + *h*. Like Dijkstra's algorithm, A* can calculate the most optimal path from *a* to *b*, and like greedy best-first search, it can do so relatively quickly.

An A* Search Algorithm

Now that you know the fundamentals, let's write code to implement the A* algorithm. This implementation will work in a two-dimensional grid. It won't allow diagonal movement at first, but I'll discuss in a bit how you can modify the code to work with diagonal movement, too.

All of the example code for this section is in the *GameHackingExamples/ Chapter11_SearchAlgorithms* directory of this book's source files. The included projects can be compiled with Visual Studio 2010, but they should also work with any other C++ compiler. Download them at *https://www.nostarch.com/ gamehacking/* and compile them to follow along. If you execute *Chapter11_ SearchAlgorithms.exe*, you'll be able to define your own 20×20 grid and watch the algorithm calculate a search path.

Creating an A* Node

To start, define an empty `AStarNode` class as follows:

```
typedef std::shared_ptr<class AStarNode> AStarNodePtr;
class AStarNode
{
public:
};
```

This code defines the `AStarNode` class and a `std::shared_ptr` type definition called `AStarNodePtr` to make it easier to create safe pointers to the class.

Next, within the public scope of this class, declare member variables for the node's x-position, y-position, cost, and node's score:

```
int x, y;
int g, score;
```

Additionally, you need a public member of type AStarNodePtr that references the parent node:

```
AStarNodePtr parent;
```

After declaring all member variables, declare a public constructor that initializes them upon instance creation, as follows:

```
AStarNode(int x, int y, int cost, AStarNodePtr p, int score = 0)
    : x(x), y(y), g(cost), score(score), parent(p)
{}
```

Now, to make creating safe pointers easier, add a static helper function like this:

```
static AStarNodePtr makePtr(
    int x, int y, int cost,
    AStarNodePtr p,
    int score = 0)
{
    return AStarNodePtr(new AStarNode(x, y, cost, p, score));
}
```

This makePtr() function creates a new instance of AStarNode and returns the instance wrapped inside of an AstarNodePtr.

Let's recap. The AStarNode class has member variables x, y, g, score, and parent. When the class is constructed, all of these members are initialized from values passed to the constructor, with the exception of score, which is optional (because you use it only when making copies of an AStarNode instance) and set to 0 if not provided.

Next, define a public member function to calculate the heuristic when given the destination coordinates:

```
int heuristic(const int destx, int desty) const
{
    int xd = destx - x;
    int yd = desty - y;
❶  return abs(xd) + abs(yd);
}
```

This function returns the *Manhattan distance heuristic* ❶, a distance calculation designed for grids where diagonal movement is not possible:

$$|\Delta x| + |\Delta y|$$

To calculate a path that allows diagonal movement, you'd need to modify this function to use the *Euclidean distance heuristic*, which looks like this:

$$\sqrt{(\Delta x \times \Delta x) + (\Delta y \times \Delta y)}$$

The class also needs a function to update score. You add that function to the public scope as follows:

```
#define TILE_COST 1
void updateScore(int endx, int endy)
{
    auto h = this->heuristic(endx, endy) * TILE_COST;
    this->score = g + h;
}
```

Now, score should change to g + h when given destination coordinates to calculate h.

To wrap up, the node class also needs a function that can calculate all of its child nodes. The function could do this by creating new nodes for each tile adjacent to the current node. Each new node refers to the current node as its parent, so the class needs to be able to create an AStarNodePtr to a copy of the current node as well. Here's how all that works:

```
AStarNodePtr getCopy()
{
    return AStarNode::makePtr(x, y, g, parent, score);
}
std::vector<AStarNodePtr> getChildren(int width, int height)
{
    std::vector<AStarNodePtr> ret;
    auto copy = getCopy();
    if (x > 0)
❶       ret.push_back(AStarNode::makePtr(x - 1, y, g + TILE_COST, copy));
    if (y > 0)
❷       ret.push_back(AStarNode::makePtr(x, y - 1, g + TILE_COST, copy));
    if (x < width - 1)
❸       ret.push_back(AStarNode::makePtr(x + 1, y, g + TILE_COST, copy));
    if (y < height - 1)
❹       ret.push_back(AStarNode::makePtr(x, y + 1, g + TILE_COST, copy));
    return ret;
}
```

This function creates child nodes at (x − 1, y) ❶, (x, y − 1) ❷, (x + 1, y) ❸, and (x, y + 1) ❹. Their parent is the node that called getChildren, and their g is the parent's g plus TILE_COST.

To allow for diagonal movement, this function needs to add children at (x − 1, y − 1), (x + 1, y − 1), (x + 1, y + 1), and (x − 1, y + 1). Additionally, if moving diagonally would cost more—that is, if the character requires more time to do it—you'd also need to do the following:

1. Change TILE_COST to 10.

2. Define a constant DIAG_TILE_COST as TILE_COST multiplied by the time increase. If a diagonal step takes 1.5 times as long, DIAG_TILE_COST would be 15.

3. Give diagonal children a g of the parent's g plus DIAG_TILE_COST.

To finish off AStarNode, declare operators for comparing the priority and equality of two nodes. You could place these declarations outside the class in global scope like this:

```
❶ bool operator<(const AStarNodePtr &a, const AStarNodePtr &b)
  {
      return a.score > b.score;
  }
❷ bool operator==(const AStarNodePtr &a, const AStarNodePtr &b)
  {
      return a.x == b.x && a.y == b.y;
  }
```

These operators allow std::priority_queue to sort nodes by score ❶ and std::find to determine node equality by location ❷.

Writing the A* Search Function

Now that you've completed the AStarNode class, you can code the actual search function. Start by defining the function prototype:

```
template<int WIDTH, int HEIGHT, int BLOCKING>
bool doAStarSearch(
    int map[WIDTH][HEIGHT],
    int startx, int starty,
    int endx, int endy,
    int path[WIDTH][HEIGHT])
{ }
```

The prototype accepts the game map's width and height, as well as the value that signifies a blocking tile on the map, as template parameters. The doAStarSearch() function also takes the map itself (map), the starting coordinates (startx and starty), the destination coordinates (endx and endy), and a blank map (path) where it can fill the calculated path when it finishes.

NOTE *The first three parameters are template parameters, so you can pass them as compile-time constants. I've done this for the example code to allow explicit array size declarations for the map and path parameters and to allow a definite value to signify blocking tiles on the map. In practice, the map you read from a game will have a dynamic size, and you'll probably need a more robust way to pass this data.*

Next, the doAStarSearch() function needs a sorted list to hold the frontier and a container to track all created notes so you can update the score and parent of an existing node if it's opened as a child of a different parent. You can create these as follows:

```
std::vector<AStarNodePtr> allNodes;
std::priority_queue<AStarNodePtr> frontier;
```

The frontier is defined with std::priority_queue since it can automatically sort the nodes based on their score. The node container, allNodes, is defined as a std::vector.

Now, let's create the first node:

```
auto node = AStarNode::makePtr(startx, starty, 0, nullptr);
node->updateScore(endx, endy);
allNodes.push_back(node);
```

The first node is a no-cost orphan node at the position (startx, starty). The node is given a score based on what the updateScore() function returns, and then it's added to the allNodes container.

With a node in the container, it's time to write the meat of the A* algorithm, starting with a simple loop:

```
while (true) {
}
```

Until otherwise specified, the rest of the code in this section will appear inside of this loop, in the order shown.

From here, the first step is to check the *goal state.* In this case, the goal is to find a path for the player to follow to the next waypoint, which happens when the node object's position is (endx, endy). Thus, to check the goal state, the program needs to check whether node has reached those coordinates or not. Here's how that check should look:

```
if (node->x == endx && node->y == endy) {
    makeList<WIDTH, HEIGHT>(node, allNodes, path);
    return true;
}
```

When the goal state is met, the program reports true back to the caller and fills path with the final path. For now, assume a function called makeList() can fill in path for you; I'll show you this function shortly. If the goal state isn't met, you need to expand the children of node, which is actually a pretty complicated process:

```
auto children = node->getChildren(WIDTH, HEIGHT);
for (auto c = children.begin(); c != children.end(); c++) {
❶    if (map[(*c)->x][(*c)->y] == BLOCKING) continue;
```

```
        auto found = std::find(allNodes.rbegin(), allNodes.rend(), *c);
❷       if (found != allNodes.rend()) {
❸          if (*found > *c) {
                (*found)->g = (*c)->g;
                (*found)->parent = (*c)->parent;
                (*found)->updateScore(endx, endy);
            }
        } else {
            (*c)->updateScore(endx, endy);
❹          frontier.push(*c);
❺          allNodes.push_back(*c);
        }
    }
}
```

After calling node->getChildren to generate a list of nodes that can be added to the frontier, the code iterates over each child and ignores any that are on blocking tiles ❶. Next, for each child, the code checks whether a node has already been opened at the same coordinates ❷. If so, and if the score of the existing node is greater than the score of the new child, the existing node is updated to the parent, cost, and score of the new child by the if() statement at ❸. If the new child doesn't have a brother-from-another-mother, it will be added as is to the frontier ❹ and the node list ❺.

Also notice that std::find uses the reverse begin and reverse end iterators of allNodes instead of the regular iterators ❶. The example does this because new nodes are appended to the end of the vector and duplicate nodes will be close together, so duplicates will usually be closer to the end of the vector. (This step could also be done directly against the frontier, but std::priority_queue doesn't allow iteration over nodes and writing the sort in place would make the code too large for print.)

Eventually, the function will run out of new children to add to the frontier; the following if() statement handles that situation:

```
   if (frontier.size() == 0) return false;
❶ node = frontier.top();
❷ frontier.pop();
```

This code points node to the cheapest node from the frontier ❶, removes it from the frontier ❷, and lets the loop repeat. If the frontier ends up empty, the function reports false back to the caller, since there's nothing left to search.

Creating the Path List

Finally, it's time to implement the makeList() function:

```
template<int WIDTH, int HEIGHT>
void makeList(
    AStarNodePtr end,
    std::vector<AStarNodePtr> nodes,
    int path[WIDTH][HEIGHT])
```

```
{
    for (auto n = nodes.begin(); n != nodes.end(); n++)
❶      path[(*n)->x][(*n)->y] = 2;
    auto node = end;
    while (node.get() != nullptr) {
❷      path[node->x][node->y] = 1;
        node = node->parent;
    }
}
```

This function updates path with both a list of closed nodes ❶ and the calculated path ❷. For this example, the value 2 represents the closed nodes and 1 represents the path nodes. The program calculates nodes in the path by following parent nodes from the goal node until it reaches the starting node, which is an orphan with nullptr as a parent.

When A* Searches Are Particularly Useful

Make sure to play with the example code and executable for the previous section, because that's the only way you'll really get acquainted with the behavior of A* searches. In most newer games, you should be able to just send a packet with the destination or even emulate a click on the map at the desired spot, but when you come across a situation where you need to calculate a path, you'll be glad you learned A*.

There are actually many situations where calculating a path can be useful:

Selecting targets
When your bot is selecting targets to attack, you may want to check whether your character can actually reach them. Otherwise, if an enemy is isolated in an unreachable room, you might get stuck in place trying to target them forever!

Selecting corpses
As your looting state(s) determine which corpses to open, you can optimize by always trying to loot the closest corpse first.

Emulating mouse movements
Very rarely, some heavily protected games actually correlate in-game actions with mouse movements to ensure that there's no bot running. In this case, you might need to emulate the mouse. Using a modified version of A* where the screen is the map, there are no blocking tiles, and node costs are slightly randomized, you can calculate human-like paths for your mouse to follow when you simulate movement.

Kiting monsters
If you ever need to write code to kite monsters, you can implement A* with a goal state of being *N* units away from all creatures. Using the same cost mechanism shown in this chapter, play with the heuristic

to give a higher cost to nodes that are closer to creatures. Kiting isn't exactly a conventional use case, and the heuristic will require a bunch of tweaking, but it works amazingly once you've got it going. Some implementations can kite any number of monsters better than a human!

Predicting enemy movements

If you're writing a bot that fights other players, you can use A* to predict their movements and act accordingly. For instance, if your enemy starts running away, your bot can assume they are running to their base, calculate their route, and use a spell to block their path or even teleport to a location where it expects them to be.

These are just a few use cases for A* searches, and you'll definitely find many more as you improve your bots. For the rest of the chapter, I'll describe some popular automated hacks that you can implement using the techniques described in this book.

OTHER USES FOR A* SEARCH

A* isn't just for calculating paths. With abstractions on top of the AStarNode class, you can adapt the same algorithm to any search problem. Realistically, A* is just a weighted iteration over a multidimensional data set that iterates until some goal object is found, and, thus, it can solve any problem that can be represented as a multidimensional data set. More advanced applications for A* include playing chess and checkers, and—when it's paired with a three-dimensional Manhattan distance heuristic and a depth-first search implementation—even solving a Rubik's cube. Sadly, I'm not going to go into these use cases; if you want to get really good with search algorithms, I encourage you to research more online.

Common and Cool Automated Hacks

Now that you've seen the design patterns and algorithms needed to create efficient, self-teaching bots, it's time to learn about some popular automated hacks that go beyond simple healing and pathfinding. Let's fly up to 10,000 feet to explore two types of bots at a high level.

Looting with Cavebots

While discussing control theory, state machines, and search algorithms, I touched on the idea of a cavebot that kills creatures, grabs loot, and walks around caves. The abilities of cavebots can vary greatly.

Depositing Gold and Restocking Supplies

If you want to leave a character botting for days on end, you'll need a *depositor* and a *refiller*. A depositor can deposit loot in your bank or vault, while a refiller refills your potions, runes, and other supplies. These features can be described with six basic states:

Leave spawn   Condition met if the character is in the spawn area or cave, if it has nothing to deposit, and if it has enough supplies. Reach this state by exiting the spawn area or cave.

Walk to town   Condition met if the character is in the spawn area or cave. Reach this state by walking from the spawn or cave to town.

Deposit   Condition met if the character is in the spawn area or cave, or if the character is in town and has nothing to deposit. Reach this state by putting loot in the bank or vault.

Withdraw cash   Condition met if the character is in the spawn area or cave, is in town with no supplies to purchase, or has enough gold to purchase supplies. Reach this state by withdrawing gold from the bank or vault.

Purchase supplies   Condition met if the character is in the spawn area or cave or if the character has enough supplies to start hunting. Reach by buying supplies.

Enter spawn   Condition met if the character is in the spawn area or cave. Reach this state by walking to the spawn area or cave.

These states would come before the states related to following waypoints (I describe a couple of those states in "A Complex Hypothetical State Machine" on page 228) in the vector of StateDefinition objects. Placing them first gives them priority over remaining in the cave, while still allowing the character to target, kill, and loot monsters on the way back to town. Depending on where you're hunting and how you want the bot to behave, you may also tell your targeting states not to attack creatures if the character isn't in the spawn area or cave, and you might add an extra state before walk to town that attacks only creatures that block the character's path to town. Specifying that extra state increases the bot's efficiency, since trips to and from town will be much quicker if the monsters on the way aren't worth killing.

Using the Character as Bait

Two other cavebot features that can make your bot awesome are *lure mode* and *dynamic lure*. You wouldn't implement these two features as actual states in a complex bot; rather, you'd have them inform the bot's targeting and walking states to help the bot make decisions.

You can control lure mode with special waypoints in your path, and its code will tell your targeting states to attack creatures only if the bot is stuck, similar to the mechanism discussed for walking to or from town. The difference is that lure mode can be switched on and off at different areas in the cave, allowing you to lure multiple mobs of monsters to certain locations before attacking them. This can make your bot much more efficient, as certain types of characters may excel at killing many monsters at once.

Dynamic lure is similar, but instead of turning it on and off at definite locations via waypoints, you can automatically turn lure mode on when there aren't enough monsters. For example, a bot with the dynamic lure feature might tell the targeting states not to attack any creature until five monsters are on screen. The targeting states would resume attacking and kiting until all five monsters are dead, and the bot would snap back into lure mode until a suitably sized mob appears again.

If your character is quick enough to outrun monsters, though, you'll need to modify your bot's walking states to walk slowly when lure mode is on and creatures are present. Otherwise, your character will leave mobs behind without killing them. You can slow down a character by adding a state before the follow path state in your state machine definition that delays movement slightly when lure mode is on and any creatures are too far away.

Allowing Players to Script Custom Behaviors

Nearly every cavebot includes a scripting interface that allows players to add their own behaviors. You could implement this interface as a way to specify custom waypoints to follow, spells to use, or items to loot. In more advanced bots, you might make your targeting, looting, walking, and luring systems as dynamic as possible so players can add unique features. If you implement your automation in Lua, third parties could easily improve and expand your bot's abilities.

Making your bot easy to write scripts for takes a lot of work off your shoulders, since other programmers who play the game might release scripts to add support for new hunting spots and improve your automation. Such scripting services are common in botting communities, and players often create and sell professional-grade scripts that integrate with bots.

Automating Combat with Warbots

Another class of automated bots is used for *player versus player (PvP)* combat. These warbots, or *PvP bots*, have many features categorized as responsive or ESP hacks, since the bots focus on responding to incoming damage or spells, revealing hidden enemies, and giving the player an information advantage.

Fully automated warbots are rare, but I've already lightly discussed how you can use some automation techniques to make smarter healers, teach bots to land more accurate skillshots, and predict players' paths to stop them in their tracks. Let's explore a few other cool hacks that fall on the fringe of responsive, ESP, and automated.

NOTE *In games that are completely PvP based, such as battlegrounds or real-time strategy games, some players might also just call these* bots, *since war or PvP is the bot's only purpose.*

Autowall Bots

If your character has a spell to create a temporary wall, you can code a bot that automatically blocks enemy players when they enter small corridors. Using error correction, the bot could learn how far ahead of the enemy to place the wall. With some really creative engineering, the bot could even learn which enemies can jump over walls by checking whether each enemy manages to get past the wall before it disappears.

Autosnipe Bots

For characters with a long-range skillshot or global execution spell, you can use automation to detect when an enemy across the map has low health and cast your spell to kill them. You can also use error correction to more accurately guess where to shoot a long-range skillshot. If you're unable to calculate exact damage amounts, error correction can also help a bot determine how much damage a spell does and tweak the casting threshold accordingly.

Autokite Bots

If you're playing a carry character that does most of its damage by attacking at a short distance, you might implement a bot to automatically kite enemies. Using a set of states similar to the ones a cavebot might use to kite monsters, you can make a bot that automatically kites enemy characters when you attack them. When you stop targeting the enemy, the bot can stop kiting. Using A* search, you can improve the kiting mechanism to avoid multiple enemies, or, if you want to escape while attacking, guide the kiting mechanism back to a safe place, such as your team's base or a neutral location.

Closing Thoughts

By this point, you should be ready to go out and make some pretty awesome bots. Don't worry if you're still not completely comfortable with the techniques in this chapter; the best way to learn is to just dive in and start hacking. Use the thousands of lines of example code provided for this book to get started without working from scratch, and most of all, have fun!

In the next chapter, I'll discuss ways that bots can hide from anti-cheat mechanisms, which are pieces of software that games use to detect and stop botters.

12

STAYING HIDDEN

Game hacking is an ever-evolving practice, a game of cat and mouse between hackers and game developers where each party works to subvert the other. As long as people make bots, game companies will find ways to hinder bot advances and ban players who use bots. Rather than making their games inherently harder to hack, though, game companies focus on *detection*.

The largest game companies have very sophisticated detection suites called *anti-cheat software*. In the beginning of this chapter, I'll discuss the capabilities of the most common anti-cheat suites. After revealing how these suites detect bots, I'll teach you some powerful ways to evade them.

Prominent Anti-Cheat Software

The best-known anti-cheat suites use the same methods as most antivirus software to scan for bots and flag them as threats. Some anti-cheat suites are also dynamic, meaning their inner workings and capabilities can change based on the game they're protecting. Anti-cheat software developers also track down and patch their suites against bypass software, so always do your own in-depth research of any anti-cheat software that you might face.

When these suites detect a botter, they flag the botter's account for banishment. Every few weeks, game company administrators ban the flagged players in a *ban wave*. Game companies use ban waves instead of instantaneous bans because banning in waves is more profitable. If botters are banned after a few weeks of playing, their familiarity with the game will make them more likely to buy a new account than if they were banned the moment their bot started running.

There are dozens of anti-cheat suites, but I'll focus on the five packages that are the most common and thoroughly understood: *PunkBuster, ESEA Anti-Cheat, Valve Anti-Cheat (VAC), GameGuard*, and *Warden*.

The PunkBuster Toolkit

PunkBuster, made by Even Balance Inc., is the original anti-cheat toolkit. Many games use PunkBuster, but it's most common in first-person shooter games like *Medal of Honor, Far Cry 3*, and several installments of the *Battlefield* series.

The toolkit uses a myriad of detection methods, the most formidable of which are signature-based detection (SBD), screenshots, and hash validation. PunkBuster is also known for imposing hardware bans that permanently ban a cheater's computer, rather than just their game account, by saving a fingerprint of the hardware's serial numbers and blocking logins from a machine that matches it.

Signature-Based Detection

PunkBuster scans the memory of all processes on a system running a game that employs it, searching for byte patterns unique to known cheat software, called *signatures*. If PunkBuster detects a signature, the player is flagged for a ban. PunkBuster carries out memory scans from user mode using the `NtQueryVirtualMemory()` Windows API function, and it sometimes runs scans from multiple hidden processes.

Signature-based detection is blind to context by design, and it ultimately suffers from a fatal flaw: false positives. On March 23, 2008, a team of hackers set out to prove the existence of this flaw by spamming public chatrooms with a text string that PunkBuster would identify as a bot signature. Since SBD blindly scans process memory for matching patterns, any and all legitimate players inside these public chatrooms were flagged as botters.

This caused thousands of fair players to be banned with no justification. A similar situation happened again in November 2013: PunkBuster falsely banned thousands of players on *Battlefield 4.* That time, no one was trying to prove a point; the company had just added a bad signature to its software.

PunkBuster resolved both of these issues by restoring the players' accounts, but these incidents show just how aggressive its flavor of SBD is. In the time since these attacks, though, PunkBuster's SBD has reduced the number of false positives by checking only for signatures at predefined binary offsets.

Screenshots

As another method of bot detection, PunkBuster also periodically takes screenshots of a player's screen and sends them to the central game server. This form of detection is a nuisance, and it's weak compared to SDB. Game-hacking communities speculate that PunkBuster implemented this feature to give game admins proof against botters who dispute bans.

Hash Validation

In addition to employing SBD and screenshots, PunkBuster detects bots by creating cryptographic hashes of a game's executable binaries on a player's system and comparing them to hashes stored on a central server. If the hashes do not match, the player is flagged for a ban. This check is carried out only on the binaries on the filesystem, not on in-memory binaries.

The ESEA Anti-Cheat Toolkit

The ESEA Anti-Cheat toolkit is used by the *E-Sports Entertainment Association (ESEA)*, primarily for its *Counter-Strike: Global Offensive* league. Unlike PunkBuster, this suite is known for generating very few false positives and being highly effective at catching cheaters.

ESEA Anti-Cheat's detection capabilities resemble those of PunkBuster, with one noteworthy difference. ESEA Anti-Cheat's SBD algorithm is carried out from a kernel-mode driver using three different Windows Kernel functions: the `MmGetPhysicalMemoryRanges()` function, the `ZwOpenSection()` function, and the `ZwMapViewOfSection()` function. This implementation makes the anti-cheat system nearly immune to memory spoofing (a common way to defeat SBD), as the functions used by the scan are much harder to hook when they're called from a driver.

The VAC Toolkit

VAC is the toolkit Valve Corporation applies to its own games and many of the third-party games available on its Steam gaming platform. VAC uses SDB and hash validation methods that resemble PunkBuster's detection techniques, and it also uses Domain Name System (DNS) cache scans and binary validation.

DNS Cache Scans

DNS is a protocol that converts between domain names and IP addresses smoothly, and the DNS cache is where that information gets stored on a computer. When VAC's SBD algorithm detects cheat software, VAC scans the player's DNS cache for any domain names associated with cheating websites. It's not certain whether a positive DNS cache scan is required for VAC's SBD algorithm to flag a player for banishment, or if the DNS cache scan simply acts as another nail in the coffin for players who are already flagged by SBD.

NOTE *To see your DNS cache, enter* `ipconfig /displaydns` *at a command prompt. Yes, VAC looks at all of that.*

Binary Validation

VAC also uses binary validation to prevent in-memory tampering of executable binaries. It scans for modifications like IAT, jump, and code hooking by comparing hashes of in-memory binary code to hashes of the same code in the binaries on the filesystem. If it finds a mismatch, VAC flags the player for a ban.

This detection method is formidable, but Valve's initial implementation of the algorithm was flawed. In July 2010, VAC's binary validation falsely banned 12,000 *Call of Duty* players. The binary validation module failed to account for a Steam update, and it banned the players when their in-memory code did not match the updated binaries on the filesystem.

False Positives

VAC has had other issues with false positives. Its initial release routinely banned fair players for "faulty memory." This same early version banned players for using *Cedega*, a platform that ran Windows games on Linux. And on April 1, 2004, Valve falsely banned a couple thousand players due to a server-side glitch. On two separate occasions, one in June 2011 and one in February 2014, VAC also falsely banned thousands of *Team Fortress 2* and *Counter-Strike* players due to bugs that the company refuses to disclose. As with PunkBuster, these incidents show that VAC is very aggressive.

The GameGuard Toolkit

GameGuard is an anti-cheat toolkit made by INCA Internet Co. Ltd. and used by many MMORPGs, including *Lineage II*, *Cabal Online*, and *Ragnarok Online*. In addition to some mildly aggressive SBD, GameGuard uses rootkits to proactively prevent cheat software from running.

User-Mode Rootkit

GameGuard utilizes a user-mode rootkit to deny bots access to the Windows API functions they use to operate. The rootkit hooks the functions at their lowest-level entry point, often inside undocumented functions in *ntdll.dll*, *user32.dll*, and *kernel32.dll*. These are the most notable API functions GameGuard hooks, and here's what GameGuard does from inside each hooked function:

NtOpenProcess()   Blocks any OpenProcess() attempts on the game being protected.

NtProtectVirtualMemory()   Blocks any VirtualProtect() or VirtualProtectEx() attempts on the game.

NtReadVirtualMemory() and NtWriteVirtualMemory()   Block any ReadProcessMemory() and WriteProcessMemory() attempts on the game.

NtSuspendProcess() and NtSuspendThread()   Block any attempts to suspend GameGuard.

NtTerminateProcess() and NtTerminateThread()   Block any attempts to terminate GameGuard.

PostMessage(), SendMessage(), and SendInput()   Block any attempts to send programmatic input to the game.

SetWindowsHookEx()   Prevents bots from globally intercepting mouse and keyboard input.

CreateProcessInternal()   Automatically detects and hooks into new processes.

GetProcAddress(), LoadLibraryEx(), and MapViewOfFileEx()   Prevent any attempt to inject libraries into the game or GameGuard.

Kernel-Mode Rootkit

GameGuard also uses a driver-based rootkit to prevent bots that work in the kernel. This rootkit has the same abilities as its user-mode counterpart, and it works by hooking ZwProtectVirtualMemory(), ZwReadVirtualMemory(), ZwWriteVirtualMemory(), SendInput(), and similar functions.

The Warden Toolkit

Warden, made exclusively for Blizzard's games, is by far the most advanced anti-bot toolkit I've encountered. It's hard to say what exactly Warden does, because it downloads dynamic code at runtime. This code, delivered as compiled shellcode, typically has two responsibilities:

*   Detect bots.
*   Periodically send a heartbeat signal to the game server. The value sent is not predefined but instead is generated by some subset of the detection code.

If Warden fails to complete the second task or sends the wrong value, the game server will know that it's been disabled or tampered with. Furthermore, a bot can't disable the detection code and leave the heartbeat code running.

Warden is formidable because you not only have no way to know what you're hiding from but also have no way to disable the toolkit. Even if you manage to avoid detection today, a new detection method might be used tomorrow.

If you plan on publicly distributing bots, you will eventually meet one of the anti-cheat solutions described in the previous sections—and you'll have to beat it. Depending on your bot's footprint, the type of detection in the game you're botting, and your implementation, the difficulty of evading one of these toolkits can range from trivial to extremely hard.

Carefully Managing a Bot's Footprint

A bot's *footprint* is how many unique, detectable characteristics it has. For example, a bot that hooks 100 functions will typically be easier to detect than a bot that hooks only 10 functions because the former makes an order of magnitude more changes to a game's code than the latter. Since a targeted detection system needs to detect only one hook, the developer of the former bot needs to spend much more time making sure all of the bot's hooks are as stealthy as possible.

Another footprint characteristic is how detailed a bot's user interface is. If a known bot has many dialog boxes that all have specific titles, a game company can just have its anti-cheat software detect the bot by searching for windows that have those titles. This same basic reasoning can be used with process names and filenames.

Minimizing a Bot's Footprint

Depending on how your bot works, there are many ways to minimize its footprint. If your bot relies heavily on hooks, for instance, you can avoid directly hooking a game's code and instead focus on hooking Windows API functions. Windows API hooking is surprisingly common, so developers can't assume a program that hooks the Windows API is a bot.

If your bot has a well-defined user interface, you can mask the interface by removing all strings from window bars, buttons, and so on. Instead, display images that show text. If you're worried about specific process names or filenames being detected by the anti-cheat software, use generic filenames and make your bot copy itself to a new, randomized directory every time it launches.

Masking Your Footprint

Minimizing your footprint is a preferred way to avoid detection, but it's not necessary. You can also obfuscate your bot, making it harder for anyone to figure out how it works. Obfuscation can prevent both anti-bot developers from trying to detect your bot and other bot developers from analyzing your bot to steal proprietary functionality. If you sell your bot, obfuscation prevents people from cracking it to bypass your purchase verification, too.

One common type of obfuscation is called *packing*. Packing an executable encrypts it and hides it inside another executable. When the container executable is launched, the packed executable is decrypted and executed in-memory. When a bot is packed, analyzing the binary to learn what the bot does is impossible, and debugging the bot process is much harder. Some common packer programs are *UPX*, *Armadillo*, *Themida*, and *ASPack*.

Teaching a Bot to Detect Debuggers

When anti-bot developers (or other bot creators) can debug a bot, they can figure out how it works and thus how to stop it. If someone is actively trying to pick apart a bot, packing the executable may not be enough to evade them. To protect against this, bots often employ *anti-debugging* techniques, which obfuscate control flow by changing the bot's behavior when a debugger is detected. In this section, I'll quickly cover some well-known methods for detecting when a debugger is attached to your bot, and in the next, I'll show you some tricks for obfuscation.

Calling CheckRemoteDebuggerPresent()

CheckRemoteDebuggerPresent() is a Windows API function that can tell you if a debugger is attached to the current process. Code to check for a debugger might look like this:

```
bool IsRemoteDebuggerPresent() {
    BOOL dbg = false;
    CheckRemoteDebuggerPresent(GetCurrentProcess(), &dbg);
    return dbg;
}
```

This check is pretty straightforward—it calls CheckRemoteDebuggerPresent() with the current process and a pointer to the dbg Boolean. Calling this function is the easiest way to detect a debugger, but it's also very easy for a debugger to evade.

Checking for Interrupt Handlers

Interrupts are signals the processor sends to trigger a corresponding handler in the Windows kernel. Interrupts are typically generated by hardware events, but they can also be generated in software using the INT assembly instruction. The kernel allows some interrupts—namely, interrupts 0x2D and 0x03—to trigger user-mode interrupt handlers in the form of exception handlers. You can take advantage of these interrupts to detect debuggers.

When a debugger sets a breakpoint on an instruction, it replaces that instruction with a breakpoint instruction, such as INT 0x03. When the interrupt is executed, the debugger is notified via an exception handler, where it handles the breakpoint, replaces the original code, and allows the application to resume execution seamlessly. When faced with an unrecognized interrupt, some debuggers even silently step over that interrupt and allow execution to continue normally, without triggering any other exception handlers.

You can detect this behavior by purposely generating interrupts within exception handlers in your code, as shown in Listing 12-1.

```
inline bool Has2DBreakpointHandler() {
    __try { __asm INT 0x2D }
    __except (EXCEPTION_EXECUTE_HANDLER){ return false; }
    return true;
}

inline bool Has03BreakpointHandler() {
    __try { __asm INT 0x03 }
    __except (EXCEPTION_EXECUTE_HANDLER){ return false; }
    return true;
}
```

Listing 12-1: Detecting interrupt handlers

During normal execution, these interrupts trigger the exception handlers surrounding them in the code. During a debugging session, some debuggers might intercept the exceptions generated by these interrupts and silently ignore them, preventing the surrounding exception handlers from executing. Thus, if the interrupts don't trigger your exception handler, then a debugger is present.

Checking for Hardware Breakpoints

Debuggers can also set breakpoints using the processor's debug registers; these are called *hardware breakpoints*. A debugger can set a hardware breakpoint on an instruction by writing the address of the instruction to one of the four debug registers.

When an address present on a debug register is executed, the debugger is notified. To detect hardware breakpoints (and thus, the presence of a debugger), you can check for nonzero values on any of the four debug registers like this:

```
bool HasHardwareBreakpoints() {
    CONTEXT ctx = {0};
    ctx.ContextFlags = CONTEXT_DEBUG_REGISTERS;
    auto hThread = GetCurrentThread();
    if(GetThreadContext(hThread, &ctx) == 0)
        return false;
    return (ctx.Dr0 != 0 || ctx.Dr1 != 0 || ctx.Dr2 != 0 || ctx.Dr3 != 0);
}
```

Printing Debug Strings

OutputDebugString() is a Windows API function that can be used to print log messages to a debugger console. If no debugger is present, the function will return with an error code. If a debugger is present, however, the function will return with no error code. Here's how you can use this function as a trivial debugger check:

```
inline bool CanCallOutputDebugString() {
    SetLastError(0);
    OutputDebugStringA("test");
    return (GetLastError() == 0);
}
```

Like the CheckRemoteDebuggerPresent() method, this method is very straightforward but also very easy for a debugger to evade.

Checking for DBG_RIPEXCEPTION Handlers

Debuggers typically have exception handlers that blindly catch exceptions with Windows' DBG_RIPEXCEPTION exception code, making that code a clear way to spot a debugger. You can detect these exception handlers in much the same way Listing 12-1 detects interrupt handlers:

```
#define DBG_RIPEXCEPTION 0x40010007
inline bool hasRIPExceptionHandler() {
    __try { RaiseException(DBG_RIPEXCEPTION, 0, 0, 0); }
    __except(EXCEPTION_EXECUTE_HANDLER){ return false; }
    return true;
}
```

Timing Control-Critical Routines

If an anti-bot developer is debugging your bot, the developer will likely place breakpoints on and single-step through parts of your code that are critical to the bot's behavior. You can detect this activity by measuring code execution times; when someone steps through code, execution takes a lot longer than usual.

For example, if a function only places some hooks, you can be sure that the code shouldn't take more than a tenth of a second to do the memory protection. You could check the execution time for memory protection with help from the GetTickCount() Windows API function, as follows:

```
--snip--
auto startTime = GetTickCount();
protectMemory<>(...);
if (GetTickCount() - startTime >= 100)
    debuggerDetectedGoConfuseIt();
--snip--
```

Checking for Debug Drivers

Some debuggers load kernel-mode drivers to assist their operation. You can detect these debuggers by attempting to get a handle to their kernel-mode drivers, like this:

```
bool DebuggerDriversPresent() {
    // an array of common debugger driver device names
    const char drivers[9][20] = {
        "\\\\.\\EXTREM", "\\\\.\\ICEEXT",
        "\\\\.\\NDBGMSG.VXD", "\\\\.\\RINGO",
        "\\\\.\\SIWVID", "\\\\.\\SYSER",
        "\\\\.\\TRW", "\\\\.\\SYSERBOOT",
        "\0"
    };
    for (int i = 0; drivers[i][0] != '\0'; i++) {
        auto h = CreateFileA(drivers[i], 0, 0, 0, OPEN_EXISTING, 0, 0);
        if (h != INVALID_HANDLE_VALUE) {
            CloseHandle(h);
            return true;
        }
    }
    return false;
}
```

There are a few common kernel-mode driver device names to check for, like \\\\.\\EXTREM and the others shown in the drivers array. If this handle-fetching code succeeds, then there's a debugger running on the system. Unlike with the previous methods, though, obtaining a handle to one of those drivers doesn't always mean the debugger is attached to your bot.

Anti-Debugging Techniques

Once you detect a debugger, there are multiple ways to obfuscate your control flow. For instance, you might try to crash the debugger. The following code crashes OllyDbg v1.10:

```
OutputDcbugString("%s%s%s%s");
```

The string "%s%s%s%s" contains format specifiers, and OllyDbg passes it to printf() without any extra parameters, which is why the debugger crashes. You could place this code in a function that gets called in response to detecting a debugger, but this option works only against OllyDbg.

Causing an Unavoidable Infinite Loop

Another obfuscation method to try is overloading the system until the person debugging your bot is forced to close the bot and debugger. This function does the trick:

```
void SelfDestruct() {
    std::vector<char*> explosion;
    while (true)
        explosion.push_back(new char[10000]);
}
```

The infinite while loop just keeps adding elements to explosion until the process runs out of memory or someone pulls the plug.

Overflowing the Stack

If you want to really confuse the analyst, you can make a chain of functions that eventually cause a stack overflow, but in an indirect way:

```
#include <random>
typedef void (* _recurse)();
void recurse1(); void recurse2();
void recurse3(); void recurse4();
void recurse5();
_recurse recfuncs[5] = {
    &recurse1, &recurse2, &recurse3,
    &recurse4, &recurse5
};
void recurse1() { recfuncs[rand() % 5](); }
void recurse2() { recfuncs[(rand() % 3) + 2](); }
void recurse3() {
    if (rand() % 100 < 50) recurse1();
    else recfuncs[(rand() % 3) + 1]();
}
void recurse4() { recfuncs[rand() % 2](); }
void recurse5() {
    for (int i = 0; i < 100; i++)
        if (rand() % 50 == 1)
```

```
        recfuncs[i % 5]();
    recurse5();
}
// call any of the above functions to trigger a stack overflow
```

In a nutshell, these functions randomly and infinitely recurse until there's no room left on the call stack. Causing the overflow indirectly makes it hard for the analyst to pause and examine previous calls before they realize what's happened.

Causing a BSOD

If you're serious about obfuscation, you can even trigger a Blue Screen of Death (BSOD) when you detect a debugger. One way to do that is to set your bot's process as critical using the SetProcessIsCritical() Windows API function and then call exit(), since Windows will trigger a BSOD when a critical process is killed. Here's how you might do that:

```
void BSODBaby() {
    typedef long (WINAPI *RtlSetProcessIsCritical)
        (BOOLEAN New, BOOLEAN *Old, BOOLEAN NeedScb);
    auto ntdll = LoadLibraryA("ntdll.dll");
    if (ntdll) {
        auto SetProcessIsCritical = (RtlSetProcessIsCritical)
            GetProcAddress(ntdll, "RtlSetProcessIsCritical");
        if (SetProcessIsCritical)
            SetProcessIsCritical(1, 0, 0);
    }
}

BSODBaby();
exit(1);
```

Or maybe you're evil, in which case you can do this:

```
BSODBaby();
OutputDebugString("%s%s%s%s");
recurse1();
exit(1);
```

Assuming you've implemented all of the techniques described in this section, this code would cause a BSOD, crash the debugger (if it's OllyDbg v1.10), overflow the stack, and exit the running program. If any one of the methods fails or gets patched, the analyst still has to deal with the remaining ones before they can continue debugging.

Defeating Signature-Based Detection

Even with amazing obfuscation, you won't easily beat signature detection. Engineers who analyze bots and write signatures are very skilled, and obfuscation is, at best, a nuisance that makes their job marginally harder.

To completely evade SBD, you need to subvert the detection code. This requires knowing exactly how the SBD works. PunkBuster, for instance, uses NtQueryVirtualMemory() to scan the memory of all running processes for any signatures. If you want to bypass this, you can inject code into all PunkBuster processes with a hook on the NtQueryVirtualMemory() function.

When the function tries to query memory from your bot process, you can give it whatever data you want, like this:

```
NTSTATUS onNtQueryVirtualMemory(
    HANDLE process, PVOID baseAddress,
    MEMORY_INFORMATION_CLASS memoryInformationClass,
    PVOID buffer, ULONG numberOfBytes, PULONG numberOfBytesRead) {

    // if the scan is on this process, make sure it can't see the hook DLL
    if ((process == INVALID_HANDLE_VALUE ||
        process == GetCurrentProcess()) &&
        baseAddress >= MY_HOOK_DLL_BASE &&
        baseAddress <= MY_HOOK_DLL_BASE_PLUS_SIZE)
❶          return STATUS_ACCESS_DENIED;

    // if the scan is on the bot, zero the returned memory
    auto ret = origNtQueryVirtualMemory(
        process, baseAddress,
        memoryInformationClass,
        buffer, numberOfBytes, numberOfBytesRead);
    if(GetProcessId(process) == MY_BOT_PROCESS)
❷      ZeroMemory(buffer, numberOfBytesRead);
    return ret;
}
```

This onNtQueryVirtualMemory() hook returns STATUS_ACCESS_DENIED ❶ when NtQueryVirtualMemory() tries to query the hook DLL's memory, but it gives zeroed memory ❷ when NtQueryVirtualMemory() tries to query the bot's memory. The difference isn't for any specific reason; I'm just showing two ways you can hide from the NtQueryVirtualMemory() function call. If you're really paranoid, you can even replace the entire buffer with a random byte sequence.

Of course, this method works only for SBD that happens from user mode, like the SBD in PunkBuster or VAC. SBD that happens from the driver, like ESEA's, or that isn't predictable, like Warden's, isn't as easy to bypass.

In those cases, you can take precautions to eliminate unique signatures in your bot. If you're distributing the bot to more than a dozen or so people, however, removing all distinguishing properties is tricky. To throw analysts off the scent, each time you give somebody a copy of the bot, you could try some combination of the following:

- Compiling the bot using a different compiler
- Changing the compiler optimization settings
- Toggling between using __fastcall and __cdecl

- Packing the binaries using a different packer
- Switching between static and dynamic linking of runtime libraries

Varying these elements creates a different assembly for each user, but there's a limit on how many unique versions of the bot you can produce that way. Past some point, this method doesn't scale to demand, and eventually, game companies will have signatures for every incarnation of your bot.

Apart from obfuscation and code mutation, there aren't many ways to defeat advanced SBD mechanisms. You could implement your bot in a driver or create a kernel-mode rootkit to hide your bot, but even those methods aren't foolproof.

NOTE *This book doesn't cover implementing a bot in a driver or creating a rootkit to hide a bot, as both topics are pretty complex. Rootkit development alone is a subject that dozens of books have covered already. I'd recommend Bill Blunden's* The Rootkit Arsenal: Escape and Evasion in The Dark Corners of The System *(Jones & Bartlett Learning, 2009).*

Some game hackers try to cover every single base, hooking every memory-reading function and the entire filesystem API, but still get caught by determined systems like Warden. In fact, I recommend staying away from Warden and Blizzard at all costs.

Defeating Screenshots

If you encounter a detection mechanism that uses screenshots as additional proof to nail botters, you're in luck. Bypassing screenshot mechanisms is easy: don't let your bot be seen.

You can subvert this type of detection by keeping a minimal UI and making no visibly distinguishable changes to the game client. If your bot requires a HUD or other distinctive UI displays, though, don't fret—you can have your cake and eat it, too. As long as you can intercept the screenshot code, you can hide your fingerprints while a screenshot is taken.

In some versions of PunkBuster, for example, the Windows API function GetSystemTimeAsFileTime() is called just before a screenshot is taken. You can use a hook on this function to quickly hide your UI for a few seconds to ensure it's not seen:

```
void onGetSystemTimeAsFileTime(LPFILETIME systemTimeAsFileTime) {
    myBot->hideUI(2000); // hide UI for 2 seconds
    origGetSystemTimeAsFileTime(systemTimeAsFileTime);
}
```

Just hook GetSystemTimeAsFileTime() using the techniques described in "Hooking to Redirect Game Execution" on page 153, write a hideUI() function, and call the hideUI() function before execution resumes.

Defeating Binary Validation

Defeating binary validation is as simple as not placing hooks inside game-specific binaries. Jump hooks and IAT hooks on Windows API functions are extremely common, so wherever you can, try to get away with using those methods instead of using jump or near-call hooks in a game binary. In cases where you must directly hook a game's code, you can trick the anti-cheat software's binary validation routines by intercepting the binary scan and spoofing the data to match what the software expects to see.

Like SBD, binary validation often uses NtQueryVirtualMemory() to scan memory. To trick the validation code, start with a hook on that function. Then, write a function like this one to spoof the data when NtQueryVirtualMemory() is called:

```
NTSTATUS onNtQueryVirtualMemory(
    HANDLE process, PVOID baseAddress,
    MEMORY_INFORMATION_CLASS memoryInformationClass,
    PVOID buffer, ULONG numberOfBytes, PULONG numberOfBytesRead) {

    auto ret = origNtQueryVirtualMemory(
        process, baseAddress,
        memoryInformationClass,
        buffer, numberOfBytes, numberOfBytesRead);
    // place tricky code somewhere in here
    return ret;
}
```

Inside this hook, you'll need to watch for any memory scans over memory that has been modified by one of your hooks.

NOTE   *This example assumes the bot has only one hook and that variables prefixed with HOOK_ already exist and describe the code the hook replaces.*

Listing 12-2 shows some scan-monitoring code.

```
// is the scan on the current process?
bool currentProcess =
    process == INVALID_HANDLE_VALUE ||
    process == GetCurrentProcess();

// is the hook in the memory range being scanned?
auto endAddress = baseAddress + numberOfBytesRead - 1;
bool containsHook =
    (HOOK_START_ADDRESS >= baseAddress &&
     HOOK_START_ADDRESS <= endAddress) ||
    (HOOK_END_ADDRESS >= baseAddress &&
     HOOK_END_ADDRESS <= endAddress);
❶ if (currentProcess && containsHook) {
    // hide the hook
}
```

Listing 12-2: Checking whether hooked memory is being scanned

When a memory scan over the hooked code happens (which makes currentProcess and containsHook become true at the same time), code inside the if() statement ❶ updates the output buffer to reflect the original code. This means you must know where the hooked code is within the scanned block, taking into account the fact that the block may span only a subset of the hooked code.

So if baseAddress marks the address where the scan starts, HOOK_START_ADDRESS marks the spot where the modified code starts, endAddress marks the address where the scan ends, and HOOK_END_ADDRESS marks the address where the modified code ends, you can use some simple math to calculate which parts of the modified code are present in which parts of the buffer. You do so as follows, using writeStart to store the offset of the modified code in the scan buffer and readStart to store the offset of the scan buffer relative to the modified code, in case the scan buffer starts in the middle of the modified code:

```
int readStart, writeStart;
if (HOOK_START_ADDRESS >= baseAddress) {
    readStart = 0;
    writeStart = HOOK_START_ADDRESS - baseAddress;
} else {
    readStart = baseAddress - HOOK_START_ADDRESS;
    writeStart = baseAddress;
}

int readEnd;
if (HOOK_END_ADDRESS <= endAddress)
    readEnd = HOOK_LENGTH - readStart - 1;
else
    readEnd = endAddress - HOOK_START_ADDRESS;
```

Once you know how many bytes you need to replace, where to put them, and where to get them, you can do the spoof with three lines of code:

```
char* replaceBuffer = (char*)buffer;
for ( ; readStart <= readEnd; readStart++, writeStart++)
    replaceBuffer[writeStart] = HOOK_ORIG_DATA[readStart];
```

Completely assembled, the code looks like this:

```
NTSTATUS onNtQueryVirtualMemory(
    HANDLE process, PVOID baseAddress,
    MEMORY_INFORMATION_CLASS memoryInformationClass,
    PVOID buffer, ULONG numberOfBytes, PULONG numberOfBytesRead) {
    auto ret = origNtQueryVirtualMemory(
        process, baseAddress,
        memoryInformationClass,
        buffer, numberOfBytes, numberOfBytesRead);
    bool currentProcess =
        process == INVALID_HANDLE_VALUE ||
        process == GetCurrentProcess();
```

```
auto endAddress = baseAddress + numberOfBytesRead - 1;
bool containsHook =
    (HOOK_START_ADDRESS >= baseAddress &&
     HOOK_START_ADDRESS <= endAddress) ||
    (HOOK_END_ADDRESS >= baseAddress &&
     HOOK_END_ADDRESS <= endAddress);
if (currentProcess && containsHook) {
    int readStart, writeStart;
    if (HOOK_START_ADDRESS >= baseAddress) {
        readStart = 0;
        writeStart = HOOK_START_ADDRESS - baseAddress;
    } else {
        readStart = baseAddress - HOOK_START_ADDRESS;
        writeStart = baseAddress;
    }

    int readEnd;
    if (HOOK_END_ADDRESS <= endAddress)
        readEnd = HOOK_LENGTH - readStart - 1;
    else
        readEnd = endAddress - HOOK_START_ADDRESS;

    char* replaceBuffer = (char*)buffer;
    for ( ; readStart <= readEnd; readStart++, writeStart++)
        replaceBuffer[writeStart] = HOOK_ORIG_DATA[readStart];
}
return ret;
}
```

Of course, if you had multiple hooks that you needed to hide from
binary validation scans, you would need to implement this functionality
in a more robust way that would allow it to track multiple modified code
regions accordingly.

Defeating an Anti-Cheat Rootkit

GameGuard and some other anti-cheat suites come with user-mode rootkits
that not only detect bots but also proactively prevent them from running.
To defeat this type of protection, rather than think outside the box, you can
completely copy the box and work inside that copy.

For example, if you want to write memory to a game, you must call
the WriteProcessMemory() function, which is exported by *kernel32.dll*. When
you call this function, it directly calls NtWriteVirtualMemory() from *ntdll.dll*.
GameGuard hooks ntdll.NtWriteVirtualMemory() to prevent you from writing
memory. But if NtWriteVirtualMemory() is exported from, say, *ntdll_copy.dll*,
GameGuard won't hook that function.

That means you can copy *ntdll.dll* and dynamically import all of the
functions you need, as follows:

```
// copy and load ntdll
copyFile("ntdll.dll", "ntdll_copy.dll");
```

```
auto module = LoadLibrary("ntdll_copy.dll");

// dynamically import NtWriteVirtualMemory
typedef NTSTATUS (WINAPI* _NtWriteVirtualMemory)
    (HANDLE, PVOID, PVOID, ULONG, PULONG);
auto myWriteVirtualMemory = (_NtWriteVirtualMemory)
    GetProcAddress(module, "NtWriteVirtualMemory");

// call NtWriteVirtualMemory
myWriteVirtualMemory(process, address, data, length, &writtenlength);
```

After copying *ntdll.dll*, this code imports the `NtWriteVirtualMemory()` from the copy with the name `myWriteVirtualMemory()`. From there, the bot can use this function in place of the `NtWriteVirtualMemory()` function. They're effectively the same code in the same library, just loaded under different names.

Copying a function that anti-cheat software hooks works only if you call that function at its lowest-level entry point, though. If this code copied *kernel32.dll* and dynamically imported the `WriteProcessMemory()` function, an anti-cheat rootkit would still stop the bot, because *kernel32_copy.dll* would still rely on `ntdll.NtWriteVirtualMemory()` when calling the `WriteProcessMemory()` function.

Defeating Heuristics

In addition to all of the advanced client-side detection mechanisms we've just discussed, game companies will employ server-side heuristics that can detect bots simply by monitoring a player's behavior. These systems learn to distinguish between human and autonomous player behavior through machine-learning algorithms. Their decision-making process is often internal and incomprehensible to humans, so it's difficult to pinpoint exactly what features of gameplay lead to detection.

You don't need to know how such algorithms work to trick them; your bot just needs to act human. Here are some common behaviors that are distinguishably different between humans and bots:

Intervals between actions

Many bots perform actions unreasonably fast or at consistent intervals. Bots will seem more human-like if they have a reasonable cooldown period between actions. They should also have some form of randomization to prevent them from repeating an action at a constant rate.

Path repetition

Bots that farm enemies automatically visit a preprogrammed list of locations to kill creatures. These waypoint lists are often extremely accurate, indicating each location as an exact pixel. Humans, conversely, move in less predictable ways and visit more unique locations along the way to a familiar area. To replicate this behavior, a bot might walk to a random location within a certain range of a target location, rather than to the target location itself. Also, if the bot randomizes the order in which it visits target locations, the variety of paths it takes will increase further.

Unrealistic play

Some botters run their bots in the same location for hundreds of consecutive hours, but humans can't play a game that long. Encourage your users to refrain from botting for more than eight hours at a time and warn them that doing the same thing for seven straight days will definitely trigger alarms in a heuristic system.

Perfect accuracy

Bots can hit a thousand head shots in a row without firing a single extra bullet, and they can hit every skill shot with consistent precision. But it's virtually impossible for a human to do the same, so a smart bot should be intentionally inaccurate at times.

These are just a few examples, but in general, you can sneak past heuristic checks if you just use common sense. Don't try to have a bot do something a human can't, and don't have the bot do any single thing for too long.

Closing Thoughts

Game hackers and game developers are engaged in a constant battle of wits. Hackers will keep finding ways to subvert detection, and developers will keep finding better ways to detect them. If you're determined, however, the knowledge in this chapter should help you defeat any anti-cheat software you encounter.

INDEX

CS register, 85
C-style operators, OllyDbg, 34–35
custom behaviors for cavebots, scripting, 243

D

dark environments, lighting up, 190–192
data modification instructions, 89
data structures, 71–73
data types, 66
    classes and VF tables, 74–78
    numeric data, 67–69
    OllyDbg, 36
    string data, 69–71
    unions, 73–74
DBG_RIPEXCEPTION handlers, checking for, 253
debugging. *See also* OllyDbg
    anti-debugging techniques, 255–256
    debug drivers, checking for, 254
    debug strings, printing, 253
    detecting debuggers, 251–254
    Process Monitor, 52–53
__declspec(naked) convention, 168
decode() function, hooking, 172–173, 174–175
Decreased Value By scan type, Cheat Engine, 7
Decreased Value scan type, Cheat Engine, 7
dependencies, DLL, 145
dependency loading, 160
depositor, 242
destination operand, 80
detection, avoiding. *See* anti-cheat software
device->SetRenderState() function, 192
Dijkstra's algorithm, 233–234
Direct3D 9, 176
Direct3D hooking, 175–176. *See also* extrasensory perception (ESP) hacks
    detecting visual cues in games, 205–206
    drawing loop, 176–177

finding devices, 177–181
    optional fixes for stability, 184
    writing hook for EndScene(), 182–183
    writing hook for Reset(), 183–184
directional lighthacks, 190–191
disabling ASLR, 128
disassembler pane, OllyDbg, 27–29, 42
Disassembly column, OllyDbg disassembler pane, 28
dispatchPacket() function, 210
display base, 27
DLL (dynamic link library), injecting, 142–146
DllMain() entry point, 144–145
DLLs option, Process Explorer pane, 57
Domain Name System (DNS) cache scans, 248
DOS header, 160–161
DrawIndexedPrimitive() function, 194, 195, 196, 200
drawing loop, Direct3D, 176–177
DS register, 85
dump pane, OllyDbg, 29–30
DWORD data type, 67, 145–146
dynamically allocated memory, 6, 11, 12
dynamic link library (DLL), injecting, 142–146
dynamic lure, 242–243
dynamic structures, 105
    std::list class, 110–113
    std::map class, 114–118
    std::string class, 105–108
    std::vector class, 108–110

E

EAX register, 81
EBP register, 83
EBX register, 82
ECX register, 82, 157
EDI register, 83
EDX register, 82
EFLAGS register, 84, 92
EIP register, 83, 139

N

named pipes, locating, 60
name of specific player, pausing
    execution when printed,
    37–38
Names window, OllyDbg, 29
near calls, 153–154
near function call, 39
.NET processes, 59
Network event class filter, 52
new addresses, determining after
    game updates, 101–104
next scan, running in Cheat
    Engine, 7
nodes, 233, 234–238
no-operation (NOP) commands,
    31, 32
NOPing, 150–152
    lighthacks, 192
    zoomhacks, 197–198
NtQueryVirtualMemory() function, 246,
    257, 259
NtWriteVirtualMemory() function,
    261–262
null terminator, 70
numeric data types, 67–69
numeric operators, OllyDbg, 34–35

O

obfuscation, 251, 255–256
observing game events
    detecting visual cues, 205–206
    intercepting network traffic,
        206–211
    monitoring memory, 204–205
obstaclcs, searches disrupted by,
    233–234
offset, 54
OllyDbg, 23–24
    assembly code, 27–29, 32–33
    call stack, viewing, 30
    code patches, creating, 31–32
    command line for, 43–44
    control windows, 25–26
    CPU window, 26–30
    crashing debuggers, 255

dealing with game updates, 104
debugger buttons and
    functions, 25
expression engine, 33–37
memory, viewing and searching,
    29–30
memory dump of numeric data,
    68–69
memory dump of string data, 70
packet parser, finding, 207–208
Patches window, 31–32
patching if() statements, 46–47
pausing execution when health
    of character drops,
    39–42
pausing execution when name
    of player is printed,
    37–38
plug-ins, 42–46
register contents, viewing and
    editing, 29
Run trace window, 32–33
supported data types, 36
translating code cave assembly
    to shellcode, 135–136
user interface, 24–26
zoom limitation code,
    finding, 198
OllyFlow plug-in, 45–46
opcodes, 78
OpenProcess() function, 121–122
OpenThread() function, 142
operands
    binary arithmetic
        instructions, 90
    IDIV instruction, 92
    MOV instruction, 89
    syntax, 80–81
    unary arithmetic instructions, 90
operations, 79
operators, using in OllyDbg
    expression engine, 34–35
optimizing memory code, 22
ordering, little-endian, 67
order of variables, in data structures,
    70–71
OutputDebugString() function, 253

P

packets
    intercepting, 206–211
    sending, 215–217
packing, 251
padding, 68
page protection, 125–126
pages, 124
parsing packets, 206–211
Patches window, OllyDbg, 26, 31–32
patching, multiclient, 30
patching if() statements, 46–47
Path column, Event Properties
    dialog, 55
pathfinding with search algorithms,
    232–234. *See also* A* search
    algorithm
path list, A* search algorithm,
    239–240
Pause button, OllyDbg, 25
pausing execution, 37–38, 39–42
pausing threads, 184
PEB (process environment block)
    structure, 146
PeekMessage() function, 184
PE header, 160–161
pick-phase HUDs, 201
PID (process identifier), 120–122
pipes, locating named, 60
Play button, OllyDbg, 25
player health, finding with OllyDbg,
    99–101
player versus player (PvP) combat,
    243–244
plug-ins, OllyDbg, 42–46
pointer chains, 11–12
pointer path, 11
Pointerscanner Scanoptions dialog,
    Cheat Engine, 14–16
pointer scanning, 11
    basics of, 12–14
    with Cheat Engine, 14–18
    pointer chains, 11–12
    rescanning, 17–18
Pong, 46–47

Popup trainer on keypress field,
    Trainer generator
    dialog, 9
predicting enemy movements, 241
prewritten hooking libraries, 169
printf() call, 72, 73–74, 75
printing debug strings, 253
Process32First() function, 120
Process32Next() function, 120–121
process access flags, 121
PROCESS_ALL_ACCESS flag, 121
Process and thread activity event
    class filter, 52
PROCESS_CREATE_THREAD flag, 121
process environment block (PEB)
    structure, 146
Process Explorer, 49–50, 55–56
    configuring colors, 56
    handle manipulation options,
        59–60
    hotkeys, 57
    Properties dialog, 57–59
    user interface and controls,
        56–57
process handles, obtaining, 121
process identifier (PID), 120–122
processInput() function, 215–216
processKeyboardInput() function, 216
Process Monitor, 49–50
    configuring columns in, 51
    debugging, 53–55
    event class filters, 51–52
    high-score file, finding, 55
    hotkeys, 52
    inspecting events in event log,
        52–53
    logging in-game events, 50–52
Process Monitor Filter dialog, 50
Processname field, Trainer generator
    dialog, 9
processNextPacket() function, 210
processor registers, 81–86
Process profiling event class
    filter, 52
PROCESS_VM_OPERATION flag, 121, 122
PROCESS_VM_READ flag, 121
PROCESS_VM_WRITE flag, 121

U

unary arithmetic instructions, 90
unavoidable infinite loops,
     causing, 255
Unchanged Value scan type, Cheat
     Engine, 7
unions, 73–74
Unix syntax, 80
Unknown Initial Value scan type,
     Cheat Engine, 6
updates, determining new addresses
     after, 101–104
user interface, Process Explorer,
     56–57
user-mode rootkit, GameGuard
     toolkit, 248–249

V

VAC toolkit, 247–248
Value Between scan type, Cheat
     Engine, 6
Value Type directive, Cheat Engine, 6
VF (virtual function) tables
     class instances and, 76–78
     finding Direct3D devices,
          177–181
     hooking, 156–160, 182–183
     traversals, 156
VirtualAllocEx() function,
     136–137, 138
virtual functions, classes with, 75–76
VirtualProtectEx() function, 126–128
VirtualProtect() function, 127

W

WaitForSingleObject() function, 129, 138
wallhacks, 192
     creating for Direct3D, 194–197
     rendering with z-buffering,
          193–194
warbots, 243–244
Warden toolkit, 249–250
waypoints, 222, 229
wchar_t data type, 67
window handle, fetching, 120

Windows window, OllyDbg, 26
WM_CHAR messages, 213–214
WORD data type, 67
WriteProcessMemory() function,
     122–124, 136–137, 138
write protection, 125–128
writing to game memory, 119
     accessing memory, 122–124
     address space layout
          randomization, 128–130
     code caves, 136–137
     memory protection, 124–128
     process identifier, obtaining,
          120–122

X

x86 assembly language, 78–79
     arithmetic instructions, 90–92
     branching instructions, 92–94
     call stack, 86–88
     command syntax, 79–81
     data modification
          instructions, 89
     function calls, 94–95
     jump instructions, 92–94
     NOPing, 150–152
     processor registers, 81–86
x86 Windows memory protection
     attributes, 125–126

Z

z-buffering, 192–195
zoom factor, 197
zoomhacks, 197–198

RESOURCES

Visit *https://www.nostarch.com/gamehacking/* for resources, errata, and other information.

More no-nonsense books from  **NO STARCH PRESS**

BLACK HAT PYTHON
Python Programming for Hackers and Pentesters
by JUSTIN SEITZ
DEC 2014, 192 PP., $34.95
ISBN 978-1-59327-590-7

THE CAR HACKER'S HANDBOOK
A Guide for the Penetration Tester
by CRAIG SMITH
MAR 2016, 304 PP., $49.95
ISBN 978-1-59327-703-1

THE IDA PRO BOOK, 2ND EDITION
The Unofficial Guide to the World's Most Popular Disassembler
by CHRIS EAGLE
JUL 2011, 672 PP., $69.95
ISBN 978-1-59327-289-0

PRACTICAL FORENSIC IMAGING
Securing Digital Evidence with Linux Tools
by BRUCE NIKKEL
FALL 2016, 256 PP., $49.95
ISBN 978-1-59327-793-2

IOS APPLICATION SECURITY
The Definitive Guide for Hackers and Developers
by DAVID THIEL
FEB 2016, 296 PP., $49.95
ISBN 978-1-59327-601-0

PRACTICAL MALWARE ANALYSIS
The Hands-On Guide to Dissecting Malicious Software
by MICHAEL SIKORSKI *and* ANDREW HONIG
FEB 2012, 800 PP., $59.95
ISBN 978-1-59327-290-6

800.420.7240 OR 415.863.9900 | SALES@NOSTARCH.COM | WWW.NOSTARCH.COM